Courtesy of Buck Taylor

All About
COWBOY ACTION SHOOTING

BY RONALD HARRIS

STOEGER PUBLISHING COMPANY

TITLE

All About Cowboy Action Shooting

STAFF

Project Coordinators: Studiocrafts & LN Design
Design & Production Director: Dominick S. Sorrentino
Editorial Consultant: William S. Jarrett
Design & Electronic Page Makeup: Lesley A. Notorangelo
Color, Black & White Electronic Imaging:
    Mark Cocce/DSS and Lesley A. Notorangelo
Cover Photography: Ray Wells
Book Jacket Design: Stephen McKelvain, *Director of Brand Marketing & Communications, Stoeger Industries*

LIBRARY OF CONGRESS

CATALOGING-IN-PUBLICATION DATA

Copyright 2001 by Ronald Harris

Published by Stoeger Publishing Company
17603 Indian Head Highway
Accokeek, Maryland 20607

ISBN: 0-88317-227-5
Library of Congress Control No.: 00-135059
Manufactured in the United States of America

Distributed to the book trade and to the sporting goods trade by
Stoeger Industries, 17603 Indian Head Highway, Accokeek, MD 20607

*For **Cimarron Sue***

A well regulated militia being necessary to the security of a free state, the right of the people to keep and bear arms shall not be infringed.

THE SECOND AMMENDMENT
BILL OF RIGHTS
THE CONSTITUTION OF THE UNITED STATES

ACKNOWLEDGEMENTS

It is said that no book is ever written by one person alone. This general overview of Cowboy/Western Action Shooting activities is but a brief summary of our decade of cowboy actioneering observations and experiences, intended only as an introduction to our beloved sport and lifestyle. Every shooter, vendor and sponsor we've met along the trail has, to some degree, contributed to this book. So have the authors of other material on Cowboy Action related matters. It's impossible to acknowledge them all.

Some, however, have contributed so greatly they must be thanked by name. Without their cooperation, this book wouldn't be possible. First among these, of course, is the Single Action Shooting Society's board of directors, The Wild Bunch. Individual board members shared information and viewpoints, but Ken The Chiseler Amorosano, the SASS Media/Public Relations ramrod, bore the brunt of my pestering for permissions, pictures and the latest SASS data.

The images provided by SASS photographer Ron Dances With Wolfson greatly enrich the illustration of our colorfully unique game. The Old West watercolors of cowboy, actor and artist Buck Taylor are a special blessing. Cowboy actioneers are fans of Taylor and his art, on film and canvas. His collection of scenes from the SASS film favorite, Tombstone, are avidly collected by lovers of Western art.

Many images and much research material were contributed by makers and purveyors to the burgeoning Cowboy Action/Living History market. We acknowledge them with inclusion in our appendix and thank Maria Uberti, the ladies of Taylor's & Co., Dixie Gun Works' Sharon Cunningham and Cimarron's Mike "Texas Jack" Harvey for their extra effort.

The We we've been using throughout refers to my wife Suzy. We took up Cowboy Action Shooting together and made this book together.

We tried to make it useful and a good read for Old Hands and Greenhorns alike. It has been a labor of love.

FOREWORD

If you were intrigued by the cover and title of this book, chances are you are already a Western fan, or you're wondering "what the heck is cowboy action shooting all about?" Well, this book provides everything you ever wanted to know about Cowboy Action and Cowboy Mounted shooting. You'll learn what these exciting western shooting and riding sports are all about, how to play them and what equipment you'll need. Most of all, it offers a colorful glimpse of the fun you and the entire family will share as you relive our western experience.

Author Ron "El Escritor" Harris has accomplished what no other writer has. He starts by tracing the sport from its humble beginnings and brings you up to date on the guns, gear and rules of the game. He takes the reader on a brief historical journey, back to the very roots of our desire to "play cowboy." Armed with this book, you'll travel back to the real Old West for a brief look at the folks who inspired the "reel" West of the big and small screens. These were, after all, the mediums that inspired generations of kids to idolize the cowboy, and to help perpetuate the legend of this truly American icon throughout the world.

In his book, Ron provides the low-down on the firearms used in cowboy action shooting, complete with a bit of historical background. He also explains how best to play in this fast-paced but friendly competition, regardless of whether you favor strictly authentic guns of the frontier era or the modernized renditions of traditional western arms. Every aspect of the sport has been laid out for you, along with explanations of Cowboy Action's exciting Old West scenarios, including all the post-competition festivities. This book also serves as a reference to help readers decide on the "hardware" they'll be totin' and the types of gunleather available from today's top makers. Ron offers a thorough look at the myriad of old-timey outfits that can be put together, bringing to reality your very own Wild West fantasy.

Ron and his wife Suzy have done a tremendous job in assembling a wealth of background information and artistic, yet real, images of cowboy action shooters, cowboy mounted shooters, the firearms, clothing and other cowboy gear, used in this fast-growing sport. During the past few years, I've observed this tireless couple at a variety of cowboy action and mounted shooting matches and have always found them hard at work interviewing competitors and vendors, all the while taking pictures embodying every aspect of this fascinating and exciting pastime.

This is not the sort of book that almost anyone can put together. Cowboy action shooting is a unique sport involving many facets. It's a sport featuring old-time guns, colorful Western outfits, historical frontier accessories—even horses and saddles for those who are into the mounted shooting game. Ron Harris' credentials for undertaking this work are impressive. They start with a lifelong passion for the outdoors, working and playing there for most of his 62 years. He has worked as a surveyor for the Bureau of Land Management, as a cowboy in Utah's rugged Escalante wilderness, and pursued the sport of Hunt Racing and Fox Hunting in the rolling hills of Virginia. Ron's personal involvement in the cowboy shooting sports dates back more than a decade. He holds a distinguished position as a Regulator of the Single Action Shooting Society (SASS) and is a Charter Life Member of the Cowboy Mounted Shooters Association (CMSA).

No stranger to the field of journalism, Ron has pursued a 40-year career in broadcasting, working as a television and radio announcer, TV cameraman, director and writer. In addition, he has served as film and video editor for Advertising & Marketing magazine and is currently a member of the Western Writers of America, the Outdoor Writer's Association of America and the Society of Environmental Journalists (he founded Arizona's first Trout Unlimited Chapter and the Zane Grey Chapter of Phoenix). His writings earned him the Arizona Game & Fish Department's "Outdoor Writer of the Year" award in 1997.

It takes someone like Ron Harris to create a book that encompasses all the various cowboy action shooting venues. He knows and loves all the various components that make up the sport. He did not simply jump into this corral and decide that writing a book on Cowboy Action Shooting would be a good way to spend some time while making a fast, easy buck. Shucks, anyone who's ever written a book knows better than that. Ron Harris is a fella who's played the game. He's a shooter, a horseman and a western aficionado with a great deal of knowledge on the subject. He talks the talk and he walks the walk. He's been there and done that. With his experienced eye and the lens of his camera, along with a passel of research and hard work, he has fulfilled his mission by telling the story of this fun, family-oriented, exciting venture. Read on. I'm confident you'll agree that Ron Harris is the man; and Cowboy Action Shooting is the game!

— *Phil Spangenberger*

Table Of Contents

CHAPTER ONE

AT LEFT.
Owen Wister
(July 14, 1860-
July 21, 1938),
author of **The**
Virginian.

OUR COWBOYS HAVE ALWAYS BEEN HEROES

W hen Owen Wister's novel, **The Virginian: A Horseman of the Plains**, was published in 1902, the author described the Wyoming of his book as a "vanished world" and his hero as one of the "last romantic figures" America would produce. The frontier had been pronounced closed, perhaps prematurely, by historian Frederick Jackson Turner in 1892, in a speech delivered in Chicago. Wister's work was to be the first verse of an endless eulogy for the American frontier. Now, a hundred years later, we are poised to renew a worldwide fascination with the epic story of America's West.

Wister, who agreed with Jackson that the frontier was a defining influence in the development of America's unique national character, chose this honest cowboy from Virginia as a model for his readers. He could not have predicted the widespread success of his literary formula, nor the never-ending influence his work would continue to exert on the arts. As Wister biographer Darwin Payne put it:

"What The Virginian ultimately did was create a nearly insatiable appetite in the American Public for cowboy heroes whose hearts were pure as gold, whose intentions for their women were beyond reproach and whose quiet courage made them feared by all." Far more than the Wild West shows, dime novels and magazine serials, Wister's book perpetuated public perception of the "cow boy" as heroic.

It still does. So classic a tale is *The Virginian* that the title role has been played on stage, screen and television by Dustin Farnam, William S. Hart, Kenneth Harlan, Gary Cooper, Joel McCrae and, most recently, Bill Pullman. The original, starring Gary Cooper in 1929, was the first feature-length Western with sound. After several remakes in the years that followed, *The Virginian* appeared as a teleplay by Larry Gross and produced and directed by Bill Pullman, who spoke the version truest to Wister, including the hero's best known and most misquoted line:

"When you call me that—smile."

Perhaps Owen Wister began the transition from Real West to Reel West, but the West of history and the West of myth was already synthesizing by the time he wrote *The Virginian* (his only

ABOVE. *Runnin' For It!*

bestseller). It remained only for writers like Zane Grey, Stuart Lake and Luke Short, and artists like Russell, Remington and Wyeth to create more mythical images with which to document Western history.

By the time moviemakers joined the writers, photographers and painters racing to record the West, it was almost too late for anything like an accurate portrayal. The frontier had been effectively fenced off into mere real estate and was completely populated by the advent of World War II. It was then fictionalized and romanticized on film. As the remaining true cowboys and cowgirls of the 19th century finally rode off into the sunset and sage, the Old West had lost its only remaining eyewitnesses. Histories turned into stories, stories grew into legends, and legends passed into the mist of mythology.

Edwin S. Porter's *The Great Train Robbery*, released in 1903, is considered by most film historians to be the first western movie. The film's flickering ten minutes of mute, black and white images, while primitive by today's high tech standards, were nonetheless compelling enough to sound the death knell for the Wild West shows of Buffalo Bill and a hundred others. The camera took the Wild West to places where the Wild West Shows could never play.

Close-up lenses conveyed audiences into scenes in a way that watching from the bleachers never could. Film captured forever the action and romance of every Frontier moment—to be shared with audiences around the world and watched again and again. Little wonder that the first film projectors were called *Magic Lanterns*.

HI YO, SILVER, AWAY!

So it was that the children of the first half of the 20th century grew up watching Tom Mix, Roy Rogers, Gene Autry, John Wayne and all the others ride and shoot their way through Hollywood's Western fantasies. Radio, with its low fidelity speakers, was listened to religiously, portraying an even more exciting Old West. The movies we watched and the radios we listened to were as real as youthful imaginations could produce and direct. For many of us, the Lone Ranger still rides the romantic ranges of our childhood fantasies. The Reel West dreamed up by radio and motion pictures may have been mythical, but it taught whole generations to love and learn about the Real West.

Where movies took audiences to the Old West in theaters, television brought the Old West home. On television, the Frontier was exposed to yet another generation and in numbers undreamed of by early Western myth makers. By 1960, when the baby-boomers were impressionable teenagers, they were already addicted to television. Eleven of the top 20 Neilsen-rated programs that year were Westerns, and all are now considered *"Classic TV"*. Millions watched every episode of *Gunsmoke*, *Have Gun, Will Travel* and *Bonanza*! We watched *Maverick* for the humor and *The Rifleman* the morals. Families gathered around the TV set for *Wagon Train*, *Death Valley Days*, *Wyatt Earp* or *Wanted: Dead or Alive*. Like the theatrical Western movies and serials produced long before and now enjoying a second generation

of TV addicts, these same popular episodes spun wholesome tales of good over evil and the triumph of the human spirit. They promulgated that wonderful philosophy born of the independent, self-reliant spirit of the American Frontier—what we called The Cowboy Way or The Code of the West.

Reflecting our rapidly changing society, TV Westerns began to change, revealing new historical facts along with the creation of more myths. Black cowboys, soldiers and mountain men were deemed important figures of the frontier; but not until recently were they depicted incidentally, if at all, in literature or film. From Herb Jeffries' 1935 *Harlem on the Prairie* (1938)—the first all-Black Western made for an all-Black audience—until Woody Strode's dramatic *Sergeant Rutledge* (1960), the contributions of Blacks on the frontier were largely neglected. The Western myth makers were indifferent to the roles of Blacks on the frontier. They were downright libelous to Native Americans and Hispanics. But our national interest in and love of the Old West doesn't cotton to mere myth. Actually, the true history of our frontier emerges from its cocoon of fabrication. Truth can be stranger than fiction and students of the Old West are forever fascinated with its genuine, recorded history. The more we know of our country's frontier days, the more we strive to learn. So proud are we of our Golden Age—when America's infancy was spent "winning" the West—we 've come to love the history *and* the myth. Folks who actively pursue both fact and fiction with equal abandon are called *occihistoriophiles*; i.e., those who love the magnificent "mythtory" of the Great American West.

The story of that place and time we call the Old West, or Wild West, has involved many heroic protagonists, beautiful co-stars and vicious villains.

Historians constantly researching folklore to support a favorite theory, and writers forever rummaging through history for untold tales, can choose from a huge cast of qualified character types, well known to aficionados of Western literature and film.

The American Frontier lasted perhaps a century and a quarter, from the country's Independence to roughly 1900. Before 1775, remember, our frontiers belonged to England, Spain, France and Russia. The letters, journals and books of westering frontiersmen and women, some of which are still coming to light, join the legends and histories of Native Americans in a long and colorful chorus. Even so, it's the polite, soft-spoken voice of a straight-shootin' cowboy from Virginia that speaks to us even now of the Odyssey of the Plains in that lost and fabled age.

Like all ages, it was a time of war and, as ages go, it was short. Most historians agree that the Wild West started with the end of the Civil War and ended before the beginning of World War I. In the interim, we fought Buffalo Wars, Range Wars, Indian Wars and the Spanish American War. For a while, we even meddled in the Mexican Revolution. Many consider this era the most interesting in Western American history, and it is certainly the period most exploited by writers, artists and filmmakers. The cowboy, the schoolmarm and the badman make an entertaining and exciting version of literature's eternal triangle. Indeed, the many variations on this fundamental human theme have elevated the cowboy to the status of folk hero, the tragi-comic symbol of an era gone, but never forgotten.

LIGHTS, CAMERA, RE-ENACTION!

To those whose love of our Western Heritage is so deep and strong, it compels more than just the study of books, movies and TV. Since childhood, we've yearned to recreate as closely as possible the thrill of ridin' and shootin', battling evil and injustice or gathering a herd and trailing it north to Dodge, fightin' off the rustlers 'n hostiles. The Frontier is gone, buried beneath subdivisions, shopping centers and parking lots; but still it lives on in our hearts and imaginations. We're not happy unless we're wearing the clothes, using the equipment and shooting the guns of the Old West. In our dedicated, if humorous pursuit of a nostalgic past, we hope that re-enacting the history of our heritage will help keep it alive. Thus the phenomena of Cowboy Actioneering has come to pass—a combination of activities and events calculated to emulate life in both the historical and mythical Old West.

The symbols of the cowboy, of course, include his horse and gun, without which he would be unemployed, defenseless and worse. A man without a horse is afoot, and an unarmed person is, well, unarmed. Our symbolic cowboy—whether a Vaquero or Texican, a Californio or Montana ranch hand—is armed and mounted, a horseman of the plains, riding into the sunset of the American frontier. It is this legendary cowboy, with his Peacemaker, rifle and shotgun, who is so central to the sports, games and lifestyles of Cowboy Action Shooting, Cowboy Mounted Shooting and Cowboy Re-enaction. In Cowboy Actioneering, our 100-year love affair with the Old West finds full flower. At

HARPER *JUDGE ROY BEAN CREIGH*: FOUNDER

Harper H. Creigh is the acknowledged founder of Cowboy Action Shooting and co-founder of the Single Action Shooting Society and End of Trail, the World Championships and Wild West Jubilee. "The Judge", as he is called, was the first recipient of the SASS Top Hand Award, the Guns of August Spirit of the Game Award and the Carolinas State Championship Spirit of the Game Award. He is a lifetime member of the National Rifle Association and an ardent supporter of the U.S. Constitution and the Second Amendment.

In years past, Creigh has sought out adventure of all kinds, from hunting and skydiving to motorcycling and dunebuggies. But shooting was always the most fun. Until the fall of 1978, he shot Trap & Skeet, IPSC and Soldier of Fortune matches. But when he, Gordon Davis and Bill Hahn hosted the world's first Cowboy Action Match at Coto de Caza, California, Harper Creigh knew he had a new mission in an already interesting life. He had fished Alaska and taken two Cape Buffalo on safari in Africa, but it was his first End of Trail experience that he fondly calls "the greatest moment of my life". This transplant from southern California was born and reared in Houston, Texas, and served nine years in the Marine Corps. Supposedly in retirement now, he realizes he is finally doing his life's work, traveling extensively to SASS events around the world on behalf of the game and the organizations he started.

events that are part shootin' match, part re-enactment and part Wild West Show, folks of all ages, genders and walks of life come together from all over the world to celebrate the heroes and heroines of America's real and imaginary Old West.

JUDGE ROY BEAN 'N THE BOYS

The shooter picked off the bad men expertly but casually, like it was almost too easy. First with his single action revolver and then with an 1866 Winchester Yellowboy Carbine, he drew fine beads on the obnoxious outlaws through three Saturday afternoon TV Western movies. From the comfort and safety of his living room, Southern California businessman Harper Creigh kept the bad guys off Roy Rogers' back, saved the heroes of a mountain-man movie and battled *banditos* alongside The Wild Bunch. This was back in 1981, when Creigh owned an architectural model-making firm. Firearms, shooting and Western movies offered relief from his tedious, demanding profession. Afternoons spent on these rigorous sight acquisition exercises rendered Creigh an epiphany of sorts. He envisioned action shooting matches

ABOVE. *SASS Founding Father Harper* **Judge Roy Bean** *Creigh sits on the porch of the "Jersey Lily" at End of Trail 2000. More than most cowboy actioneers, "The Judge" personifies his alter ego.*

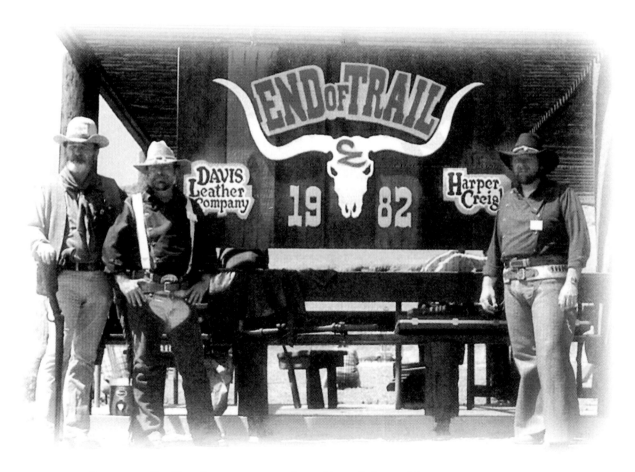

ABOVE. *Buckles, firearms, gear and trophies, all donated by supporting sponsors, are the grand prizes competitors shoot for in Cowboy/Western Action Shooting.*

SHOOTERS HANDBOOK

EIGHTH EDITION
July, 1999
© COPYRIGHT 1987, 1989, 1992, 1995, 1996, 1997, 1999
Single Action Shooting Society®, Inc.
All Rights Reserved

ABOVE. *The 43-page SASS Shooter's Handbook contains the philosophy and rules governing SASS-sanctioned matches and events.*

much like the popular International Practical Shooting Confederation (IPSC) style of shooting enjoyed by many wild west aficionados, complete with the guns of the Old West and dressed in cowboy gear.

"All my shootin' buddies had these old guns around, we just never shot 'em much anymore", says Creigh. "It seemed like a fun idea for a shootin' match." Like Owen Wister, he couldn't have known what he was starting, but he was about to learn. The time had come for his "fun idea" to become reality. He telephoned fellow shooter and Western History enthusiast Gordon Davis about his ideas for a shooting match. Davis, an internationally known holster and saddle maker, was excited about the match and helped Creigh decide upon some basic rules of engagement. The most important of these was the stipulation that all firearms used must have been generally available to the cowboys and frontier folk during the last half of the 19th century. It was further ordained that all shooters must wear Old West outfits of the period and shoot lead ammunition at steel reactive targets using legal firearms. These included single action revolvers, Derringers, single-shot or lever-action rifles and appropriate shotguns. No "race guns", laser sights, running shoes, T shirts or baseball caps were allowed.

Creigh and Davis gathered a dozen or so pals for a weekend shoot, but were rained out. Their enthusiasm wasn't dampened, however, and they retired to nearby Coto de Caza (CA) to slake their thirst and make plans for another match. So it was that the world's first Cowboy Action Match was held there in the fall of 1981. Creigh, Davis and the other men—all destined to become famous for their new sport—were joined by 20 or so other shooters. They blazed away all day and had such a good time that nobody can recall who won. "Most of us were in

Levis and snap button shirts," Creigh remembers, "but a couple of folks showed up in chaps n' spurs n' full cowboy gear! We all just shot whatever we brought—.38's, .30-.30s, .44s, everything old time. Boy, was it fun!"

The seed of Harper Creigh's idea was nourished occasionally by similar cowboy matches until March, 1982, when he was seized by yet another stroke of genius. Creigh had just attended his first *Mountain Man*, or *Buckskinner Rendezvous*, and had come away completely charmed. "There were clubs for Civil War re-enactors, muzzle-loader clubs for students of the early 19th century and, of course, many kinds of modern firearms and target shooting organizations," he recalls. "The Society for *Creative Anachronism* re-enacts the medieval period, but there was nothing for us American cowboys who wanted to shoot for fun with a frontier gun. So right then, I decided to start one."

Harper Creigh started more than a shooting match—and even more than a shooting club. He started a whole movement and a shooting sport phenomena, aided and abetted by the Founding Fathers of Cowboy Action Shooting. Gordon Davis was recruited once again, joined by Marine Captain Bill Hahn, IPSC Champion Jerry Usher and the chief executive of EMF Arms Company, Boyd Davis. This formidable five, among others, conceived and produced the first Cowboy Action matches and the first World Championship of Cowboy Action Shooting, known as "End of Trail."

"I came up with that name," Creigh explains, "and Bill Hahn designed, built and handled all the artwork and such for the sets and props."

Creigh is quick to acknowledge the efforts of many others who contributed to the rearing of his brainchild, which doubtless would have died aborning without a dedicated Board of Directors. "We (i.e., the Board) were given the name 'The

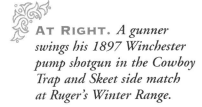**AT LEFT.** *Volunteers of the Arizona Territorial Company of Rough Riders built this humorous set with its false front for the National Championships at Ruger's Winter Range '99.*

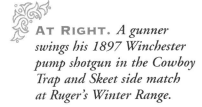**AT RIGHT.** *A gunner swings his 1897 Winchester pump shotgun in the Cowboy Trap and Skeet side match at Ruger's Winter Range.*

ABOVE. *Proper eye protection is mandated by all Cowboy/Western Action Shooting organizations. Ear protection is also strongly recommended.*

Wild Bunch' at 'End of Trail '86," Creigh recalls. "I set up a team event of 75 targets, and the only rule was that they all had to be knocked down safely. I called the stage, 'The Wild Bunch'. After every team had shot the stage, the shooters all insisted that the Board of Directors shoot it, too. Well, we did, and we won the event. Some wag yelled out 'The Wild Bunch has won the Wild Bunch shoot,' and the name stuck."

By 1988, Creigh and Boyd Davis were the only original board members still serving, but by then the sport had grown large enough to require a governing body. In 1989, the nine-member Wild Bunch organized the Single Action Shooting Society (SASS), with Harper Creigh assigned

SASS badge Number One. Choosing his registered alias to honor the hero of his favorite film, Creigh became his alterego: *Judge Roy Bean.*

As the number of SASS affiliated local clubs grew, so did the need for local representation in the development of match and club rules and policy. This led to the creation of the Territorial Governors, who were elected from among the members of local SASS clubs. A consensus of this august body is required in order to effect changes in SASS rules. With over 250 local SASS clubs at this writing, consensus is not always easily achieved.

SASS members are informed, advised and entertained bi-monthly by *The Cowboy Chronicle,*

ABOVE. *Misses are counted by the timer. OWSA Shootout on the Santa Fe Trail, NRA Whittington Center, Raton NM.*

the journal of the Single Action Shooting Society. Much more than a clubby newspaper, *"The Chronicle"* has become an institution to its thousands of readers, many of whom first learned about the Cowboy Action movement from its pages. Virtually all the major related businesses now advertize in *The Cowboy Chronicle*, whose readers have come to trust its recommendations and reportage. The SASS publications staff also produces the *SASS Rule Book, End of Trail* publications and the *Territorial Governor Bulletin.* Many cowboy actioneers learn about the sport from the SASS Web Site (www.sassnet.com), which averages over a million visits a year. Cyber Space Cowboys (and girls) communicate and conspire via the SASS Bulletin Board, which further promotes fellowship and membership growth. Since *The Judge* and his co-founding fathers started the Single Action Shooting Society, the organization has grown to over 30,000 members in all 50 states and 18 foreign countries. Hundreds of membership applications and requests for new local club start-ups pour in to SASS headquarters monthly.

In response to the game's mushrooming popularity, SASS expanded its national Cowboy Action Shooting Championship program in 1999 to include seven SASS regional events: Northwest, Southwest, High Plains, South-Central, Midwest, Northeast and Southeast. This annual cycle of matches begins in May in Gainseville, Georgia, with the Southeast Regional, known as "The Shootout at Mule Camp." The Winter Range National Championships are held in February at Phoenix, Arizona, and the year ends in April with the World Championships in Norco (CA) at Colt's End of Trail.

Called by gun and outdoor writers and the shooting industry, "The fastest growing shooting sport in the country," Cowboy Action Shooting— or Western Action Shooting, as it is sometimes called by other organizations—now influences

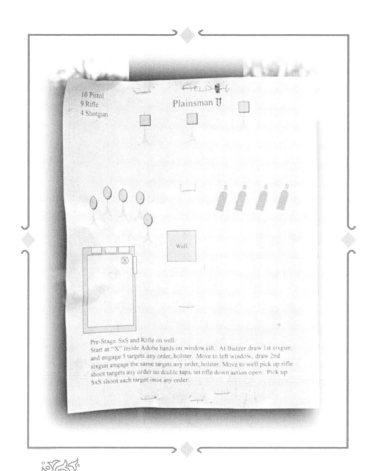

ABOVE. *In this posted Plainsman Side Match scenario, shooters must memorize the instructions before shooting the stage.*

whole industries in the areas of fashion, firearms, ammunition and related items. With the sponsorship of major players throughout the industry, End of Trail has matured into one of the premier shooting matches in the world. "To keep the game from getting too serious, we require period clothing and gear and the use of aliases," says Harper Creigh. Humor is a major component of this relaxing and therapeutic game and central to its burgeoning popularity. It was decided early on that no money would ever be awarded at the End of Trail World Championships or other SASS sanctioned matches. This was surely "Judge Bean's" most Solomon-like decision.

Since that Saturday afternoon two decades ago, the Father of Cowboy Action Shooting has helped guide the growth of his brainchild into maturity and a new century. It's important to him that his creation remain the safe, fun-filled and educational amateur family recreation that he helped design. While the shooting match remains the nucleus of a Cowboy or Western Action event, and whereas the old-time firearms are first-rate fun for serious (and not-so-serious) competitors, Cowboy Actioneering encompasses many other activities representing a critically important and deeply held Western philosophy—the Cowboy Way, the Code of the West, the Spirit of the Game. These qualities represent Harper Creigh's philosophy and the guiding principle of Cowboy Actioneers. May it always be so.

"The hardest part is keeping it pure and honest," says Judge Roy Bean, sounding vaguely like Paul Newman, "...'n runnin' off the cheaters n' complainers. A few years ago, somebody called me 'The Conscience of Cowboy Action Shooting'. It's a hair shirt I wear proudly, because I feel that Cowboy Action Shooting is my child and I want it to grow straight and true. With all the great godfathers and godmothers it has, it can't go any other way."

THEM'S THE RULES!

The SASS Handbook, which is updated periodically by the Territorial Governors, contains the current rules for SASS-sanctioned Cowboy Action matches, both Ground and Mounted. The rules, which are all equally important, are too numerous for listing individually. The discussion here is philosophical, its intent solely meant to inspire in shooters a desire to read and consider with care the rules of Cowboy/Western Action Shooting, including its organization and events. Ignorance of the rules, as any Range Officer or competitor will tell you, is no excuse for breaking them. The first concern of the rules, of course, is **safety**. Except for Cowboy Mounted Shooting, in

which only blackpowder blanks are used, Cowboy Action Shooting is carried on with live ammunition (see also the section on Mounted Shooting). No breach of safety regulations is ever tolerated. The SASS Handbook quite correctly begins its rules section with a critical paragraph entitled: *The Spirit of the Game*

> *"As the game of Cowboy Action Shooting has evolved, our members have developed and adopted a certain attitude towards their participation that we call The Spirit of the Game. Competing in these games requires the shooter to participate fully in what the competition asks. Participants do not look for ways to create advantages from what is, or is not, stated as a rule or shooting procedure. Some would call The Spirit of the Game nothing more than good sportsmanship. Whatever you call it, if you don't have it, Cowboy Action Shooting is not your game."*

The Handbook continues with an egregious example of failing to play in *The Spirit of the Game,* or what we call *Failure to Engage.* A failure to engage occurs when a competitor willfully or intentionally disregards the stage instructions in order to obtain a competitive advantage (i.e., taking the penalty would result in a lower score or faster time than following the instructions). In such cases, in addition to any procedural penalty and penalties from misses, a 15-second "failure to engage" penalty may also be assessed.

For example, a shooting problem at a club match called for the competitor to start the stage by knocking over a "stick of dynamite" with a bullwhip. This procedure required swinging the whip across a dynamite stick just a few feet away. It was impossible to miss, but many did. They had to keep swinging until they got the dynamite. One shooter, who decided he could shave some time by taking a penalty rather than trying to knock over

✦ ABOVE. *Loading and unloading tables can be plain or elaborate structures, similar to this one at Colt's End of Trail.*

the dynamite, simply threw the bullwhip to the ground and went after the targets. In Cowboy Action Shooting we call this *Failure to Engage*. It definitely is not in keeping with the *Spirit of the Game*.

As the old saying goes: "Cheaters never win and winners never cheat". In Cowboy Actioneering, as in life, attitude is everything. This spirit involves more than simply not cheating or manipulating the rules to "get an edge" on the competition. The *Spirit of the Game* means helping to run stages when you're not shooting, loaning equipment to fellow shooters in need and cheerfully abiding by the calls of the officials. It's the soul of Cowboy Action Shooting.

SAFETY: FIRST, LAST AND ALWAYS!

The model for the rules of virtually all Cowboy and Western Action Shooting organizations is the SASS Shooter's Handbook. It lists 30 distinct rules regarding safety, all critically important. No shooter should enter any event without first reading and understanding all the rules governing the competition. According to the Handbook, "Our sport, by its very nature, has the potential to be dangerous. However, the history of SASS affiliated matches is free of any serious accident."

This happy circumstance is due largely to the fact that all participants in Cowboy Action matches are required to take the role of a safety officer and be responsible for their own actions as well as any unsafe behavior by other shooters. As the Handbook states: "Any range officer or shooter may confront any participant about an observed unsafe situation, and it is expected the matter will quickly be corrected and not repeated. Any argument by any shooter concerning the correction of a safety related matter can be expected to result in that shooter's ejection from the range."

Here, then, are the safety rules to which all shooters must adhere at all times:

1. Treat and respect every firearm at all times as if it were loaded.

2. All firearms will remain unloaded except while you are under the direct observation of a range officer on the firing line or in the loading area.

3. All loading and unloading will be conducted only in the designated areas. NOTE: Percussion revolver shooters must exercise care to ensure that they maintain safe muzzle direction during loading and have fired or cleared all capped chambers prior to leaving the unloading area.

4. Six-guns are always loaded with only five rounds (five shooters with four), the hammer lowered and left resting on the empty chamber.

5. Long guns will have their actions open with chambers and magazines empty and muzzles pointed in a safe direction when being carried to and from the designated loading and unloading areas for each range. Chambers and magazines must be empty and actions open for all firearms transported in gun carts.

6. Long guns will have their actions left open and the magazine/barrels empty at the conclusion of each shooting string (i.e., whenever the gun leaves the shooter's hands during or at the end of a stage).

7. Rifles may be "staged" down range from the shooter with the magazine loaded, the action closed, hammer down and chamber empty.

8. Shotguns are always "staged" open with magazine and chambers empty and are loaded on the clock unless the stage is begun with the shotgun in the shooter's hands. It is permissible for mule-eared, (exposed hammer) shotguns to be "cocked" at the beginning of a scenario, whether staged or in the shooters hands.

AT LEFT. *Percussion and black powder cartridge revolvers are loaded at an End of Trail loading table. Percussion pistol shooters may cap only five loaded chambers, leaving the hammer down on the uncapped chamber.*

AT RIGHT. *A shooter loads under the supervision of a Range Officer. He cannot leave the table until called to shoot the stage.*

ABOVE. *Claudia Feather unloads at the unloading table after completion of a stage. Range Officer Mountain Lady watches. All firearms are inspected and no shooter may leave the firing line until all firearms are emptied and inspected by an RO.*

9. Handguns are returned to leather (re-holstered) with hammer down on a spent case at the conclusion of the gun's immediate use, unless the shooter has been specifically directed otherwise. There can be no live rounds in the pistol when reholstering. For example, when changing from handgun to rifle in a two-gun stage, the handgun will be holstered before the rifle is picked up.

10. All shooters must demonstrate rudimentary familiarity and proficiency with the firearms being used. SASS matches are not the forum in which to learn basic firearms handling.

11. Alcoholic beverages are prohibited in the range area for all persons, shooters, guests, range officers, and others, until the range is closed and shooting is done for the day.

12. No shooter will consume any alcoholic beverage until he or she has completed all shooting for the day and stored all of their firearms.

13. No shooter will ingest any substance that may affect his or her ability to participate with a maximum state of awareness and in a completely safe manner. Both prescription and non-prescription pharmaceuticals that may cause drowsiness or any other physical or mental impairment must be avoided.

14. Eye and hearing protection must be worn by all competitors when in the loading area or on the firing line. Such protection is recommended for everyone when in the range area, and eye protection is **mandatory** for spectators when within direct line of sight of steel targets.

15. SASS affiliated matches **are not** fast draw competitions. Any unsafe gun handling in the course of a draw from the holster or any "fanning" will result in the disqualification of the shooter from that stage. "Slip-hammering" is not the same as fanning and is legal.

16. Although cross-draw holsters are legal, they represent a significant safety concern. Cross-draws may not depart from the vertical by more than 30 degrees. Extreme care must be exercised when drawing a firearm from a cross-draw holster or returning the firearm to leather. Users must twist their bodies to ensure the muzzle never breaks the 170 degree safety rule during the process. Failure to ensure the muzzle is always down range is grounds for an immediate stage disqualification. A second infraction during the same match is grounds for match disqualification. (Note: The 170-degree safety rule means the muzzle of the firearm must always be straight down range +/- 85 degrees. If a competitor even comes close to breaking the 180-degree safety plane, the 170-degree safety rule has been violated, and the competitor is at fault.)

17. Holsters must be located on each side of the belly button and separated by at least the width of two fists.

18. No cocked revolver may ever leave a shooter's hand.

19. When changing location during a stage, all firearms being carried must either have the hammer down on an empty chamber or spent case, or have the action open.

20. Shooters are expected to perform within their capabilities at all times, with particular concern about controlling the muzzle direction of the firearms being used. The shooter must never violate the "170-degree safety rule."

21. A dropped gun will result in the shooter's disqualification from the stage and, perhaps, from the match, depending upon local match rules. A "juggled" gun that breaks the 170-degree safety rule will result in a disqualification. A shooter may not pick up a dropped gun. The range officer will recover the gun, examine it, clear it, and return it to the shooter.

22. The shooter will not cock his revolver until the firearm is pointed safely down range. Any

ABOVE. *A timer indicates a shooter's time to a posse member who is keeping score. Decisions of the officials are final and arguing with Range Officers is grounds for ejection from the match.*

ABOVE. *A scorekeeper fills out a shooter's score card at Ruger's Winter Range. Scorecards are more than records; they identify the competitor for door prizes and other benefits.*

Our Cowboys Have Always Been Heroes **29**

accidental or premature discharge of any firearm determined by the range officer to be unsafe will result in the shooter incurring a safety penalty, disqualification from the stage, or disqualification from the match. A second such incident on the same day shall certainly result in the shooter's ejection from the match. A safe practice is to develop the habit of cocking handguns with the "weak" or off-hand after the gun has cleared leather and is pointed safely down range.

23. Ammunition dropped by a shooter in the course of reloading any firearm during a stage is considered "dead" and may not be recovered until the shooter completes the course of fire. For example, if a round of shotgun ammo is dropped while reloading, the round must be replaced from the shooter's person or counted as a missed shot. No attempt may be made by the shooter to pick up the dropped round, as to do so prompts loss of control of muzzle direction.

24. Shooting ammo with a muzzle velocity greater than stated within this handbook is grounds for immediate disqualification from a match.

25. It is expected the range officers will be the responsible parties for observing and resolving all safety related matters occurring in the loading, unloading, and firing line areas. However, any shooter who observes a safety infraction not seen by the range officer(s) should call the infraction to the range officer's attention, at which time the matter will be resolved.

ABOVE. *A posse shoots a Team stage at Colt's End of Trail as Range Officers watch. Note the large array of bowling pins that must be shot down in order to stop the clock.*

ABOVE. *A large posse begins a Team stage. When all targets are down, the team must shoot the star out of the target (upper right) before the clock will stop. It's more difficult than it looks.*

AT RIGHT.
The air is filled with blackpowder smoke as a posse shoots a Team stage at Colt's End of Trail. Note the fallen steel and bowling pins.

ABOVE. *A "mounted shooter" blazes away from the saddle at Colt's End of Trail.*

ABOVE. *SASS Wild Bunch member and editor of The Cowboy Chronicle, Don Tex Ormand, armed with an 1851 Navy Colt in each hand, shoots a Colt's End of Trail stage in gunfighter style.*

26. Minor safety infractions occurring during a course of fire that do not directly endanger persons will result in a ten-second penalty being added to the shooter's time for that stage. "Minor" safety infractions are occurrences such as an accidental discharge impacting within ten feet, but not closer than five feet, of the shooter and failure to open a long gun's action at the conclusion of a shooting string.

27. Major safety infractions will result in the shooter's disqualification from the stage or the match. A second major infraction in the match shall result in the shooter's ejection from the range. "Major" infractions are a dropped gun, an accidental discharge that impacts within five feet of any person, violation of the 170-degree safety rules, "sweeping" any person with the muzzle of a firearm, and similar acts that have high potential for personal injury.

28. Muzzle direction is important between, before, during and after shooting a stage. A muzzle must not be allowed to 'sweep' the other participants between stages or when moving the firearms to and from the gun cart. The muzzles of all long guns must be maintained in safe direction, even when returning to the unloading table. Failure to manage safe muzzle direction is grounds for disqualification from the stage and, for repeated offenses, from the match.

29. All firearms **MUST** be inspected by the unloading officer or range officer before leaving the shooting stage. All rifles must have their action cycled for the inspecting official. All six-guns, whether used or not in the stage, must also be inspected.

30. Only registered competitors may wear firearms.

Note: Other rules, such as those governing Mounted Shooting, Clothing and Accouterments, will be discussed in later chapters.

ABOVE. *Posse members prepare to shoot a team event that requires pistol, rifle and shotgun. Most Team stages afford the opportunity to use several guns.*

CHAPTER TWO

An illustrious posse from an early Winter Range National Championship sponsored by Ruger includes members of the Red Sash Cowboy gang from the film Tombstone.

AT RIGHT. *A stage set-up at the Shootout on the Santa Fe Trail (NM).*

THE WHOLE SHOOTIN' MATCH

From high on the driver's seat of the stagecoach, the scenery ahead looked lovely—until the robbers attacked. After that, the view was all to the rear. Turning to battle the bandits, Tutler plugged three of the thugs, but the six rounds it cost were the last in his Winchester. Meantime, five more outlaws were gaining ground and spreading out. It took all five .45's from Tutler's Colt Peacemaker to neutralize the ne'er-do-wells. Suddenly, the remaining four felons appeared at the side of the creaking Concord coach, certain of success. Tutler was still riding shotgun, but with only four 12 gauge "howdys!" left to defend against the masked marauders. Firing and reloading and firing again, Tutler luckily ran out of ammo and adversaries simultaneously. Quite literally, the stage was saved.

If that reads like a familiar scene from a John Wayne or other Western movie, you're close. It describes the scenario of a course of fire, or Stage, as they are called, from a recent Colt's End of Trail, the World Championships of Cowboy Action Shooting. The three gun 15-round course of fire took World Champion Tom "Tutler" Filbeck just 22.72 seconds, from the starter's beep to his last, clock-stopping shotgun shot. While not all stages utilize multiple firearms, most are designed to afford shooters the opportunity to shoot two or more 19th century firearms at reactive steel, and occasionally cardboard, balloon or clay targets.

It's the *action* in Cowboy Action Shooting that propels the perennial popularity and growth of this exciting game. Shooters face the same challenges of time, space and movement as in other action three-gun disciplines, but in difficult and usually humorous scenarios. These sometimes silly scenes are plagiarized from western movies, novels, documented history and/or the fertile imaginations of diabolical match officials.

At major Cowboy Action events like End of Trail and Ruger's Winter Range Nationals, stage configurations can rival the movie sets and props of Hollywood westerns. Shooting bays are disguised as saloon false fronts, adobe pueblos, mining operations and other frontier locales. Besides stagecoaches and celerity wagons, there are freight wagons and buckboards from

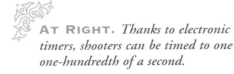

AT RIGHT. Thanks to electronic timers, shooters can be timed to one one-hundredth of a second.

ABOVE. Knockdown targets must be hit solidly and fall down completely or count as a miss. Ropes are pulled to re-set the targets after each shooter.

AT RIGHT. A shooter fights his way down a Colt's End of Trail stage. Range Officers and a timer follow to observe any errors and misses.

which to shoot over, around or under. Comical, old-time set decorations frequently interfere with one's concentration, while procedural instructions usually include reciting lines and performing distracting chores before, during or after a course of fire. Contestants may have to shoot from standing, kneeling, sitting and prone positions or any combination thereof. The stages may occasionally be simple, but they're never easy.

QUIET ON THE SET!

Imagine shooting a typical Stage scenario, with a couple of (real) dummies sitting around a poker table playing cards. A Derringer, a jigger of "whiskey" and saddlebags are among the props.

The Range Officer wants to know if you understand the course of fire.

"I do," you yell. But suddenly, you're not so sure.

"Is the shooter ready?" his voice sounds far away.

"I am!" you reply, hoping it's true.

There follows a moment of breathless silence while time stands still. Then **BEEP!** The electronic timer startles you, and for an instant your mind goes completely blank and your arms refuse to move. Then, somehow, you're galvanized into action.

"Yew varmints have cheated me fer the last time!" you holler, hurling the contents of a jigger into the face of a dummy. You grab your Derringer and shoot two paper targets attached to the dummies seated at the other side of the table. Drawing your six-gun, you shoot the next five outlaws (steel targets), 12 feet or so downrange. Holstering your pistol, you scoop up the money left on the table, stuff it in the saddlebags, bust through the swinging doors of the saloon, and throw the loot over the saddle of your plastic Paint pony. Drawing your rifle from its scabbard, you twice sweep the five "villains" (16-inch steel targets) who now threaten you from way

BRAD *HIPSHOT* MYERS SASS 7

Hipshot has been a Cowboy Action shooter for 19 years and , since 1988, Match Director of SASS End of Trail. He's a co-founder of SASS, a winner of the SASS Top Hand Award in 1992 and past president of the Coto Cowboys. Myers recently developed the SASS Supporting Dealer Program, a net work of firearms and clothing stores run by SASS members. These shops provide ideal points of contact for those interested in learning about Cowboy Action Shooting and events.

Hipshot is an original, one of the games earliest practioners. His avowed intent, he says, is to maintain the sport in the spirit in which it began. His wife, Blue Eyes, SASS 92 and daughter Jubilee Montana, SASS 888, participate with him in their cowboy lifestyle.

ABOVE. *Remembering that there's no such thing as a target too big or too close to miss, a Buffalo Soldier takes aim at Ruger's Winter Range targets with his nickel Peacemaker.*

off yonder. Replacing the long gun, you snatch up your shotgun, which is open and empty, leaning against the hitching post. You load it and engage the last four card sharps—all 10-inch, spring-loaded "pepper popper" targets—until they're all knocked down, stopping the clock.

Fun like that doesn't just happen. The Rules of the Game, legislated by the Territorial Governors, determine how and with what equipment the Cowboy Action game is played. Matches sanctioned by the SASS are governed by these rules, which are published in the organization's Handbook and issued to each new member along with his registered alias, SASS badge and number. The SASS Handbook details the following General Match Guidelines:

• *Electronic timing devices are recommended, but stop watches may also be used.*
• *Targets are set at close to medium range.*
• *Metal, paper and cardboard targets ("of generous size") are used. Rifles and shotguns may engage clay pigeons, while balloon targets are fun for Derringers at close range. Balloons are also ideal for Mounted Shooting stages. Reactive targets—including "pepper poppers" and falling plates—are used when practical to enhance shooter feedback and spectator appeal.*

The SASS handbook emphasizes another point central to the success of the sport: *Cowboy Action Shooting is not intended to be a precision shooting competition. . . . . . Small targets and long distances take the action out of the game and discourage newer shooters.*

All shooters want to hit their targets; some folks just hit (or miss) faster than others. The sport is designed to be safe fun, while at the same time developing proficiency with firearms. According to the SASS Handbook:

There's no such thing as a target too big or too close to miss!

(continued on p. 45)

GEORGE GLENN: FOUNDER OF NCOWS

George Glenn has been involved in various shooting sports for 40 years, primarily muzzleloading, buckskinning, Revolutionary War re-enactments, and most recently Western Action Shooting. In 1969, he founded a muzzleloading club, the Turkey Foot Longrifles, in Cedar Falls, Iowa.

When members of the TFL got wind of the new Western Action shooting game, it began hosting a bi-annual match, which proved quite popular. In the fall of 1993 Glenn proposed the formation of an organization that would combine the historical authenticity and accuracy of buckskinning and re-enactments with the excitement of Western Action Shooting and the romance of Period guns. Thus was the National Congress of Old West Shootists born.

Since every organization needs a newsletter or journal, Glenn started writing, editing and publishing NCOWS' official magazine, The Shootist. It was the first bi-monthly magazine devoted solely to Western Action shooting, with most articles, both fact and fiction, written by NCOWS members. A retired professor of theatre, Glenn resides in Cedar Falls, Iowa, with his wife, Sandra. Their grown children are all NCOWS members and are busily raising a third generation of Western Action Shooters.

ABOVE. *Each shooter uses three guns, with all shooting restricted to the driver's seat of the wagon.*

AT RIGHT. *At some shooting facilities, such as Arizona's Ben Avery Range, stages are set up side-by-side in large, open bays. This encourages lateral movement by shooters but precludes forward travel while shooting.*

ABOVE. *Stages and shooting bays are usually decorated with humorous Old West folk art as exemplified by the OWSS Shootout on the Santa Fe Trail.*

ABOVE. *The stage scorekeeper records all times and penalties for misses and procedural errors, etc., in the match book and each shooter's scorecard.*

Shooting ranges are different. No absolute rules are set down, but the Handbook suggests the following distances (assuming targets measure 16x16 inches).

- *Derringers & Pocket Pistols: point blank to three meters. Paper, cardboard or balloons only may be used (it's far too close for shooting steel targets).*
- *Revolver: 7 to 10 meters.*
- *Shotgun: 8 to 16 meters.*
- *Rifle: 13 to 50 meters.*
- *Decisions of the Range Master/ Match Director are final.*
- *Ammunition suspected of exceeding velocity restrictions stated herein may be examined by the Range Master, who has final authority in determining ammunition*

acceptability. Shooters may be held responsible for damages to targets or injuries to personnel due to bounce-back created by the use of illegal ammunition. This major safety violation is grounds for instant disqualification and ejection from the match.

- *Firearms of all approved types should be maintained in their original exterior condition as much as possible. No visible external modifications other than non-rubber grips, recoil pads on shotguns and leather wrapping (e.g., rifle levers) are allowed. Minor exterior modifications and cosmetic engravings are acceptable so long as the overall outward appearance of the firearm is not altered. The firearm must look "Period".*
- *Ammunition required for reloads during the course of any stage must be carried on the shooter's person*

ABOVE. *Five-time SASS World Champion Dennis China Camp Ming shoots a stage at Ruger's Winter Range National Championships.*

in a bandoleer, belt, pouch or pocket. Rifle and pistol ammunition may not be carried in a shotgun loop, nor in one's mouth, ears, nose, cleavage or any other bodily orifice.

- *Bandoleers, cartridge belts and pouches must be of traditional design. Modern drop pouches, "combat-style" shotgun loops, wrist or forearm bandoleers and such are not allowed. Pouches must carry their contents loose, with no special provisions for organizing their contents for rapid retrieval. Leather belt slide ammo loops are acceptable.*
- *Cartridge loops may not contain metal or plastic liners.*
- *Ammo belts must be worn around the waist, at or below the belly button.*
- *Shotgun ammo loops must conform to the shooter's contour and not tilt out from the belt for ease of retrieval.*
- *Cartridge loops mounted on a firearm's stock or forearm are not allowed.*

Finally, the SASS Handbook offers some general "Spirit of the Game" guidance: If you have to ask permission to use something simply because it offers a competitive advantage, the response will nearly always be "No!"

Within these guidelines, and depending upon the size and shape of the range and/or shooting bays, a large number of possible target arrays and scenario configurations are possible. Set pieces, target blinds and props are discretionary, with safety. as always, the sole overriding concern. Cleverly designed sets have an important function. Like the outfits worn by shooters and the old time guns themselves, they help create the fun and excitement of Cowboy Action Shooting.

RANGE AND SAFETY OFFICIALS

Since the safety of shooters and onlookers alike is the first and most stringent rule in Cowboy Action Shooting, each and every participant must become a safety officer. Behavior that is in any way

unsafe is grounds for immediate disqualification and/or dismissal. Each stage and side match has an "R.O." (Range Officer), whose word regarding safety, rules, regulations, timing and scoring disputes is absolutely final. In addition to being utterly futile, taking up arguments with the R.O. is considered very bad form and definitely not within the spirit of the game.

Competitors shoot stages grouped into teams called "Posses." Posse members volunteer to take on the duties of an R.O. by watching over the loading operations at the various stage loading tables, by operating the timer, by calling each shooter's order of fire, by keeping score, and by recording and supervising at the unloading table. Before a shooter can leave the firing line, all firearms must be cleared of ammunition.

Posses also shoot in team stages, i.e., they shoot at a field of targets simultaneously until they're all down. They may also fire at a single target, such as a thick log, until it is cut in two or demolished. Some team stages require that certain posse members be responsible for engaging specific targets in a certain order and with particular arms. Under such pressure, Posse members often form lifelong friendships—and it's enormous fun.

KEEPIN' SCORE

The 8th edition of the SASS Shooters Handbook states the following:

SASS matches are scored based upon elapsed shooting time and added penalty points, generally five seconds, for missed targets."

Additional penalties may be added for Procedural errors and omissions, such as failure to engage a target, to speak a line of dialogue correctly, or to follow stage instructions explicitly.

Each stage is scored individually and, in most club matches, the total combined score for all stages fired is ranked for place of finish, either overall or by category.

 **AT RIGHT.**
A stage at a shootout on the Santa Fe Trail is typical of the Old West Shootist Society's annual match in New Mexico. Note the range officer's extended index finger indicating the shooter has one miss.

ABOVE. *A shooter reloads his 1873 Trapdoor Springfield .45-70 carbine under the timer at Colt's End of Trail.*

At End of Trail, and at the discretion of each affiliated club, rank scoring is used. Here, each stage is ranked for each competitor's place of finish. At the conclusion of the match, a combined total for each competitor is ranked for an overall place of finish. For example, if one's place of finish in stage one is 23, stage two is 12, stage three is 5, and stage four is 33, the total rank score adds up to 73. All competitors with lower total rank scores will finish ahead of that competitor. Rank scoring is recommended when all stages in a match vary according to duration and degree of difficulty.

SIDE MATCHES
Special Events for Special Guns

In addition to the main match consisting of several stages, many local and virtually all regional and championship events offer special side matches for special firearms deemed inappropriate for use in the main match. These matches are usually conducted on separate days, generally before the Main Match of an event. As defined by the SASS Rule Book, side matches consist of:

THE PLAINSMAN

This event requires two SASS legal "traditional-style" percussion (cap & ball) revolvers, fired one-handed and unsupported. Also permitted are SASS-sanctioned single-shot rifles firing a traditional blackpowder cartridge (e.g., .45-70, not .30-30). The cartridges may be either rifle or pistol caliber, the former with spring-actuated ejectors (assuming they are standard for that rifle). Also required is an SASS legal blackpowder shotgun (side by side, with or without exposed hammers, or with lever action). In addition, blackpowder must be used in all loads (rifle, pistol and shotgun).

POCKET PISTOLS AND DERRINGERS

Pocket pistols and derringers have become popular for use in side matches and are occasionally introduced as additional firearms in main match

ABOVE. *This small but elite posse at Colt's End of Trail includes, from left: Bad As Bob, Lady L'Amour, The Governor, Mesa and the author.*

AT RIGHT.
*Saloon Sal makes a badman pay dearly for abusing a lady in this scene recreated from the film **The Unforgiven**.*

ABOVE. *A dozen or so sculptured bronze trophies await the winners of Colt's End of Trail. No money is ever awarded at SASS-sanctioned shooting events.*

stages. A pocket pistol is defined as a small frame, single or double action revolver of a design made prior to 1890 and possessing a barrel less than 4" in length. It must be at least .31 caliber. Model "P" Colts (and their reproductions) are not included in this definition. A Derringer is defined as a breechloading, small frame firearm available with one to four fixed, short barrels. The Remington-style over/under and Sharps' four-barrel pepper box are typical. Derringers are considered legal in calibers as small as .22 rimfire.

LONG RANGE
(OR PRECISION) RIFLES

The competitor may use any tube-fed, lever action or single shot rifle manufactured before 1896, or any reproduction thereof. All rifles must have external hammers and iron sights (mounted as on the original rifle) or tang-mounted peep sights. Optical and receiver mounted sights are not allowed. Typically, four categories in Long Range or Precision Rifle are permitted: single shot, lever action (rifle caliber), lever action (pistol caliber) and buffalo single shot.

Other categories may be added to any or all of the above at the option of the match director. Each category should compete within itself.

SHOOTER CATAGORIES & ARMS

Cowboy Actioneers are as individual in their taste in firearms and ammunition as they are in their selected Cowboy Action personas and preferred shooting styles. SASS and other Western Action Shooting organizations recognize this

ABOVE. *Three happy Cowboy Actioneers—Jim "William Bruce" Rodgers, John "Bronc" Peel and William "Billy Concho" Lang—proudly display their winnings at Colt's End of Trail.*

The Whole Shootin' Match **51**

ABOVE. *Jerry James Butler Tarantino carries away the magnificent bronze trophy he won at the 1996 World Championship of the Cowboy Mounted Shooters Association.*

ABOVE. *Denise "Darn It" Darr, who competes successfully in ground and mounted shooting events, poses with her 1998 SASS Top Hand Mounted Shooter award and buckle.*

The Whole Shootin' Match **53**

ABOVE. *Five-time SASS World Champion Cowboy Action shooter Dennis "China Camp" Ming shows off his 1996 trophy.*

Western personality trait and accommodate it by offering multiple classes or categories in which to compete. From the SASS Shooters Handbook:

Cowboy Action Shooters are divided into six basic categories: Traditional, Modern, Frontier (blackpowder) Cartridge, Frontiersman, Duelist and Gunfighter. A shooter's category is determined by the type of six-gun used, its propellant and shooting style.

The following is an overview of the classes:

Traditional Revolvers: These are defined by the Handbook as single action cartridge, percussion revolvers, or blackpowder cartridge conversion types manufactured prior to 1896, or reproductions thereof. Its sights are not adjustable and shooters may elect to use the classic one-handed or duelist style, or the less romantic but probably more accurate two-handed, or "Squaw" hold.

Modern is the category defined by the Handbook as: *Any single action cartridge revolver of at least .32 caliber and having adjustable sights. Again, the shooter may employ one or both hands.*

Frontier Cartridge is a blackpowder category, using "Traditional Style percussion or cartridge single action revolvers of original manufacture prior to 1896, or reproductions thereof."

Frontiersman shooters must use percussion (cap and ball) revolvers of .36 caliber or better, with blackpowder used in rifle and shotgun as well.

Duelist class, according to the Handbook, requires the following: *An SASS-legal Traditional Style single action revolver. Any propellant, (blackpowder or smokeless) may be used.* The important distinction here is that *the pistol **must be cocked and fired one-handed** and unsupported. The revolver, hand, or shooting arm may not be touched by the off hand.*

Gunfighter is a class designed for skillful veteran shooters. Novice shooters need not apply. Considered the apex of authenticity and frontier

style, this colorful category is sometimes called "Double Duelist." According to the SASS Handbook, it requires the following: *Two SASS legal Traditional Style single action revolvers, both shot Duelist style, one right-handed and one left-handed.*

COWKIDS, "WIMMIN FOLK" AND OLD TIMERS

Without obligation to do so, any match may define additional shooting categories for women, junior and senior competitors. So claims the SASS Handbook. These categories incorporate the following standards:

Juniors are defined as those competitors aged 12 through 16. This class may also be divided by gender.

Women may be subdivided further by shooting classes, such as Traditional or Modern; for example, "Lady Duelist" or "Lady Traditional".

SENIOR are defined as those shooters who have passed their 60th birthday. It's considered a very difficult class in which to compete. In addition, the **Elder Statesman** or **Woman** category honors and welcomes competitors 70 years young or over.

Overall, Cowboy Action Shooting is designed to provide safe fun and frontier excitement for all shooting styles and age levels using the great guns of the Old West.

PRIZES 'N PLUNDER

Since no cash prizes or other financial reward are offered at SASS matches, the awards for winning a match or any class, category or section thereof, include firearms and equipment, trophies, plaques, belt buckles and the like, many of which are donated by generous sponsors. And, of course, there are braggin' rights.

While it's true that many of the firearms offered as prizes are quite valuable, as are the sculptured trophies, gun leather, gun cases, ammunition and

The Tally Book™

$6.00

A Publication of
The National Congress of Old West Shootists, Inc.

ABOVE. *The Tally Book contains all the rules and regulations of the National Congress Of Western Shootists (NCOWS).*

ABOVE. *Ted "Coosie" Wolff waits for the timer's beep to begin shooting a Railhead stage, near Williams (AZ). Shooters who start with their backs to the targets must turn completely around before drawing a pistol.*

clothing so highly sought after. They are, after all, good incentives to shoot your best and try your hardest. Cowboy Action Shooting is an amateur game meant for family participation. What members really shoot for is fun and the fellowship of others who share a love of the shooting sports and the Old West.

While the Single Action Shooting Society was the first of such organizations, the appeal and popularity of the sport and its lifestyle have become so widespread, and the possible approaches to the game so varied, that other national and local clubs were bound to form around the original SASS design, albeit with certain philosophical differences.

Principal among these is the *National Congress of Old West Shootists (NCOWS)*, a largely Mid-Western organization headquartered in Cedar Falls, Iowa. It was founded in 1994 by George Glenn, a professor of theater at the University of Northern Iowa with 40 years of shooting experience. There he assembled a group of other veterans of muzzleloading, buckskinning, historical re-enacting and modern shooting disciplines. NCOWS differs from other organizations mainly in that it insists upon higher levels of authenticity in all of its activities, but without the use of aliases (although they may be used by members, if desired).

NCOWS has grown steadily since its inception and membership at this writing stands at better

ABOVE. *The NRA Whittington Center, near Raton, New Mexico, is the greatest shooting sports facility in the world and home of the Old West Shootist Association annual championships.*

than a thousand shootists. Many Cowboy/ Western Action shooters belong to both SASS and NCOWS, as well as local clubs and organizations. Member benefits include a subscription to *The Shootist*, the official bi-monthly publication of NCOWS and another creation of Professor Glenn, the magazine's editor and publisher since its first issue appeared in 1994. Most of the articles, both fact and fiction, are written by NCOWS members.

The *Tally Book* is NCOWS' official book of rules and regulations, including full details on safety, appropriate firearms, clothing and equipage. The organization's new member package even includes a handy illustrated guide to its period (1865 through 1900), along with haberdashery, hats, footwear and accessories. A short list of suppliers and purveyors of frontier provisions is included.

Officers are elected annually at the NCOWS Annual Convention and the Old West Show and Sale. Held in Des Moines, Iowa, in February, the event is hosted by NCOWS first Posse (NCOWS local clubs are called Posses), called the *Fort Des Moines Rangers*. The lingo and terminology used by SASS and NCOWS are much the same, with occasional variances in the names of shooting classes and categories. The show and sale draw visitors, venders and collectors from around the country, and the event grows larger each year.

NCOWS' national competitions take place at the Prairie Fire Range, near Ackley, Iowa. In 1996, NCOWS began a Western Action shooting complex from scratch, intending to make the 400-acre range its permanent home. Local clubs host monthly matches in several western and midwestern states.

"NCOWS is meant as a parallel alternative to SASS", says founder George Glenn. "Like SASS, we do what we can to promote the growth and development of Cowboy or Western Action Shooting which, after all, had its origins with the founders of SASS. We present NCOWS as an alternative organization for those who desire a greater level of historical authenticity and member involvement in governance. We encourage all NCOWS members to support SASS and all other legitimate shooting sports organizations."

Glenn points out other differences between the two sanctioning bodies, including penalties for missing targets. "We try to encourage accuracy by assessing 10-second penalties for misses, instead of five. And our rules regarding historical correctness are fairly rigid. We feel it's easier to relax rules than to tighten them after they're in place."

NCOWS appeals to those *occihistoriophiles* for whom "B Westerns" and black and white TV shows from the 50s hold little fascination. They do, however, love the real history along with the authentic guns and regalia of the Old West. And like SASS, they're a patriotic bunch. "Since its inception," Glenn adds, "NCOWS has been a charter organization of the National Rifle Association and strongly urges every NCOWS member and all other shooters to join the NRA."

COWBOY ACTION ON THE TRAIL

Another Cowboy Action Shooting organization bears mention here: the *Old West Shootist Society, (OWSS)*. Hardly the tightly organized outfit that SASS or NCOWS are, it staged its first Western Action Shooting event in 1986 at Cowtown, near Phoenix, Arizona. An offshoot of SASS, but with a different philosophy regarding the staging of events and competitions, OWSS was started by Bill Hahn, a retired Marine Captain. He, along with Harper Creigh, Gordon Davis and Boyd Davis, had helped create Cowboy Action Shooting, but their ideas about the sport were all their own. If the shooting matches are the nucleus around which all the other cowboy actioneering activities are staged by SASS and others, they are the single reason for the two matches Bill Hahn and his OWSS outfit put on each year.

Trailtown is a 10-stage match on the Pala Reservation, located near Tumecula, California, but The Shootout on the Santa Fe Trail is the main reason for the group's existence. This incredible event takes place at a range facility acknowledged to be the finest in the world: The NRA Whittington Center, near Raton, New Mexico. The OWSS Shootout actually happens in shooting bays at the edge of the historic Santa Fe Trail. Many shooters avail themselves of the opportunity to walk along the Trail, perhaps contemplating this wondrous heritage as they behold the vistas of the Southwest, much as the pioneers had.

The Shootout is just that: a Western Action shootin' match in the signature style of Bill *Moss Horn* Hahn. Hahn comes by his love of the Old West naturally. He was born in Witchita, Kansas, and raised in Dodge City. His philosophy is simply stated: "Our goals are safety, fun and more bang for the buck. We don't offer all the social and entertainment attractions of the big SASS events, and we charge roughly 25 percent of their entry fees." Hahn says his loosely knit Society has a nine-member Board of Directors who meet annually at the Raton match "...four days early, to set up the match." He praises the Whittington Center and the beautiful, natural setting. Still, it's the match Bill and his colleagues are most proud of, and they have every right to be.

"We only shoot one handgun, Hahn points out, "so there's less shooting per stage—but we shoot more stages." "More stages" is a huge understatement. In the year 2000, the Shootout on the Santa Fe Trail consisted of no less than 70 main match stages, 28 side matches and 10 different team matches! The shooter entry fee for such week-long fun and Old West excitement cam to $45.70 for the first shooter and $32.20 for the "significant other" second shooter. How does one become an OWSS member? By shooting the Shootout on the Santa Fe Trail. After that, you're in for good. ♣

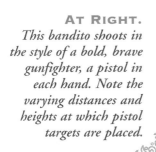

AT RIGHT.
This bandito shoots in the style of a bold, brave gunfighter, a pistol in each hand. Note the varying distances and heights at which pistol targets are placed.

Chapter Three

ABOVE. *In 1830, when he was a young man at sea, Samuel Colt carved these wooden parts. They are the first prototypical evidence of the legendary Colt revolvers which later revolutionized the firearms industry.*

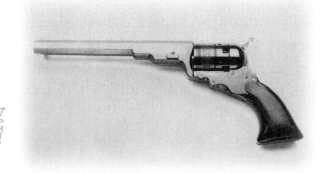

AT RIGHT. *Paterson Holster Model with charcoal blue finish*

Old Guns Win the New West: A Colt Chronology

itting on the deck of the brig Corvo in 1830, young Sam Colt could not have known that the wooden cylinder and hammer he was whittling would one day profoundly influence the course of history. In 1830 there was no firearm on earth anything like the one Colt carved from his imagination, but 17 years later, in 1847, Colt's designs for multi-firing, revolving cylinder pistols began to revolutionize the arms industry. Proven in combat against General Santa Ana and the Commanches, Colt Patterson revolvers rapidly replaced the single shot flintlock and percussion pistols for both civilian and military use.

For 1847 was the year of the Walker Colt, the first in the series of sixguns by Colt. The Walker Colt and successive generations of the revolvers it spawned have served armies and private citizens around the world and are now the basic firearms of the Single Action Shooting Society and similar Cowboy Action clubs.

It is the Walker Colt, (named for Captain Samuel H. Walker, a Texas Ranger, hero of the above conflicts and designer, with Colt, of his namesake hand-cannon), that first assumes that romantically fluid form finally finding full flower in the Single Action Army. The 4-pound, 9-ounce behemoth fired six .44 caliber lead balls from its nine-inch barrel with enormous energy and utilized the trigger guard and cam-and-lever loading rod that Capt. Walker wisely required. A huge improvement over the light caliber, five-shot Patterson model, it was the largest and most powerful pistol Colt ever made and, in fact, the most powerful

handgun in the world, until the advent of the Magnums a century later.

So call the Walker Colt 'Grandfather'; the progenitor of the clan, the once and always smoke wagon, the original six-shooter. Sam Walker, the hero of the battle of Huamantla, died shooting SASS Gunfighter style, a Sam Colt Walker model in each hand. In Larry McMurtry's *Lonesome Dove*, Augustus McCrae appropriately carries a Walker Colt. Heroes, real or mythical, deserve a pistol of heroic proportions.

The success of the Walker Colt bred the so-called Transition Walker and then the Dragoon models. These were .44 caliber like the Walker, but with 7.5 instead of 9-inch barrels, and were lighter. Colt continued to fine tune his revolvers' designs through the Dragoons and then began his first line of pocket and belt pistols with which to equip virtually everyone. America was Manifesting its Destiny all over the West,

(continued on p.67)

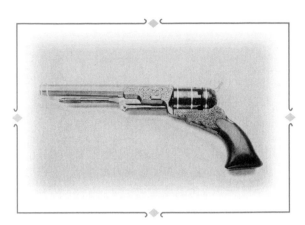

AT RIGHT. *Paterson Texas -with silver engravings*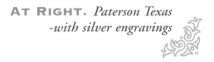

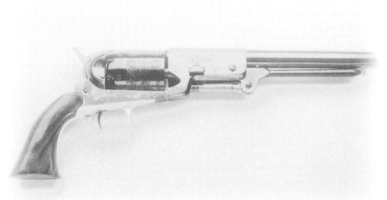

 **AT LEFT.** *Walker*

AT RIGHT. *Dragoon 1st Model*

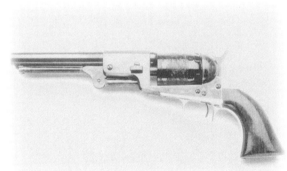

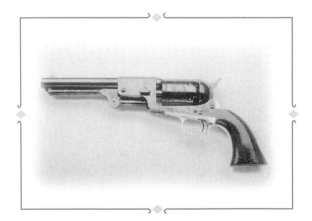

 AT LEFT. *Dragoon 2nd Model*

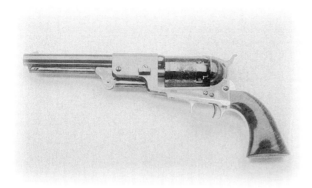

ABOVE. *Dragoon 3rd Model 'civilian'*

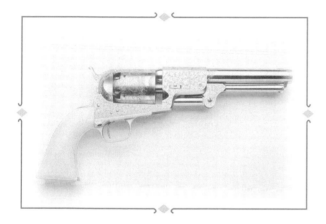

ABOVE. *3rd Model Dragoon - with special engravings and ivory grip*

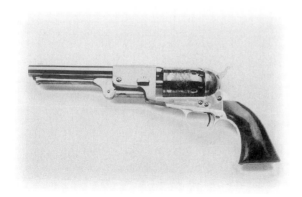

ABOVE. *Whitneyville Dragoon*

BOYD A. *U.S. GRANT* DAVIS

A General and President, Boyd U.S. Grant Davis rides herd on the Board of Directors of the Single Action Shooting Society (a.k.a "The Wild Bunch"). Not only is he its President (of SASS), he also runs the E.M.F. Company, a major supporter and sponsor of Cowboy Action Shooting since its inception. The company has been making and importing replica arms since 1956 and was the first firm in the U.S. to copy the Colt Single Action Army. Since 1986, EMF has specialized in historical reproductions. Davis is particularly proud of the EMF Hartford and Dakota models, exact clones of first generation Colt Peacemakers. As Cowboy Action Shooting grows in worldwide popularity, Davis and EMF continue to help supply the increasing demand for guns of the Old West. Their most recent addition, according to Davis, is a "true and authentic screw-for-screw reproduction" of the 1892 Winchester rifle. Boyd Davis was awarded the prestigious SASS Top Hand Award at End of Trail '91 and continues to be a guiding presence as SASS and Cowboy Action Shooting grow into the 21st Century, promoting the love of our Western Heritage and our constitutional rights to bear arms.

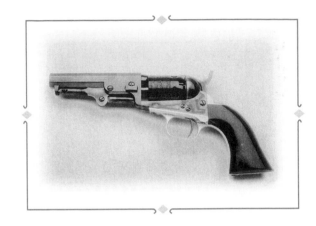

ABOVE. *Pocket 1849*

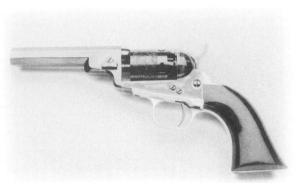

ABOVE. *Wells Fargo*

AT RIGHT. *Navy 1851 2nd Model*

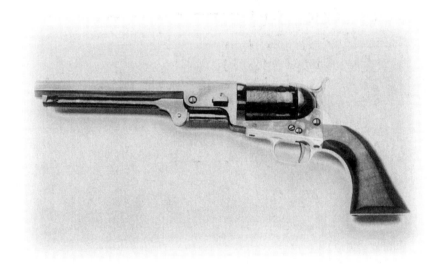

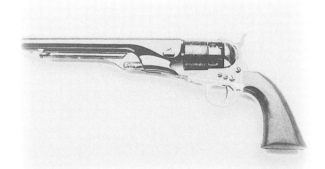

AT LEFT. *Army 1860 'military' (cut for shoulder stock)*

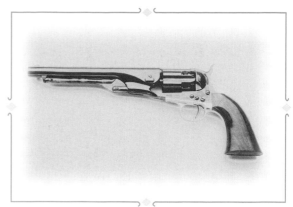

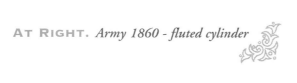

AT RIGHT. *Army 1860 - fluted cylinder*

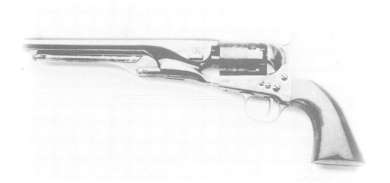

**AT LEFT.** *Navy 1861*

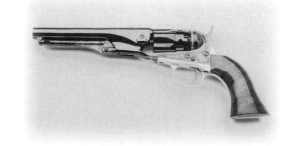

**AT RIGHT.** *Pocket Police 1862*

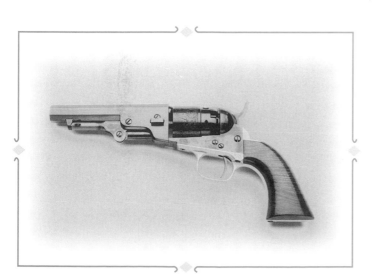

**AT LEFT.** *Pocket Navy 1862*

AT RIGHT.
*Open Top 1871 -
Early Model*

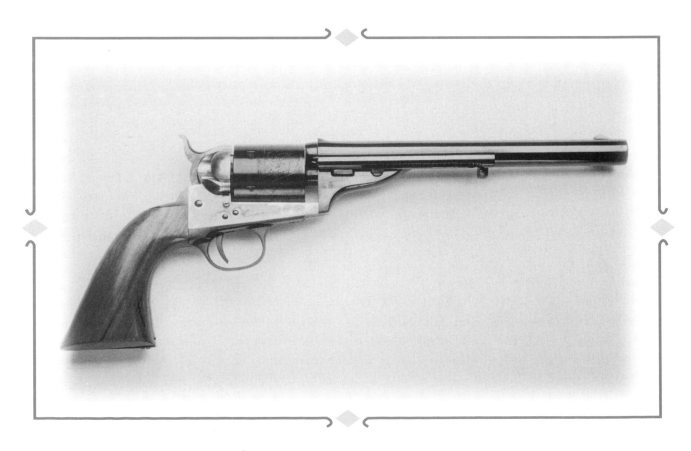

ABOVE. *Open Top 1871 - Late Model*

was in political upheaval over slavery and was everywhere rife with banditry and worse. Then as now, self-defense was a daily concern and a personal responsibility.

The Walker and Dragoon pistols, however, were impractical to be carried by most folks in normal daily use. They were military arms, generally hauled about in the field in box-like cases strapped to the pommel of a saddle, the horse bearing the burden. As the pistols were issued in pairs and carried loaded with six each .44 caliber lead balls, the eleven pounds were ponderous when added to the weight of the cavalryman's primary weapon, his sabre. To this considerable cargo was added the ball, powder, caps, canteens, blanket and other equipage constituting the tools of the horse soldier's trade.

By 1849, Colt had produced a "pocket pistol", (pockets were deeper in them days), now called the Baby Dragoon. With this first "practical pistol", all Americans could go heeled. The scaled-down 22 ounce Dragoon fired a scaled-down .31 caliber ball, had no loading lever and was just a five-shooter, but it answered the self-defense needs of private citizens and luminaries. Sam Houston was an early customer.

The model 1849 Pocket, with a loading lever added, proved even more popular. But Sam Colt's favorite was the .36 caliber 1851 Belt or Navy Model. The Navy moniker springs from the sea battle scene roll engraved onto the cylinder. It commemorates the battle of Compeche, in 1843, in which the Texas navy defeated the Mexican navy.

"The Navy Colt was", as noted gun writer and Colt historian R.L. Wilson puts it, "the .38 of its day". More '51 Navy Models were made than any other Colt arm. Reproduction '51 Navy Colts are the choice of many cap-and-ball Cowboy Shooters, just as originals were preferred by shootists like that prince of percussion pistoleers, Wm. Butler *Wild Bill* Hickock. Hickock carried his brace of Belt models as Colonel Colt intended, in his belt.

Although Colt made many other arms in those darkening days before the Civil War (most notably revolving cylinder rifles and the Sidehammer series), it was the .44 caliber 1860 Colt Army model that marked the dawn of the next era in revolver design. The '60 Army – basically a re-work of the Dragoon – was made possible by advances in steel-making. The new formula metal, called Silver Steel, produced gun parts lighteer, but much stronger than iron or the previous cast steel. Thus, the two pound, eight-and-a-half ounce 1860 Army replaced the four-pound, two-and-a-half ounce Dragoon and then went on to the Civil and Indian Wars as the official sidearm of the US Army.

And then it went West with the veterans of these wars, in the wagons of emigrants and saddlebags or holsters of cowboys. With its larger, man-sized grip and smooth, holster-friendly streamlining, the 1860 Army was literally the shape of things to come.

The 1861 Navy model was an 1851 Navy with an improved loading lever and a round barrel. Custer carried a couple. The 1862 Police and Pocket Colts were based on the 1860 Army, but in the smaller .36 caliber frame. Shorter barrels were popular, including, on special order, a two-inch snub-nose. Fluted cylinders appeared, not as aesthetics, but to insure against cylinder rupture. Then, as they transitioned from that pillar of the percussion period, the 1860 Army, into the new age of breechloading and metallic cartridges, Sam Colt was forced into the future by converting to cartridge his most successful percussion pistols.

COWBOYS AND CARTRIDGES

Perhaps the renewed interest by collectors and Cowboy Actioneers in cartridge conversion revolvers springs from the desire to own and shoot something new; most Cowboy Action Shooters begin with a pair of Single Action Army Colts or copies and then add to their armory with variations like different barrel lengths, grips,

AT RIGHT. *A 5.5-inch .45 Colt Single Action Army is typically the favorite Cowboy Western Action revolver.*

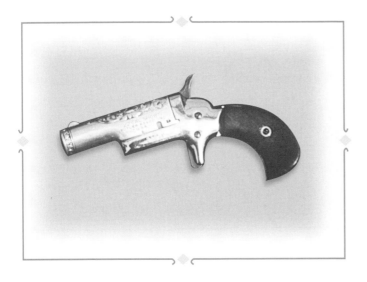

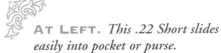

AT LEFT. *This .22 Short slides easily into pocket or purse.*

AT RIGHT.
Bond Arms' Derringer is shown open for loading.

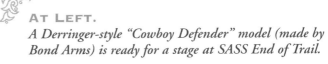

AT LEFT.
A Derringer-style "Cowboy Defender" model (made by Bond Arms) is ready for a stage at SASS End of Trail.

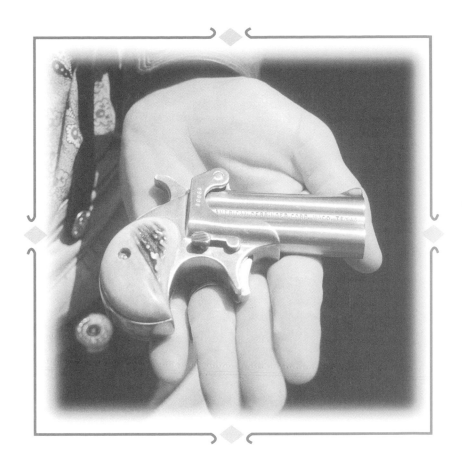

AT LEFT.
Good things come in small packages. A cowboy's stainless American Derringer packs two .38 Special rounds and wears stag grips.

calibers and finishes. But part of Cowboy Action Shooting is the love of Western history; and for many of us, the most exciting and romantic period is the era of the trail drives, the glory days of the open range, of the lawdogs and badmen, cowboys and Indians. These first years after the Civil War are the years of the Colt Conversions, the time when totin' my old .44, meant a Colt 1872 Open Top.

War is always good for business and our country's internecine conflict of the 1860s was no different. It was a boon to the nation's arms industry and technology and some firms, like Smith & Wesson, caught the wave as it formed. Others—Sam Colt was one—hesitated. While it's unclear just why Col. Colt initially missed the point of breechloading metallic cartridge ammunition, the fact is that Smith & Wesson secured a patent that effectively locked Colt out of the breechloading revolver business until it expired in 1871. The patent wasn't for

sale and metallic cartridges were, so the only way Colt could enter the exploding market was by converting his percussion revolvers to accommodate the new ammunition. With the mating of cartridge to the re-designed breech of Colt's cap-and-ball pistols, Sam Colt salvaged his inventory of percussion arms and otherwise obsolete parts and began the gestation of the Single Action Army.

Colt engineers Alexander Thuer, C.B. Richards and William Mason rebuilt virtually all Colt models, from the 1860 Army down to derringer-sized hide-a-way pistols, which were the first to be converted. So popular were these handy pocket protectors, many folks carried several. One Arizona peace officer managed, somehow, to haul eleven (!) secreted about his person. One wonders how he walked.

Small pistols continue to fascinate. SASS and other shooters enjoy target scenarios utilizing Derringers and pocket pistols, but are generally

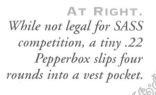 **ABOVE.** *A cowgirl carries her engraved, ivory-handled Colt .41 caliber rimfire pocket pistol in its handy holster.*

AT RIGHT.
While not legal for SASS competition, a tiny .22 Pepperbox slips four rounds into a vest pocket.

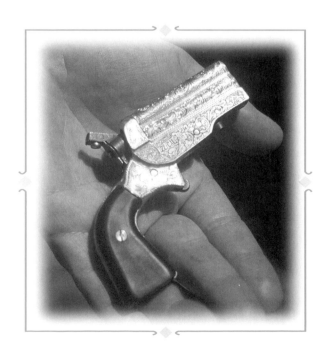

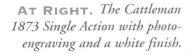

AT LEFT. *The new Colt Cowboy was designed for Cowboy Action Shooting with a 5-inch barrel, fine walnut grips and color case frame.*

AT RIGHT. *The Cattleman 1873 Single Action with photo-engraving and a white finish.*

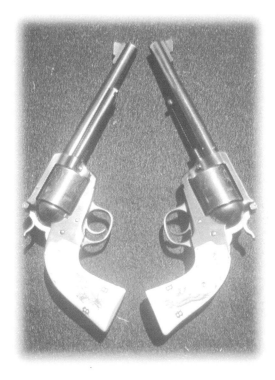

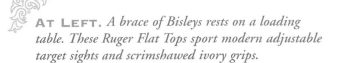

AT LEFT. *A brace of Bisleys rests on a loading table. These Ruger Flat Tops sport modern adjustable target sights and scrimshawed ivory grips.*

AT RIGHT.
*A 5-inch, .45 Colt caliber Colt Single Action
Army model, typifies the favorite Cowboy/Western
Action revolvers. The model shown was nickel-
plated by Colt's custom shop.*

AT LEFT. *Aimless Annie's 4-inch Colt
revolvers are fully engraved and feature one-
piece ivory grips inlaid with engraved silver
escutcheons.*

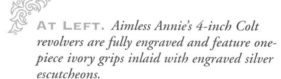

AT RIGHT.
*A 7-inch Peacemaker is completely
engraved and inlaid with gold; its grips
are carved from solid ivory.*

AT LEFT. *A brace of beauties (from Colt's Custom Shop)
features nickel-plated frames, hammers and barrels. Ejector
buttons, housings, cylinders and triggers are charcoal-blued.
Birdshead grips made of extra fancy figured wood.*

ABOVE. *A Third Generation Colt SAA is finished in an 1880's cosmetic package with case hardened frame and hammer, rust-blued barrel, cylinder and grip straps, plus one-piece ivory grips.*

limited to originals or modern reproductions of the classic design created by Henry Derringer himself. When collectors and cowboy style shooters create enough demand, reproductions of many early pocket pistols will surely be supplied.

The archetypal Colt conversion, the pistol that represents the zenith of the conversion period, is the Open Top Frontier .44 rimfire of 1872. It is the closest precursor to the Single Action Army in design and is, some feel, more attractive and pointable. Sharing the same three-piece design as the Walker, Dragoon, Army, Navy, Police and Pocket models, the Open Top featured the larger grip and smooth lines of the 1860 Army. For black powder cartridge shooters, along with those whose shooting persona lived in the 1870s, it may be the perfect pistol.

Only 7,000 Open Top models were made, but they were around long after the introduction of the Single Action Army. Firearms then were meant to last a lifetime. Few folks could afford a new pistol just because it was new, and Peacemakers didn't hit the entire frontier overnight. Colt conversions were in use well into the 20th century and are as appropriate to the period as the Single Action Army or Smith & Wesson Schofield.

Shooters and re-enactors who seek smaller grips, or merely a smaller pistol, can choose originals from the Richards and Mason conversions of 1851 Navy, 1861 Navy, and 1862 Police and Pocket models. That is, assuming they can find and afford them. In all, only 46,100 Colt cartridge conversions were made, so most collectors consider originals far too dear to actually shoot. Thanks

AT RIGHT. *This 4-inch barreled .45 is tastefully engraved and nickel plated. Note the one-piece ivory grips scrimshawed with the End of Trail logo. Colt contributed this gorgeous gun as a prize.*

AT LEFT. *A cowboy shows off his engraved 7-inch nickel-plated Colt with ebony grips overlaid with an ivory buffalo head.*

to the demand by Cowboy Actioneers, these historic and romantic six-shooters are now in re-production by major manufacturers.

THE COLT SAA

More has been written about the Colt Single Action Army revolver than perhaps any other arm in history, surely more than any other Colt firearm (the most respected works are listed in the bibliography). Call it a Peacemaker, Equalizer or Plowhandle, the SAA is known as *The Gun That Won The West* (as is Winchester's Model 1873). It is the nucleus around which organizations like the Single Action Shooting Society, the National Congress of Old West Shootists and the Old West Shootists Association have grown. More cowboy shootists shoot Colt SAAs or reproductions thereof than all other pistols combined. Even with the growing interest in cartridge conversions and Schofields, the Single Action Army is—and will

doubtless remain—the cowboy pistol that dwells in the hearts and minds of lovers of the Great American West.

Because so much attention has been paid to the Colt Single Action Army by scholars in the field, and with many accurate and profusely illustrated volumes available for serious study, we shall consider here only that which is of immediate importance to Cowboy Action Shooting. Action Shooting "the cowboy way" requires two single action revolvers, a pistol-caliber lever action rifle, and a pre-1897 shotgun. Some match stages require only one pistol, but most courses are designed for two. Most shooters acquire their pistols in matched pairs for both practical and aesthetic reasons. A decade of participation in Cowboy Action Shooting has revealed much about the relationships shooters have with their firearms. A firearm is–or should be–an indivi-

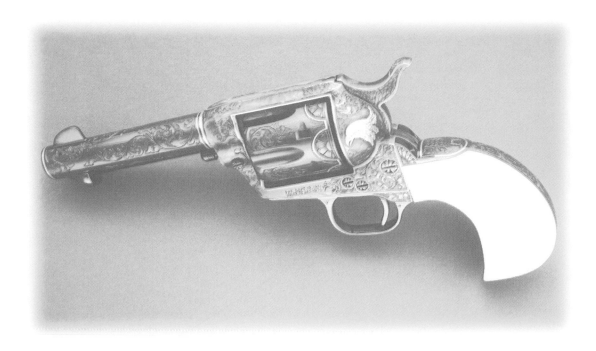

ABOVE. *This exquisite Colt .45 was fashioned at the Colt Custom Shop. It is engraved and inlaid with gold stripes and includes ivory grips and a silver and gold Bald Eagle.*

dual and intimate object, with which its owner is totally familiar and adept.

Since all Single Action Army models are basically the same, most cowboy actioneers select their first brace of pistols based on caliber, barrel length, grip size and finish. Beyond these criteria, shooters can select originals or reproductions from among standard 7," 5" and 4" Single Action Army models, or from such variants as the shorter Sheriff Models, the Bisley Colts (introduced for target shooting in 1894), or Flattop models with modern adjustable sights (which preclude their use in anything but the SASS Modern class).

Sticklers for historical accuracy may require particular models or calibers deemed correct for their period. Cowboy actioneers with such high standards are referred to *The Book of Colt Firearms*, by R.L. Wilson. Probably the most complete reference work available to shooters and Colt fanciers,

this beautiful book illustrates and enumerates virtually every Colt firearm ever made. Shooters can thus choose with confidence the exact original or reproduction Colts as to their period, place and person.

SIZE MATTERS

Barrel length is a legitimate concern for Cowboy Action Shooters, from both practical and aesthetic perspectives. A pistol must feel "right" to a shooter. Balance, pointability and handiness are largely functions of barrel length and grip size. A shooter, when confronted with a distant target, might reach for a 7-inch model because of its longer sight radius, rather than for a pair of 2-inch snubbies. Ladies and gents who insist upon shooting dressed in all their 1880s formal finery may eschew long-barreled pistols because of their tendency to become entangled in voluminous petticoats, frock coats and froufareau. Cowboy Mounted

American Western Arms' Peacekeeper revolvers are hand-tuned at the factory and available with barrels from 3 to 12 inches. An exact copy of first generation Colts, it offers a cross pin or blackpowder frame cylinder pin retainer.

AT LEFT.
Cimarron's 3-inch .38 Special Model P Jr. is 20 percent smaller than the Colt original

AT RIGHT.
The nickel-plated Cimarron Thunderer has a blackpowder frame and one-piece ivory birdshead grips.

AT LEFT. The Uberti Cattleman, a favorite on cowboy/western ranges, has a 4 -inch barrel in .44 Special caliber. It also features a first generation black-powder frame and round ejector button.

AT RIGHT. *A 5-inch Uberti Cattleman displays an old-time charcoal blue and color case hardened frame. A cross-bolt cylinder pin release and half-moon ejector button identify the pistol as a Third Generation Colt replica.*

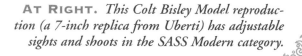

AT LEFT. *This Colt Single Action Army with 7-inch barrel in .45 Colt is Uberti's New Model featuring finely figured hardwood grips.*

AT RIGHT. *This Colt Bisley Model reproduction (a 7-inch replica from Uberti) has adjustable sights and shoots in the SASS Modern category.*

AT LEFT. *Ruger's most popular cowboy revolver is the Vaquero (shown with a 5-inch barrel). The open sights place it in the SASS Traditional category.*

shooters generally prefer the handiness of shorter barrels, but many win with 7-inch Cavalry models. Those whose adopted aliases were real people might well select arms their heroes actually carried. Barrel lengths are a matter of shooter taste.

A GRIPPING STORY

For his masterpiece, the Single Action Army, Colonel Sam Colt chose his grips from the highly successful 1851 Navy. For many Cowboy Action types, these proved ideal, but for those blessed with large hands, the grips on an 1860 Army will be a better choice. Its slightly longer handle can accommodate little fingers that must otherwise curl uselessly under the diminutive '51 Navy/ Peacemaker stock. It is possible, by the way, for a good gunsmith to mount 1860 Army grips on a Colt Single Action Army. This modification has precedence, witness Colt's own records containing orders requesting 1860 Army grips on the SAA. The slight change in appearance is hardly noticeable, and some will avow that it renders the Single Action Army even more attractive.

Some Cowboy/Western Action clubs may not see it that way, however. Shooters in such cases are advised to consult the rules regarding the legality of such grip swaps. Shooters not wanting longer grips on their Peacemakers can fill their hands by substi-

ABOVE. *Uberti's 1875 S&W Russian Model in .44 S&W Russian is replete with a unique trigger guard, lanyard ring and round butt grip.*

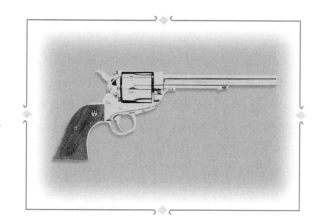

AT RIGHT. *Ruger's 7-inch Vaquero, shown in nickel, is a Third Generation Colt alternative, but with important internal changes.*

AT LEFT. *Uberti calls its 1875 Remington single 7-inch action revolver in .357 Magnum the Outlaw model.*

tuting thicker custom grips, so long as the material is period correct and the basic shape of the stocks, or scales, remains true to Colt. Like so many aspects of Cowboy Action Shooting, grips are a matter of personal taste. Shooters may choose wood, antler, bone, mother-of-pearl, ivory or hard rubber; all were used by Colt carriers in the Old West.

CALIBER COUNTS

Colt once made Single Action Army Peacemakers in many calibers now obsolete. Thanks to the phenomenal interest in Cowboy Actioneering and its ever-growing number of shooters, ammunition makers have re-introduced calibers long absent from their lines. Of most interest to cowboy style shooters are the .45 Colt, .44-40, .44 Special, .38 Special, .38-40, and .32-20.

Percussionists shoot the original .36 and .44 caliber balls. Not that other calibers—period appropriate and otherwise—aren't used. Some Colt reproductions, for example, are chambered for .357 Magnums, a caliber not introduced until 1935. Those wishing their pistol calibers to match both their rifle and their period will choose ammunition generally available during the last half of the 19th century. The .45 Colt was ubiquitous in the Wild West and is perhaps the favorite of today's Cowboy and Western Action shooters. Hardcore history buffs may want to check the *Book of Colt Firearms* before selecting their pistol/rifle caliber. The famous and popular .44-40, for example, didn't exist until 1878–the wrong choice for a shooter attempting to re-enact a 7th Cavalry horse soldier. The practical .38 Special, while SASS

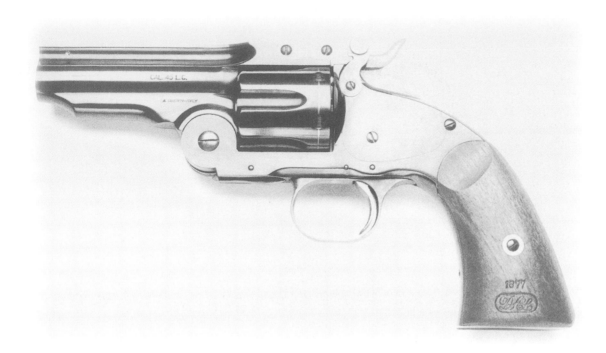

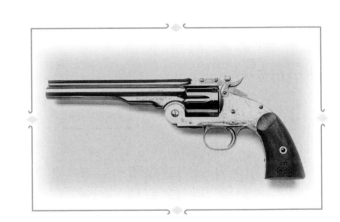

ABOVE. *Navy Arms offers these Cavalry Model S&W Schofields in "as-issued" versions with charcoal blue finish (right), case hardened frame and army grip cartouche in regulation .45 Colt caliber. A nickel plated version (bottom) is also available, as is a snubby 3-inch barreled model with blued frame (top).*

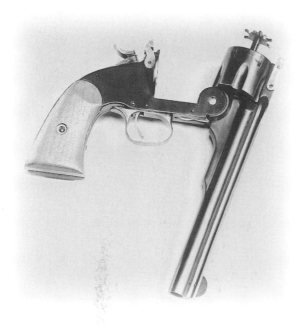

ABOVE. *The extractor on the S&W Schofield is shown in the open position (left), ready to lift empty brass for removal and reloading. The same model (right) is shown partly opened, providing a view of the frame latch cylinder face, extractor and cylinder pin.*

legal, wasn't introduced by Colt until 1930, hardly a frontier favorite. But it does substitute for the .38-40 and is a good choice for shooters who seek recoil relief.

So the choice of ammunition should match the period portrayed at matches and events, but it's even more important that it match both the shooter's rifle and pistol! Juggling different but similar calibers for one's rifle and pistols, while shooting in competition with rifle and pistol under the clock and the eyes of competitors and spectators alike, usually proves too tedious and dangerous for most contestants. Shooters do well to pick a period appropriate caliber, the recoil of which they can tolerate and practice until proficient.

It's important to remember the rules. SASS reactive targets are set to fall when squarely hit with a standard .38 Special 158 grain factory load. Other organizations have similar rules governing calibers, powder and loads; but some, including the National Congress of Old West Shootists, have more stringent ammunition requirements because their version of the sport places more emphasis on history and less on myth. Canny cowboy actioneers, many of whom belong to two or more clubs, must familiarize themselves with the rules in force at each match.

Having picked a pair of pistols with the right barrel lengths, grips and caliber to match both rifle and frontier period, there remains only the choice of finish. Practically speaking, the choices narrow to charcoal bluing, an ancient technique beautiful to behold when brand new, but so unstable that it frequently begins to deteriorate in the box and then wears off completely with any use at all. Many shooters like the antique look of well-worn Colts, but those who seek more permanent protection for their firearms will choose the standard factory hot blued finish with case hardened frames. This was the

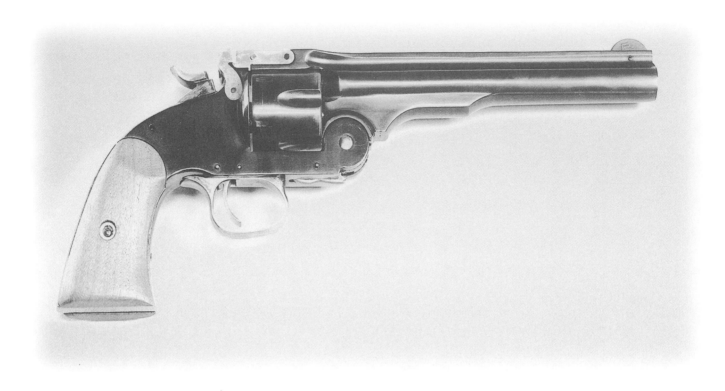

standard finish of most Colts made in the era we emulate. Those who opt to shoot period correct black powder cartridge ammunition may want their pistols nickel plated. This process, added by Colt in 1877 as a standard finish, protects against the ravages of rust and makes black powder clean-up easier. It also photographs better, adding color and drama to an already colorful and dramatic sport. Several reproducers of 19th century Colt pistols have made certain models in stainless steel. Durable and impervious to the problems of moisture and blackpowder, this material is easy to keep clean. It also imitates the nickel look as well as the worn, antique appearance which lends a touch of authenticity. Stainless steel just wasn't around in the Old West.

Many Cowboy Actioneers have their firearms engraved, while many more own pistol grips engraved, scrimshawed, carved and/or inlaid with precious metals, gems and other embellishments. Cowboys and girls have never been afraid of a little decoration, a truism today as in the Wild West. Many experts believe Sam Colt might not have met with so much success had he not bestowed so many beautifully inlaid and engraved examples of his products on important people and government officials. While such fanciful goings-on do nothing for a shooter's final score or Old West authenticity, neither do they lack authenticity; nor are they impediments to calm, cool and collected accuracy.

THE OTHER ORIGINALS

Until recently, literature, motion pictures and television would have us believe that everyone on the frontier carried Colt pistols. While most cowboys, lawmen and outlaws did indeed prefer Colts, it's also true that other makers have marketed

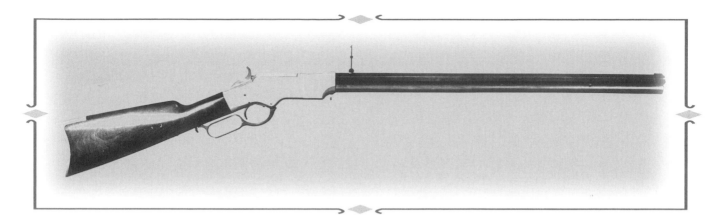

ABOVE. *The brass-framed 1860 Henry was the first Cowboy Rifle. It was often referred to as "That damned Yankee rifle you loaded on Sunday and shot all week!"*

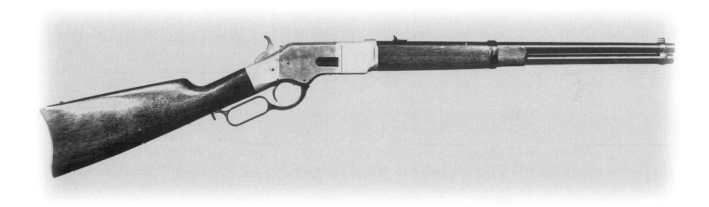

ABOVE. *The 1866 Winchester carbine was known by Indians as the "Yellowboy" because of its brass receiver. It first receiver-loading lever action rifle. The model shown is an Uberti-made .44-40 from Dixie Guns Works.*

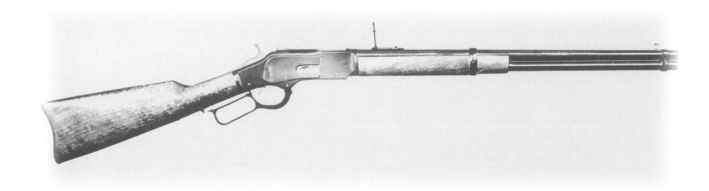

ABOVE. *This Winchester Model 1873 was made by Uberti for Dixie Gun Works. It features a blued carbine with round barrel, shotgun stock and flip-up ladder sight.*

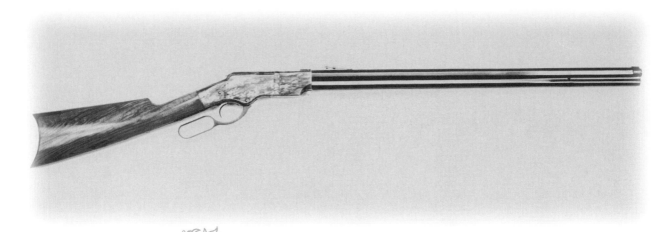

ABOVE. Uberti's "Iron Frame" Henry re-creates the first few Henrys produced. Originals are extremely rare.

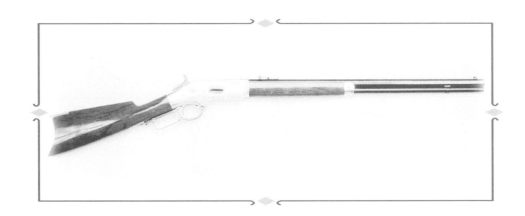

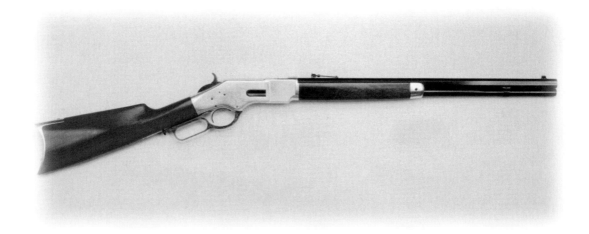

ABOVE. The 1866 "Yellowboy" Short rifle, made by Uberti (center), features an octagon barrel and ladder rear sight. The "Yellowboy" (above) is a sporting Rifle, with a 26-inch octagon barrel, brass receiver and furniture.

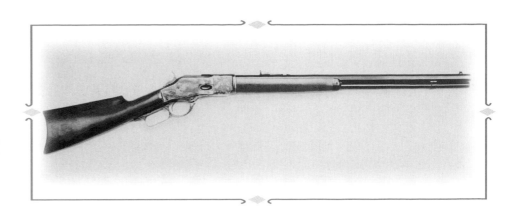

AT RIGHT. *A Cowboy/Western Action favorite—the Winchester 1873 Sporting Rifle—has a 24-inch octagon barrel, case hardened receiver and lever.*

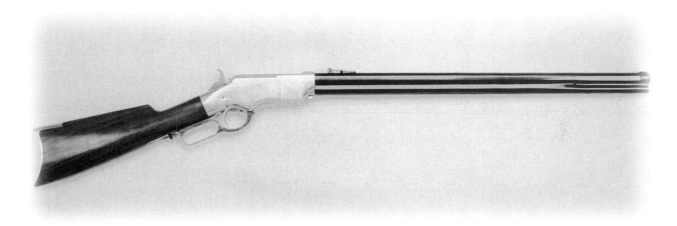

ABOVE. *With its brass receiver and butt plate, this Uberti 1860 Henry recalls the early days of the West, shortly after the Civil War.*

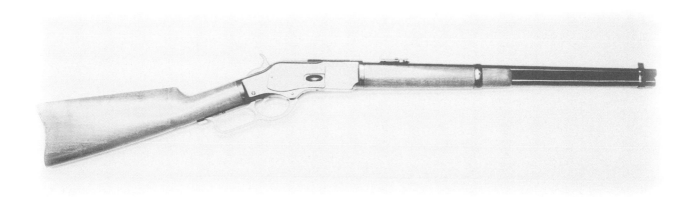

ABOVE. *The 1873 Winchester and the Trapdoor Springfield of the same year both had movies named after them. The '73 carbine shown is an accurate replication from Uberti.*

ABOVE. *Uberti's standard engraving is displayed on the brass receiver of an 1860 Henry.*

copies, variations and (in their opinions) improvements on Colt's revolvers. No overview of the sidearms in general use through the latter half of the 19th century would be complete without a look at some of the other single action six-shooters commonly available in the Old West.

Chronologically, the development of six-shooters built by others loosely parallels Colt's, and in some ways precedes it. The first cartridge revolver, for example, was a Smith & Wesson which was made in the 1850s and represented the first solid frame single action. It was an 1858 Remington, built in .36 and .44 calibers, which evolved into the 1863 .44 caliber New Model Army and .36 Navy. Both originals and reproductions are now called 1858 or Beals Models, (after the designer). During the Civil War, the U.S. Army bought a big bunch of .44 caliber 1858 Remingtons, not because they were better than

Colt's 1860 Army, but because they were cheaper. Cap-and-ball Cowboy Action Shooters who compete in the Frontiersman category or the popular Plainsman side match, sometimes employ New Model Army and Navy Remington clones, but they are less popular than Colt 1851 Navy, 1860 Army or 1861 Navy models. Several makers are now reproducing Remington single actions for import by some of the biggest names in the business.

These same arms companies also import reproduced Remingtons, Frank James' favorite model. First chambered for .44 Remington, these guns were later made available in .44-40 and .45 Colt cartridges. Their distinctive profiles feature a steel buttress under the barrel. It was dropped when this Remington model was superseded by the 1890 version, made only in .44-40. Originals of both models are rare and quite valuable.

As shooting the guns of the Old West often leads to collecting them, more Remingtons and other Colt competitors will be used in the ever-growing number of cowboy events. Chief among these are the .45 S&W Smith & Wesson Number Three American and the Schofield Model, originally in 45 S&W. S&W Top Break single actions like the Old Model Russian were recently popularized by Sam Elliot and others in film and television. From its introduction in 1870, with modifications made by cavalry Major George Schofield and its subsequent adoption by the U.S. Army in 1875 until its discontinuance in 1917, over 250,000 "Schofields" were produced and sold around the world. Many traveled west in the holsters of people like Frank and Jesse James, the Younger brothers and Buffalo Bill Cody, who also favored the Number Three American. Schofield's revolutionary design incorporated a top break feature which allowed access to the entire cylinder face. When opened, it automatically ejected all six chambers at once. Designed for easier reloading compared with other revolvers, the S&W Top Break Models quickly found favor among the officers and enlisted men of the U.S. Army as well as with civilians—the good and the bad. Available in 15 calibers, this unusual pistol served in the Indian Wars alongside the Colt .45 SAA. One rusty Schofield and some ammunition used by at least three Number Threes have been excavated from Last Stand Hill, site of George Custer's final faux pas.

In its infinite wisdom, the U.S. Army dropped the revolver when it couldn't chamber the newly approved .45 Long Colt rounds. It was cheaper than simply re-chambering their Schofields. In 1880, Wells Fargo purchased many New Model Number Threes, cut the barrels from seven to five inches, and issued them to the company's agents for use on annoying outlaws like Butch and Sundance. Ultimately, these interesting firearms became a part of the romance of the Wild West, a fact not lost on cowboy style shooters. Like the Open Top and other Colt conversions, they remain colorful examples of America's heritage while offering an additional and unique shooting experiences straight from the American Frontier. The increasingly valuable originals are highly prized by collectors, but prudent shooters shoot reproductions.

Colt, Smith & Wesson and Remington were not the only single action revolvers made during the last 60 years or so of the 19th century. Most percussion pistols manufactured during the Civil War—including the Yankee Rogers and Spencer .44 and the Confederate .36 caliber Spiller and Burr—are rather obvious copies of the Remington 1858 Army Model. These and some rare originals like the .36 caliber Leech and Rigdon, the Confederate .44 Dance Dragoon and the incredible nine-shot .44 caliber LeMat revolver/shotgun, must be considered by cowboy competitors as historical firearms esoterica. Like all original firearms of the period, they are far too valuable, both as history and investment to historians, to be subjected to the rigors of cowboy competition.

THE REPLICAS: PERCUSSION

Our overview of the reproduction guns of the Old West begins once again with Colt's first revolver: the .36 caliber, five-shot cap-and-ball Texas Paterson. While not appropriate for cowboy competition, shootists who also collect the antique arms of the frontier—and there are many of them—include the Paterson for its important first place within the genesis of Colt revolvers. Owners of such rare originals would certainly never shoot them, but replicas allow percussion shooting cowboys the experience of firing the pistol used to defend against Santa Ana and those quarrelsome Comanches.

The Paterson and the other Colt replicas are currently imported from Italian makers—Armi San Marco, Fausti Stefano, Pietta and Uberti among them—and by the oldest and most respected

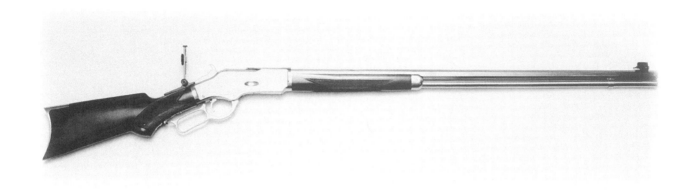

ABOVE. *Finished "in the white" (unblued), this extra grade '73 Winchester Sporter has checkered walnut stocks with pistol grip and a Venier tang rear sight, making it a fine and fancy choice for the "Lever Action Long Range Rifle" category.*

AT RIGHT. *Uberti's "1 of 1,000" Model closely replicates the Winchester originals. Here the engraved receiver has been left in white.*

ABOVE. *Winchester remade its Model 1892 Short Rifle for use by Cowboy Actioneers. This one has a round barrel, walnut stocks and an old-style crescent butt plate.*

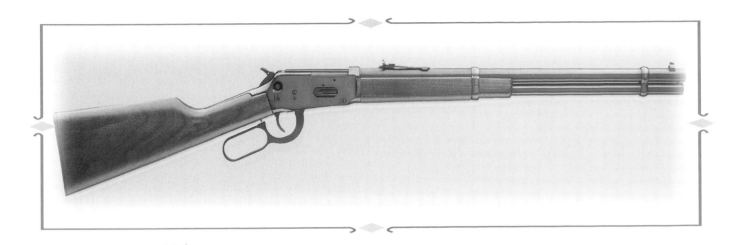

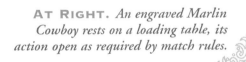*ABOVE. Winchester's best-known saddle gun is probably the 1894 carbine. This "Trail's End" reproduction is chambered for Cowboy Action and features walnut stocks.*

AT RIGHT. An engraved Marlin Cowboy rests on a loading table, its action open as required by match rules.

ABOVE. The "Legacy" is Winchester's longer Model '94 with a 22-inch barrel and checkered walnut stocks with pistol grip. It makes an excellent choice for SASS pistol-caliber Long Range Rifle shooting.

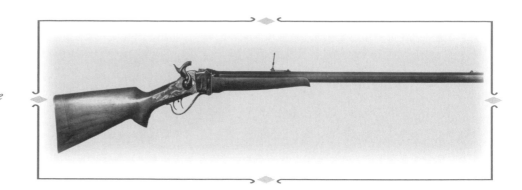

AT RIGHT. *Dixie's 1873 Springfield Cavalry Trap Door carbine was the U.S. Army's Indian War issue and the last single-shot blackpowder rifle issued to the troops.*

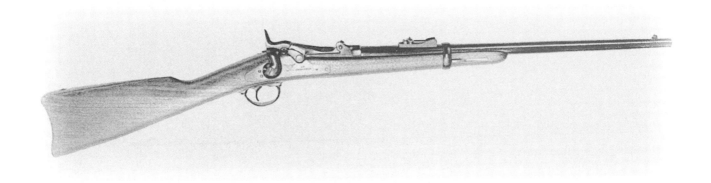

ABOVE. *The 1874 Sharps Cavalry Model in .45-70 was made by Pedersoli for Dixie Gun Works.*

dealers in black powder and Cowboy Action arms: Cimarron, Dixie Gun Works, EMF, Navy Arms, Taylor's & Co. and Uberti USA. In the U.S., Colt Blackpowder Arms assembles a complete line of Italian-made Colt percussion replica revolvers.

The same can be said of Sam Colt's other percussion progeny, including the 1847 .44 caliber Walker Model. Like the Texas Paterson, it's an unlikely cowboy competitor. It has a nasty habit of dropping its loading lever when fired, pretty much locking up the pistol until the loading lever is replaced (under the barrel, where it belongs). Add this vexation to the ten pounds or more of holstered weight, which the poor percussion pistolero must carry, and it's almost more than he can bear.

Colt Dragoons are slightly lighter and feature the loading lever latch Colt and Sam Walker somehow failed to include on the Walker Model. They are still too heavy for the average cowboy actioneer to use in matches, much less in the dramatic pistol-in-each-hand *Gunfighter* class although those who have the sand for it find the experience thrilling. Most, if not all, Dragoon Models are available through the arms companies mentioned above.

The Colt Model 1849 Pocket and 1851 Belt or Navy Model in .36 caliber were probably the first revolvers to be carried around in pockets and holsters by private citizens, lawmen and outlaws. Some say these pistols began the "Age of the Gunfighter." They were certainly easier to carry

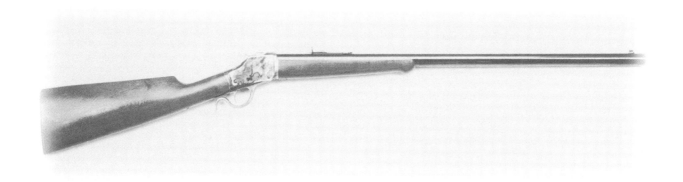

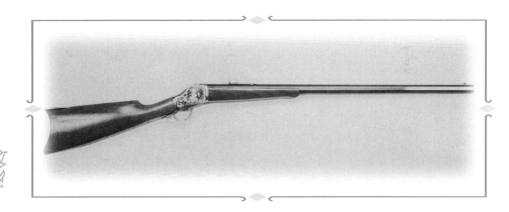

ABOVE. *Uberti's 1885 "High Wall" Single Shot carbine in .45-70 is shown with round barrel, shotgun-style buttstock and Schnabel forend.*

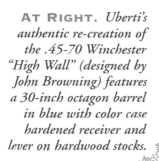

AT RIGHT. *Uberti's authentic re-creation of the .45-70 Winchester "High Wall" (designed by John Browning) features a 30-inch octagon barrel in blue with color case hardened receiver and lever on hardwood stocks.*

and deploy than previous pistols, being faster "out of the leather" than any of their predecessors. While Cowboy or Western Action Shooting is definitely not Fast Draw competition, handiness and carrying convenience rate high with cap-and-ball cowboys. Colt 1851 Navy Model replicas are not only favorites, they are readily available from most makers and dealers. For those with hands of average size, they make an historic and practical percussion pistol. They also offer less recoil than that other Cowboy Action Shooter's percussion favorite—the beautiful and equally historic Colt .44 caliber 1860 Army.

For shooters who portray the early period— around the Civil War and for some years after—

replica .44 caliber 1860 Army models are a logical choice. Other shooters simply enjoy the boom and smoke and chores intrinsic to the cap-and-ball business. It's a dirty, greasy, troublesome pursuit— the very opposite of those high tech race guns in vogue in some other shooting sports. But it does put shooters in touch with life on the frontier, teaching them to make each shot count. The 1860 Army is ideal for cowboy actioneers with larger hands and who opt to shoot a .44 caliber ball from an 8-inch barrel with its long sight radius. Those with normal-sized hands and who appreciate the lower recoil of .36 caliber often choose the 1861 Navy, a slightly smaller version of the 1960 Army model. Both offer the same smooth, elegantly

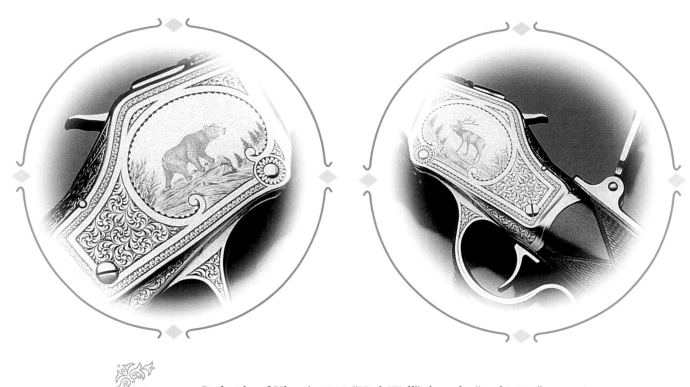

ABOVE. *Both sides of Uberti's 1885 "High Wall" show the "1 of 1,000" engraving on their receivers (left in the white). Note the tang-mounted ladder peep sight.*

sculpted barrel and loading lever assembly, the same easy in-and-out of the holster, and the same romantic history. Both are great fun, especially in the authentic *Frontiersman* category.

The same can be said for the Remington Model 1858. Very popular in its day—and chosen by cowboy style shooters for its solid frame and superior sights—the Remington was available in both .36 and .44 caliber, and in six- and eight-inch barrels. Fine replicas are sold by the major suppliers of Cowboy firearms, but apparently only in .44 caliber and with the longer barrel.

Last, but hardly least, among percussion pistols is the Ruger Old Army .44. While this superior revolver is not really a replica of a 19th century firearm, it does, with non-adjustable sights, meet SASS criteria for percussion revolvers. In stainless steel, it's as practical as it is pretty. Cleaning is simpler than with either Colt or Remington

percussion pistols, making the Ruger a favorite with SASS shooters who elect to do it the smelly, smoky way.

CENTER FIRE CARTRIDGE REVOLVERS

So far as Cowboy and Western Action Shooting is concerned, the earliest period cartridge firearms are the Colt conversions, the most recent addition to SASS legal revolvers. So new and popular are these historic six-guns that cowboy actioneers must usually wait some time for delivery. The earliest conversions offered by the major Cowboy Action suppliers are the 1851 Navy, 1860 Army and 1861 Navy Model. Already popular with shooters lucky enough to have them, these .38 and .44 caliber Richards and Mason patent parts are made by Armi San Marco in Italy and assembled in the U.S. by American Western Arms. Prototypes available for inspection

AT RIGHT.
The new Browning Traditional High Wall Hunter features a tapered octagon barrel, matching blued receiver lever and butt plate. Its checkered walnut stocks, sling swivel lugs and tang rear sight make this a contender in .45-70 and .38-55 calibers.

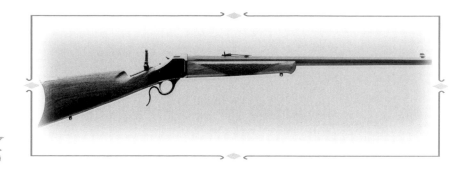

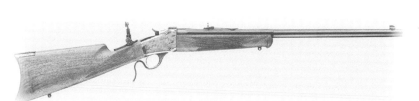

AT LEFT. *Browning's "Low Wall" Traditional Hunter comes in cowboy pistol calibers: .38/.357, .44 Magnum and .45 Colt. The half-and-half barrel and case hardened receiver/lever complement the checkered walnut rifle stocks.*

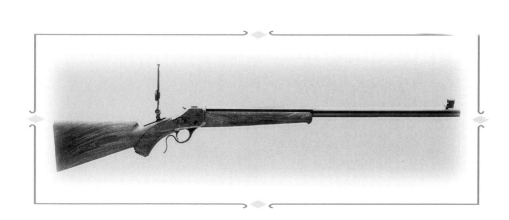

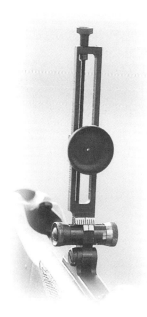

ABOVE. *At left, a Browning Black Powder Cartridge Rifle (in .45-65 and .45-70 calibers) is an 1885 "High Wall" for the serious blackpowder shooters of the Long Range Rifle, Buffalo Gun and Silueta. Amenities include the spirit level globe front sight on a half octagon-half round 30-inch blued barrel case hardened receiver with Vernier rear tang sight and extra grade pistol grip walnut checkered stocks. At right is a shooter's view of the Vernier rear sight on a Browning "High Wall" BPCR.*

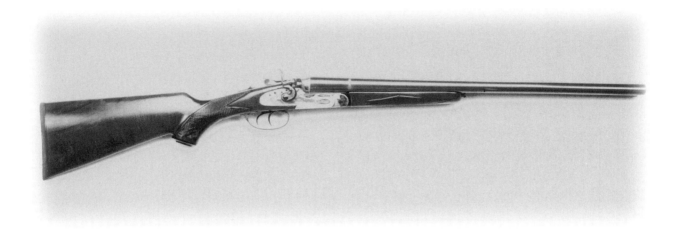

ABOVE.
Uberti's new "Mule Eared" Coach Gun has 12 gauge, 20-inch barrels on a color-case hardened receiver with double triggers, a tang-mounted, sliding safety and side-mounted, exposed hammers.

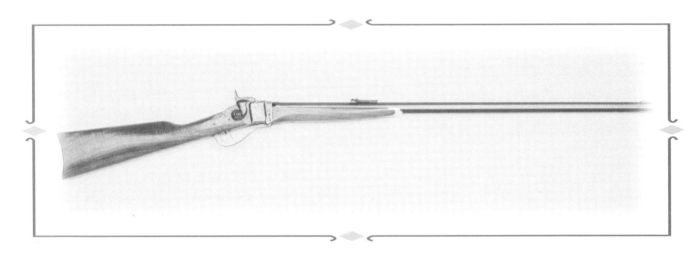

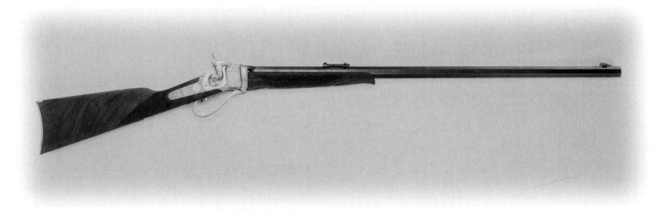

ABOVE. *A .45-70 1874 Sharps (center) with figured stocks and silver forend cap, is a fine Long Range single shot rifle. Another Armi Sport Sharps (above) features an engraved and inlaid receiver group and Schnabel forend.*

ABOVE. *The 7-shot Spencer carbine (an Armi Sport replica) was once used by both the U.S. Army Cavalry and its Indian adversaries.*

are finely fitted and finished firearms, as are the Navy Arms conversions built by Uberti. All come with 5-inch and 7-inch barrels, color case hardened frames and brass or silver-plated trigger guards. U.S. Fire-Arms Manufacturing Company builds its single Colt conversion model, an 1851 Navy replica, where the original Colts were made, under the famous blue dome of the Hartford (CT) East Armory. They come in .38 Special only and 7-inch barrels.

But the queen of the replica Colt conversion revolvers is the 1872 Open Top. These gorgeous guns are made by Uberti in Italy and are available exclusively through the Cimarron Fire Arms Company (Fredericksburg, TX). AWA offers the Open Top in both .38 and .44 caliber, either 5-inch or 7-inch barrels, blued with color case hardened frames or nickel plated. Both 1860 Army or 1851 Navy grips are available.

Cimarron sells the 1872 Colt Open Top (made by Uberti) with either Army- or Navy-sized grips, 5-inch or 7-inch barrels and four beautiful finishes: blue, charcoal blue, nickel and what is called "original finish." This last choice bears the look of an antique arm that has been well used on frontier cattle trails. Shooters will find the Cimarron replica Open Top available in .38 Colt and S&W Special, .44 Colt and Russian or .45 S&W Schofield. Using modern steel and technology, Uberti has produced an open top model that is considerably stouter than the originals. Cimarron's boss, Mike *Texas Jack* Harvey, calls it, "The finest replica to come forth in a decade." Navy Arms also offers Colt conversion revolvers, in both barrel lengths and with both '51 Navy and '60 Army grips. All are currently available in .38 Special/.38 Colt calibers.

As accurate and romantic as Colt cartridge conversion revolvers are—most will shoot two- or three-inch groups at 50 feet—a caveat is called for. Technically, all Colt conversion models are "open tops;" i.e., they have no top frame member. Made for slower burning black powder and ball ammunition, they are intrinsically less strong than solid frame revolvers with screwed-in barrels. The barrel and ejector rod assembly, which makes up the front of the frame, is held in place only by the barrel wedge and two small alignment pins. These guns, while sufficient for blackpowder cartridges and occasional shooting, were never intended for

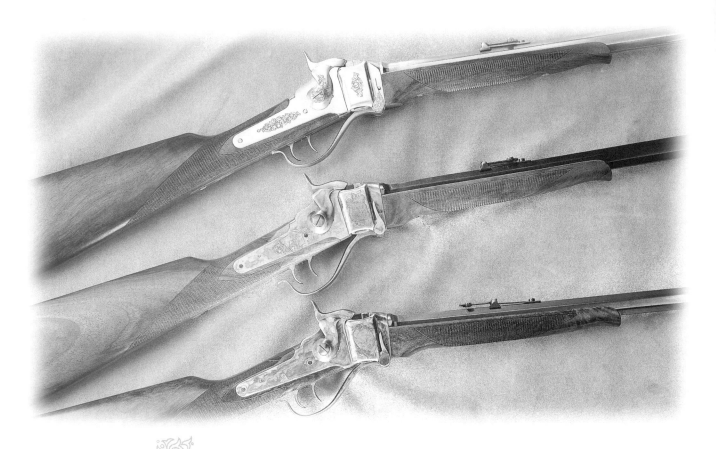

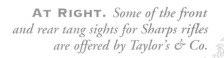

ABOVE. *A trio of extra grade 1874 Sharps rifles are from EMF Co., Inc.*

AT RIGHT. *Some of the front and rear tang sights for Sharps rifles are offered by Taylor's & Co.*

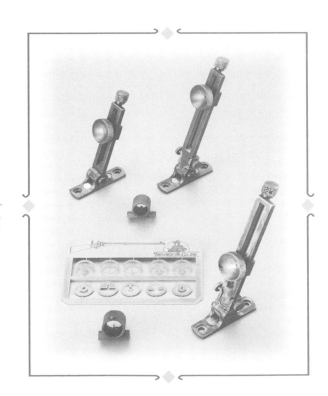

the pressures and volumes of rounds that smoke-less powder and cowboy competition requires. No matter the fine modern steel and close tolerances of computerized manufacturing, these were—and remain—black powder guns for use with black powder cartridges only.

Further, Colt conversions should not be used as a shooter's primary pistol like a Peacemaker, Remington or Schofield. Ideal for re-enactors, collectors and the occasional Cowboy stage, these delightful pistols may not withstand the pounding of thousands of rounds per year, whether in competition or practice. With light shooting with black powder cartridges, these replica guns of the "real" Old West should provide another 150 years of recreational shooting.

THE COLT SINGLE ACTION ARMY

Some 130 years later, Colt's 1873 Single Action Army is still winning the West. More has been written about Colt's SAA than perhaps any other firearm in history. It has appeared in more books, movies and TV shows than any gun ever and is easily the most replicated, best-selling sidearm in reproduction. This discussion is limited to versions of the SAA purveyed by major players in the replica field and in general use by cowboy/western action shooters. Those whose further interest has been spurred are referred to our abundant appendices and bodacious bibliography.

The Colt Single Action Army is period appropriate from 1873 forward. Perhaps the U.S. Cavalry issue of 1873 was indeed the "Gun That Won The West." In .45 Colt caliber and with a 7-inch barrel, these original Peacemakers made war in the West as the sidearm of choice with the 7th Cavalry. The model used by SASS members is reproduced by all of the aforementioned gunmakers, along with many others, sometimes with the a government inspector's signature embossed on the

ABOVE. *Three grips from Ajax Custom Grips (from left): ivory polymer, ivory and stag.*

pistol's one-piece walnut grips. A more correct and practical Cowboy/Western Action revolver cannot be found, with reproductions available in every caliber deemed legal for cowboy competition. As with all variations on the original theme, most makers market first, second and third generation Colt SAAs, in all four popular barrel lengths. A good many of them sell replica Bisley Models, Flat Top Target models with adjustable sights, and models with Birdshead grips.

Of particular interest to cowboy shootists is Cimarron's Model P, an Uberti exclusive. It's an exact replica of a first generation Colt, complete with a "pinched frame" rear sight, special springs and hardened, hand-fitted internal parts, the working surfaces of which are highly polished. Model P actions are tuned to three pounds of trigger pull. Cimarron promotes all of these features as its "Cowboy Competition" package, an out-of-the-

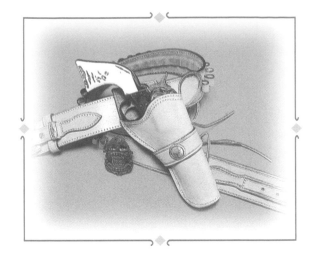

AT RIGHT.
*These authentic stag two-piece grips (left)
and those that follow (right and below) are
courtesy of Ajax Custom grips.*

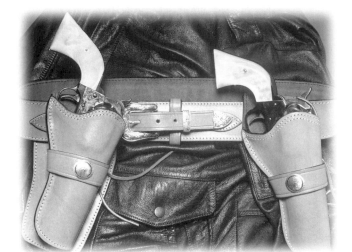

AT LEFT. *White pearlite
Ajax grips on a pair of Colts.*

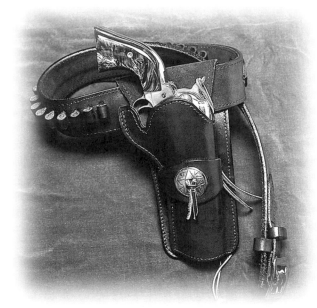

AT RIGHT.
*Ajax black pearlite on a
nickel plated Colt SAA.*

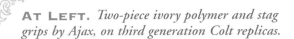

AT LEFT. *Two-piece ivory polymer and stag
grips by Ajax, on third generation Colt replicas.*

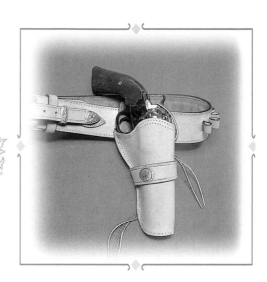

AT RIGHT. *These buffalo polymer two-piece grips, replicas of early Buffalo horn grips, were early favorites, especially on the Great Plains.*

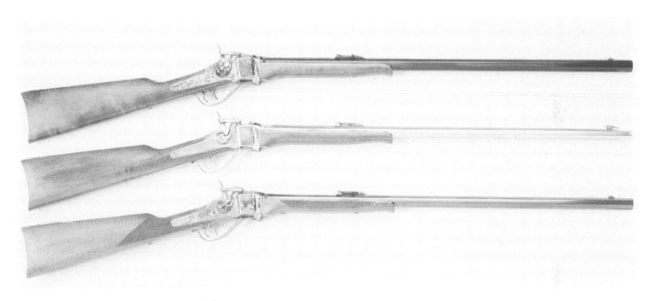

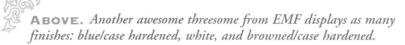

ABOVE. *Another awesome threesome from EMF displays as many finishes: blue/case hardened, white, and browned/case hardened.*

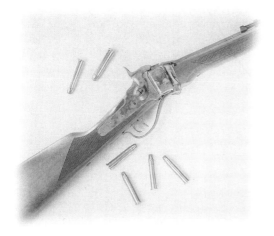

AT LEFT. *An EMF Co. 1874 Sharps, reproduced by Pedersoli, is shown with .45-70 ammunition. The semi-jacketed rounds, while ideal for hunting, are not legal for Cowboy/Western Action Shooting competition.*

Old Guns Win the New West: A Colt Chronology **99**

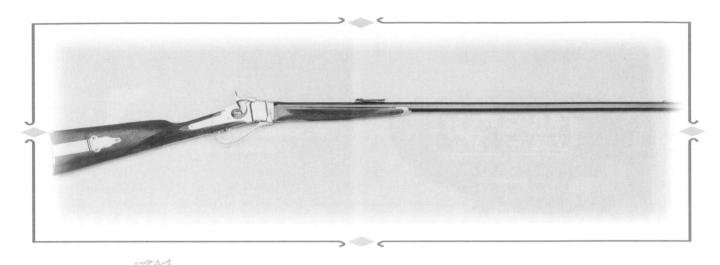

ABOVE. *A deluxe .45-70 1874 Sharps from Taylor's & Co. with blued barrel, contrasting forend cap, receiver group, patchbox and buttplate (all left in the white).*

box match pistol. The Model P comes in the usual barrel lengths and calibers, including all the popular and period-correct cowboy favorites.

Cimarron also sells a version by Uberti called the Thunderer, a company exclusive resembling the original Colt 1877 Lightning and 1878 Frontier series double action revolvers. These early Colt double actions saw action in the hands of Billy the Kid and Frederic Remington, among others. The Thunderer, especially with the shorter barrels, is a favorite of cowboy shootists who carry one or more of these dandy boomers in their shoulder holsters, a la Doc Holiday in the film *Tombstone*. The important difference is that the Cimarron special is a single action revolver, hence legal in the eyes of SASS. Even though it's not a replica of an original Colt model, the Thunderer is a Colt-based gun with a grip design that Cimarron boss Mike Harvey claims makes this "The gun that Colt should have made." In .45 Colt, .44 WCF and .38/.357 Magnum, Cimarron's Thunderers are great options for shootists who favor the Birdshead butt.

More important than grips or luxury finishes, however, are the requirements that replica single

actions shoot decent-sized groups (2-3 inches) to point of aim at pistol range. In cowboy competition, that computes to roughly 50 feet or closer. Equally critical, the gun's internal mechanism must be smooth and finished sufficiently to be reliable, to time correctly, cock easily and boast a light but crisp trigger pull (three pounds or so). Sadly, the most affordable reproductions rarely come out of the box with these important qualities and must usually be tuned by qualified single action gunsmiths. As simple as Peacemakers are, most cowboy actioneers have neither the inclination nor skill to perform action jobs and barrel twisting on their shooters, whether they're Colts or some other models.

As with everything, demand and competition increase both quality and prices. In the early days of cowboy sport shooting, shooters used whatever guns they could lay hands on, which were frequently Colt look-alikes requiring serious gunsmithing to set them right for competition or even casual shooting. Fortunately, the arms offered today by major firms are light years ahead of those early reproductions. As a result, some can be taken out of the box and straight to the

AT RIGHT.
*A 5- inch barreled SAA
replica from Taylor's &
Co. is shown with charcoal
blued barrel, cylinder, trigger
guard and backstrap, plus
a color case hardened First
Model frame. Grips are
one-piece walnut, same as
the original.*

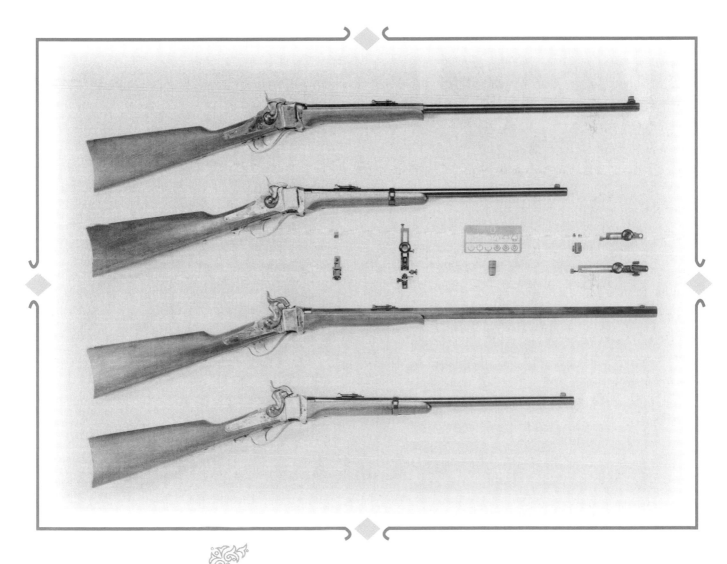

ABOVE. *EMF Sharps carbines and rifles pose
with an assortment of sights and front sight inserts.*

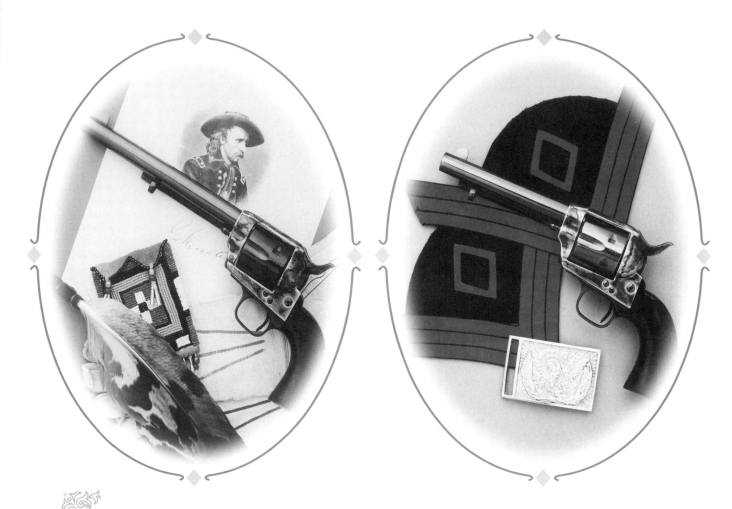

ABOVE. An exact copy of a .45 caliber Colt Cavalry model issued to the 7th Cavalry was made exclusively by Uberti for Cimarron F.A. in Fredericksburg, TX. It is shown in charcoal blue and color case hardened frame (left) with one-piece walnut grips. The same model is pictured in a 5-inch Artillery Model (right).

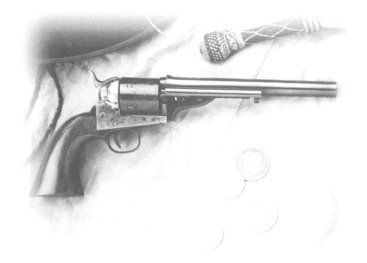

AT LEFT. This Cimarron Fire Arms Colt 1872 Open Top Cartridge Conversion made by Uberti is blued with color case hardened frame and 1860 Army Model grips. Calibers are .44 Colt, .44 Russian, .45 Schofield and .38 Special.

cowboy match without expensive hospital stays at the gunsmith's. Examples of today's higher quality reproductions are made by American Western Arms at their Armi San Marco factory. Introduced at SASS *End of Trail 2000*, these Open Top, Single Action Army replicas impressed shooters with their smooth actions and finish. Top-flight cowboy shooters who were chosen to compete in the Master Gunfighter stage all praised AWA's Peacemaker model as the #1 pistol in the championship scenario. Readers should look for AWA conversions and Peacekeeper SAA models may figure strongly in future Cowboy and Western Action events.

The EMF Company, which dates back to 1953, has been (along with Dixie Gun Works and Navy Arms) a pioneer in replica arms. A huge supporter of SASS and other Cowboy/Western Action Shooting clubs, EMF also distributes Single Action Army models made by Uberti, along with at least as many variations in barrels, frames, grips and calibers as any purveyor of Peacemakers. Navy Arms offers several models of Colt Single Actions, in .45 Colt and .44-40, also made by Uberti and available in blue with color case frames or with nickel plating. Navy Arms also offers an entry level economy model, complete with brass trigger guard and backstrap. Barrels from 3- to 7-inches are available, all one-piece walnut grips. Taylor's & Company sells the Cattleman Model Uberti with 4-inch , 5-inch and 7-inch barrels, and in calibers .38-40, .357 Magnum, .44-40, .44 Special and .45 Colt. These SAAs can be bought standard blue or charcoal blue finishes with case-hardened frames or nickel plated. All sport nicely grained one-piece walnut grips.

Uberti is the old and highly respected Italian gunmaker, contributed greatly to the re-popularization of the Peacemakers after Aldo Uberti replicated Colts for the Clint Eastwood-inspired Sergio Leone spaghetti westerns. Uberti arms are imported by the late Signor Uberti's daughter Maria and her firm, Uberti USA. As original Colts were locked away in the safes and display cases of collectors and museums, the film industry turned to companies like Uberti to arm the lawdogs and badmen of their movies. Uberti SAA replicas, especially after being "slickened" by gunsmiths, perform quite well in cowboy competitors. And unlike the movies, cowboy competitors must shoot the scene right the first time.

Those with more to spend, or who wish to shoot real Colt Single Action Army models for the sake of authenticity, can purchase them from the Colt's Manufacturing Company. These "real Colts" are available in .45 and .44-40 calibers and in 4-inch and 5-inch barrels. They have a blued/color case or nickel plated finish and come with black plastic Colt grips. Other calibers, barrel lengths, finishes and grips can be ordered through Colt's Custom Shop. The company's newest model, inspired by the exploding interest in Cowboy Action Shooting, is the Colt Cowboy. Designed specifically for cowboy actioneers, it is offered in .45 Colt caliber with a 5-inch barrel, black plastic Colt logo grip scales and a device no 19th century cowboy ever heard of: a transfer bar safety. Until the development of this device, "six-guns" were actually five-guns, because folks hesitated to carry six rounds. Should the gun ever drop directly on its hammer, the round directly under it could be fired with tragic results. It's doubtful that soldiers, cowboys, lawmen and outlaws actually handicapped themselves before a fight by omitting one round for safety's sake. Even so, rules is rules. Transfer bar safety or not, each cowboy competitor must carefully lower the hammer on an empty cylinder chamber after loading up to shoot a stage. It's a good rule. Nothing is as safe as an empty chamber and safety is a behavior, not a device.

The transfer bar safety, while affording peace of mind to those carrying a Colt Cowboy for self defense, means little to the serious competitor. Other than a lower price (offset somewhat by the cost of a gunsmith's tuning) one wonders why the need for this redundant addition to the Colt line.

Then one remembers the Vaquero, the first single action revolver built by Sturm, Ruger & Company. It was created in response to the popularity of Colt revolvers and their clones and the wildfire growth of cowboy/western shooting. Ruger introduced the Vaquero (Spanish for cowboy) in 1993 to widespread acceptance by cowboy shootists and single action lovers. It is, after all, less expensive than Colt's Single Action, and yet well-made and accurate. It does look a lot like a Colt—but it doesn't act like one. Ruger's "improvements" include a mechanism that allows the cylinder to rotate when the loading gate is opened. Colt replicas require the hammer to be drawn to half-cock in order to free the cylinder. The Ruger system, on the other hand, makes for faster unloading and may be a little safer, since the hammer need not be touched until ready to fire.

Then, too, there's that hammer bar safety for non-cowboy shooting users who wish to carry a full six-pack in their Vaquero. These single action firearms are available in the most popular cowboy calibers (.38-.357, .44-40 and .45 Colt) and barrel lengths (4-inch, 5-inch and 7-inch). The blued and color-cased combination is standard, but Ruger also offers a high gloss stainless model that rivals nickel plate for appearance and resistance to rust and corrosion. It can't flake off and makes a great choice for black powder cartridge shooters. The Vaquero also comes in a Bisley format, with a more vertical grip frame, a lower, wider hammer and a target trigger (but not offered in .44-40 caliber). Bisley replicas are popular with those who prefer the straighter grips and whose chosen

"persona period" is the 1890s. Bisley Colts, by the way, were designed for target shooting in England. The model is named after the place where the major shooting matches were held. Bisleys were hardly commonplace in the Old West. Because of their adjustable sights, Bisley replicas must shoot in the SASS Modern category.

Other Rugers that shoot in the SASS Modern stages are the Single-Six and Blackhawk models, which sport fine adjustable sights and a heavy Flat Top frame. These excellent revolvers boast a faithful following among cowboy shootists for whom period authenticity is less important. Some clubs, for whom authenticity is everything, proscribe the use of modern Rugers in their matches.

Other manufacturers make "Colt-style" revolvers, of course, but the builders cited above, who make either Colt Single Action Army models or close clones thereof, require the most attention. Cowboy Action Shooting should rightly require that shooters stick to their guns: The guns actually used in the Old West.

While safety mechanisms are well and good, they are no substitute for careful gun handling and the obedience of range and match rules. Part of the beauty of single action revolvers is that they are so deliberately simple in their operation. Carried with the hammer down on an empty chamber, they are as safe as any loaded firearm can be, each round fired requiring the hammer to be cocked and the trigger pulled. If only all pistols were so sensible.

THE REMINGTONS

E. Remington & Sons responded to the success of Colt's Single Action Army in 1875 with what many feel was a superior design. With its heavier frame and steel barrel buttress, the 1875 Model was, as they say, "hell for stout." Replicated by Uberti, these first Remington Single Action models are available from both EMF and Navy Arms. EMF offers 1875 Remingtons in .45 Colt,

AT LEFT.
Cimarron's Model P, an exact replica of the earliest Colt SAA, features a blackpowder frame. This makes an ideal Cowboy Action Shooting six-gun.

AT RIGHT. *The Cimarron Thunderer, with Mike Harvey-designed Birdshead grips, is considered by some as "The gun Sam Colt should have made." It remains quite popular with cowboy actioneers.*

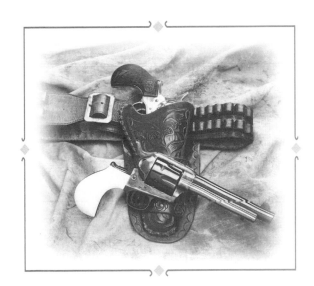

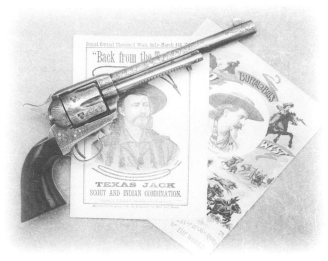

ABOVE. *An engraved 7-inch Cavalry Model Colt replica from Cimarron appears in its "original finish," making it difficult to distinguish from an old Colt, especially with a blackpowder frame.*

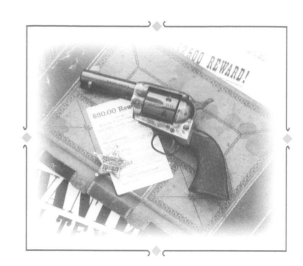

AT RIGHT. *The Cimarron 3-inch Sheriff's Model was made by Uberti. An ideal SAA Snubby, it's a good choice for close range targets and SASS Mounted shooters.*

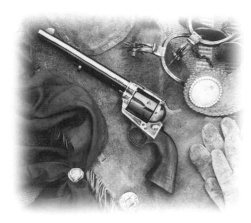

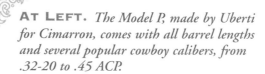

AT LEFT. *The Model P, made by Uberti for Cimarron, comes with all barrel lengths and several popular cowboy calibers, from .32-20 to .45 ACP.*

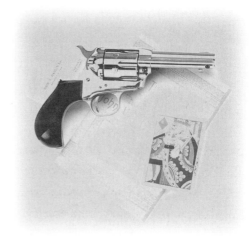

AT RIGHT.
The Cimarron Model P Junior is ideal for lady shootists and anyone with small hands. It's available with regular or birdshead grips.

AT LEFT. *Two examples of engraving styles on Cimarron Single Actions, plus a rare photo of Dr. & Mrs. Albert Einstein shot while visiting the Navajo Nations. The ivory-gripped 5-inch first generation replica at bottom bears the initials of U.S. General George Patton, who carried a similar pair.*

.44-40 and .357 Magnum, with 5- and 7-inch barrels. Finish choices are blue/color case, nickel and engraved. Navy Arms' 1875 Models are in blue with case hardened frames and are available in .45 Colt or .44-40, with barrels measuring the original 7 inches. Both have walnut two-piece grip scales and are considered accurate replicas.

In 1890, Remington updated its single action by removing the steel web from under the barrel (overkill for the already strong construction), changing the rear sight to a more Colt-like configuration and adding a lanyard ring to the grip butt. EMF sells the most variations of the replicated 1890 Remington, but in .45 Colt only. EMF offers a nickel-plated edition as well as an all-blued version with brass trigger guard. The Navy Arms model is blued throughout and is sold in .44-40 as well as .45 Colt. Both versions feature walnut grips standard on the originals. The Remington 1890 Model is an interesting option for those whose chosen characters lived in the 1890s, and who are comfortable with the different feel and balance of these Colt alternatives.

THE SMITH & WESSON SCHOFIELD

The Smith and Wesson breaktop single action revolvers of 1875 are quite different in both use and appearance. A transitional design between the traditional Colt/Remington single action and the swing-out cylinder revolvers that came later, the S&W Schofields represented a step toward the future. Looking very little like the Colt Peace-maker, these businesslike six-shooters are nonetheless historic. Billy the Kid's pal, Pat Garret, carried a version of the S&W Schofield, as did Colonel George Custer, at least for a while. His troopers might have had better luck at the Greasy Grass fight if they'd been armed with Schofields. Cowboys carried them, and the Wells Fargo agents used the same models with shorter barrels. Lawmen, too, praised these revolvers for their practicality. Admirers of Colt Peacemaker's

fluid lines won't find the Schofields very attractive, but "pretty is as pretty does," and some Cowboy/ Western Action shooters who do pretty well with Schofields.

The idea behind the Schofield and its predecessor, the 1874 New Model Russian (or S&W Third Model) was the ease with which cavalry troopers could unload and reload, both at the gallop and under fire. Cowboy actioneers don't have such requirements, thankfully, for the Schofield's operation takes some getting used to and the competition clock adds pressure enough. The pistol cocks and fires just like any single action, but reloading is totally different. The shooter first pulls the hammer to half-cock, then releases the catch at the top of the frame with the thumb. The barrel is then tipped down, causing the ejector to rise out of the cylinder, carrying empty brass high enough to be removed by fingers. The ejector then drops back into the cylinder face and the cylinder is ready for reloading. When all pills are in place, the barrel is swung back up and re-latched, ready to be cocked and fired. Cowboy competitors must learn to position the cylinder so that the hammer will rest on an empty chamber.

Some of us find the Colt design faster and easier to reload: Hammer to half cock, swing out the loading gate with the same thumb, rotate the cylinder and eject all brass with the ejector rod. Reload one round, skip a chamber, load four more rounds. Close the gate, pull the hammer to full cock, and CAREFULLY let the hammer down on the empty chamber. You're now ready to cock and fire.

Currently, S&W Breaktops are supplied by the Cimarron F.A. Company, the EMF Company, the Navy Arms Company, Uberti USA and now from the original maker, Smith and Wesson. Cimarron specializes in two models: the 7-inch barreled 1875 Cavalry Model in .45 Colt, .45 S&W Schofield, .44 WCF and .44

Russian. As built by Uberti for Cimarron, this Cavalry Model bears the imprimatur of the inspector impressed upon its walnut grips. Like the originals, it is blued throughout, the same as issued to some of Custer's ill-fated troops.

Cimarron's other version is the Wells Fargo Model, with the same 5-inch barrel favored by the company's agents. When carried against such scofflaws as The Hole-in-the-Wall Gang, this short version of the Schofield revolver is chambered for the same calibers as the Cavalry Model and stamped with the Wells Fargo name and number. Cimarron boasts that its Schofield parts are interchangeable with the originals. EMF Schofields, also made by Uberti, come with the shooter's choice of 7-inch or 5-inch barrels. It also is beautifully blued (but only in .45 Colt caliber).

Navy Arms offers the most variations on the Schofield theme. Aficionados of the arcane may want their unique New Model Russian in the original .44 Russian caliber. This distinctive foot-long firearm features an unusual grip design—a spur for the middle finger on the trigger guard. It's an eye-catcher, but unless a cowboy competitor can find a lever action rifle or carbine in .44 Russian, it might not be the best choice. A better option for the Schofield may be the Navy Arms Cavalry and Wells Fargo Models with their 5- and 7-inch

Major Cowboy Action events are a good place to shop for guns of the Old West. This display features replicas of Sharps, a Springfield cavalry carbine, an 1873 Winchester and an 1885 Winchester High Wall.

barrels in .44-40 and .45 Colt calibers. Peculiar to the Navy Arms Schofield line, by the way, is the snubby 3-inch barrel on its "Hideout" Model. With a short sight radius and additional recoil, this model is not ideal for those 50-foot range stages; but it would make a fine belly gun for self defense and it does have a certain intimidating, bulldog-like appearance.

The increasing influence of activities and lifestyles–like Cowboy and Western action shooting, re-enacting, history adventure vacations and replica arms collecting—has caused some arms and ammunition makers to alter their product lines. Thus it is that Smith & Wesson has re-introduced its 125-year old Model Three Schofield in its original configuration. Cowboy shootists may now shoot Schofields with "Smith & Wesson" on the barrels. Blued, with a case hardened trigger, hammer and an early model latch, this reproduction Third Model Schofield in .45 S&W has a 7-inch barrel and the same fixed notch and half-moon post sights found on the originals. The sight plane atop the barrel is grooved full-length and the grips are walnut. Cowboy *pistoleros* prefer .45 Colt and .44-40, original calibers or not. It's impossible to recommend a firearm sight unseen, but with the addition of cowboy calibers, these "real" Schofields are sure to be blazing away in cowboy competitions across the country.

ABOVE.
A Mexican Two-Loop rig holds a Colt Peachmaker replica. The 1875 S&W Schofield is nickel plated, as is the deluxe 1873 Winchester with tang peep sight. The brass receiver at top is on an 1866 Yellowboy carbine.

Please note: Because replica/reproduction arms vary somewhat from time-to-time and dealer-to-dealer in terms of price, maker and specifications, buyers should consult the listing of firearms dealers in the appendix, along with current gun catalogues and related information.

COWBOY LONG GUNS

Historically, the West was won with rifles. Famous pistol fights, Hollywood walkdowns and genuine duels notwithstanding, frontiersmen and women looked to their long guns first, for both meat and defense. Rifles have their uses and heroes in both categories; Buffalo Bill earned his name and reputation with the 1866 Allen Conversion Springfield he lovingly dubbed Lucrezia Borgia. Cody and fellows like Billy Dixon, with his Sharps, helped rid the Plains of most of the Indians and virtually all the buffalo.

Settlers for whom the West was being won reached for their Winchester or shotgun when danger threatened. Pistols were almost a last resort, just before axes and knives. They reached for rifles again to put meat in the pot; wild game made up much of the frontier diet. Rifles are central to the iconography of the Old West, accounting for at least as many rounds fired in Cowboy/Western Action matches as do revolvers. Riflecraft is requisite for success and a full load of fun in this increasingly competitive sport.

THE HENRY

Cowboy Action means lever action and the earliest period lever guns practical for cowboy competiton are the Henrys. B. Tyler Henry worked for Oliver Winchester in 1860 when he received his patent for his lever operated, cartridge ammunition rifle. The revolutionary rifle held 15 of the new .44 Henry rimfire rounds and it was said that a man armed with a Henry couldn't be captured. In those days, it might have been true.

The Henry was a force to be reckoned with through the Civil War. Most combatants were armed with muzzle loading percussion arms. Henry's were known as "that damned Yankee rifle you loaded on Sunday and shot all week", the fifteen bullets in their magazine tubes an overwhelming advantage in combat. After the war, Henry's became the first of the Winchesters to be one of the guns that won the West.

Cowboy shootists can choose Henry replica models made by Uberti and marketed by Cimarron, Dixie Gun Works, EMF, Navy Arms, and Taylor's & Co. Cimarron's version is perhaps the most detailed replica, bearing the original inspection stamps of a government inspector and B. Tyler Henry himself. The fidelity of reproduction doesn't end there; Cimarron Henrys come with brass receivers and buttplates, ladder type rear sights and sling hardware. The 24 inch octagon barrels come charcoal blued or in the white (untreated), and in .44-40 and .45 Colt calibers.

Dixie Gun Works Henrys, iron frame or brass, are also chambered for these cowboy calibers, weigh about the same, (9+ lbs.), but have blued barrels and levers. In addition, Dixie offers a Trapper, (carbine), with a 16.5 inch barrel. The shortened magazine holds but seven rounds, however, effectively curtailing its use as Cowboy Action equipment. The 24¼ inch rifle tube holds twelve, two more than most match stages usually require.

From EMF, shooters can select either of two Henry rifles in .44-40 or .45 Colt, with barrels in the white or blued. Navy Arms offers three brass frame Henry models, all with blued barrels of .44-40 or .45 Colt and richly oil-finished walnut stocks. But Navy Arms also has "Iron Frame Henrys", replicas of those very few—400 or so—first models built in 1860 with case hardened steel receivers. Originals are scarce as hen's teeth, but Navy Arms has replicas both color case hardened and deep gloss blued. These beauties are chambered for .44-40 only, with a thirteen round magazine capacity. The brass frame carbine holds eleven rounds

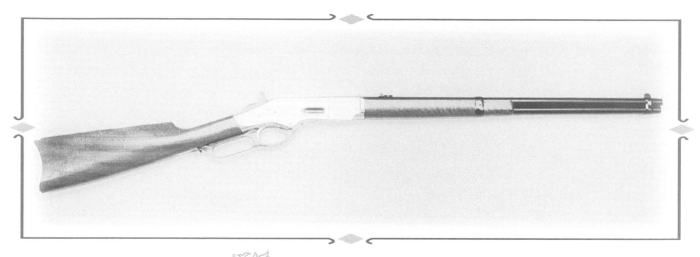

ABOVE. *1866 Yellowboy Carbine*

and the short Trapper, eight. The most practical models for Cowboy shootists are their military models, which are specially reinforced to withstand the rigors of cowboy action and skirmishing. Both brass and iron frame Henry models are for sale at Taylor's Company with both blued barrels and flip-up ladder rear sights. Calibers are .44-40 and .45 Colt.

While Henrys are a fine choice for shooters whose persona lived in the 1860s and early 1870s, they come with considerations. Henrys load from the front of the magazine tube, there being no provisions for loading through the receiver. The rifles are thus handicapped in stages of fire requiring rifle reloads. And Henrys have no wooden forend, and those barrels heat up quickly in rapid fire. But the most important concern is that of safety. The magazine follower, which compels by spring-loaded energy the movement of cartridges to the receiver, must always be released gently against the rounds in the magazine, and NEVER be allowed to slam home as a result of spring tension. This could—and very well might—result in one or more rounds being fired straight from the end of the magazine. It has happened. Henrys are eye-catching, however, and they remain the only lever gun correct for most of the 1860s.

THE 1866 WINCHESTER YELLOWBOY

Those who want to shoot an early period carbine or rifle with a brass receiver might choose the 1866 Model Winchester Yellowboy. It was the first firearm sold under the Winchester name and became an instant success—especially in the West, where both cowboys and Indians snapped them up one way or another. Greatly improved over the Henry, the Yellowboy features a loading gate located on the right side of the receiver and a walnut forearm for improved handling. The rifle could now be reloaded while the butt was at the shoulder, a huge advantage. Winchester 1866 Yellowboys are as appropriate for "Old West" scenarios as one can get and are extremely popular with cowboy actioneers. Decorated with tribal-like brass tacks, Yellowboys make a colorful sight at cowboy events.

Cimarron's 1866 Model Winchester is a 24-inch barreled Sporting Rifle with a flip-up long range rear sight and a brass forearm tip. The 19-inch barrel carbine, with its buckhorn rear sight and near-side carbine ring, is just like Red Ryder's. Both are available in either .45 Colt or .44 WCF caliber. Dixie Gun

Works' Yellowboys come only in .44-40 with blued barrels and furniture on both carbines and rifles. EMF offers the same Yellowboys in .44-40 and .45 Colt as well as engraved versions (for special order) in brass and nickel. Navy Arms sells its 1866 Model in .38 Special as well as the standard cowboy calibers .44-40 and .45 Colt. Taylor's & Company offers only the carbine in .38 Special.

THE WINCHESTER '73

Perhaps the rifle that comes closest to being truly "The Gun That Won The West" is the Winchester Model 1873. Originally chambered for the .44 WCF, Winchester reverted back to its steel receiver with removable side plates for ease of

AT LEFT. *The Navy Arms Border Rifle, nicknamed "The Texas Special," was popular throughout the Southwest. With the same 20-inch barrel as the carbine, but with a heavier, octagon barrel, it made a fine saddle rifle that held steady. Pictured here with "Mother Hubbard"-style Santa Fe saddle.*

cleaning and repair. Other calibers—namely, the .44-40, .38-40 and .32-20—were added, whereupon the frontiersmen began the practice cowboy actioneers continue today; carrying the same caliber for both pistol and rifle.

Winchester continued to develop its lever action line through the 1876 Model in .45-70 and the 1886 Model in both .45-70 and .45-90, but these rifles were designed strictly for buffalo and big game. Tom Horn used an '86 Winchester, although not on poor Willy Nickell, and "Teddy" Roosevelt was also a fan of the big gun. The '86 Winchesters are not currently replicated and originals are pricey and hard to come by. Should they ever be reproduced, however, these rifles would be fun to shoot in long range side matches.

The Winchester '73s are probably the second most popular rifle in Cowboy/Western Action Shooting. They are also "period correct" for any time from 1873 up to 1920, when the model was finally discontinued. Today's cowboy competitors can choose from among several variations of the 1873s built by A. Uberti of Italy. Cimarron offers shooters a dream collection of no less than eight versions of the famed rifle (in .44 WCF and .45 Colt). Included are 24-inch barrel Sporting rifles, Long Range rifles with 30-inch barrels, a 19-inch round-barreled Saddle Carbine, a 20-inch octagon-barreled Short Rifle and an accurate replication of the original limited edition beautifully engraved, "1 of 1,000.." All but this rifle and the carbine have color case hardened receivers. Deluxe versions feature gentle pistol grips and fine-grained checkered walnut stocks.

Dixie Gun Works offers a handsomely blued, 10-shot saddle carbine '73 in .44-40 and .45 Colt, a 24-inch octagon-barreled Sporting Rifle (same calibers), a deluxe pistol grip version of the above, an engraved model and the half magazine (six-round capacity) Deluxe Sporter. This last is blued, with a color case

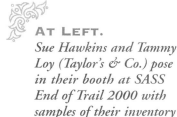

hardened receiver and an octagon-to-round barrel. Unfortunately, it's four rounds short of a Cowboy ten-pack. EMF sells three examples of the 1873 model: all-blued carbine, a carbine with color case hardened receiver, and an octagon-barreled/case hardened rifle, all in .44-40 or .45 Colt.

Navy Arms' Winchester '73s include two blue and case hardened rifles, one with fancy wood and a pistol grip, the other an all-blued carbine. The rifles feature octagon barrels; the carbine is round. Navy Arms has a "Border Model" Short Rifle with a 20-inch octagon barrel. It was popular in the Old Southwest for its heavier barrel and the ease with which it could slide in and out of a saddle scabbard. All models are available in .44-40, .45 Colt or .357 Magnums, with bead and blade front and ramp buckhorn rear sights. Taylor's & Company offers only one 1873 Winchester, but it is easily the most popular model used in Cowboy/Western Action Shooting. Thousands of these 24-inch octagon-barreled rifles (in .44-40 and .45 Colt) were built and used throughout the West by nearly everybody.

The three rifles discussed above—the 1860 Henry, the 1866 Winchester Yellowboy and the 1873 Winchester Sporting Rifle—were made for blackpowder cartridges. Shooters and re-enactors who use these models ought properly to shoot blackpowder ammunition, both for the sake of authenticity and to minimize the pressures of smokeless powder and heavy usage. These toggle action guns are precursors to the later and much stronger vertical locking block actions found on lever guns built by Winchester and Marlin. Blackpowder is the appropriate propellant for such guns; indeed, for any firearm manufactured prior to the general introduction of smokeless powder in the 1890s.

THE MODEL '92 WINCHESTER

The most frequently used lever action rifle and carbine in Cowboy Action Shooting is the Winchester Model 1892 designed by John Browning. It's the rifle most of us grew up thinking that it (along with the Colt Peacemaker) was *the* cowboy gun. With its vertical locking block lever gun design, the Winchester '92 (and '94) are also the *only* Old West rifles and carbines used properly with modern smokeless powder. The '92 was the lever action John Wayne carried in virtually

AT LEFT. *Buffalo and Indian War rifles from Dixie Gun Works include (from right): 1873 Springfield Trapdoor .45-70 Gov. Infantry rifle, Springfield Cavalry Carbine; 1874 Sharps in .45-70; and a Kodiak Mark IV .45-70 Double Express rifle with external hammers.*

AT RIGHT. *Schofield 1875 and Cattleman 1873 S.A. with standard engraving and white finish*

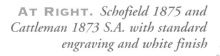

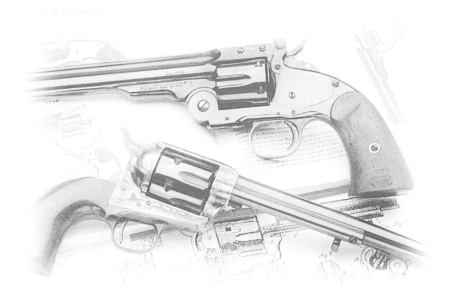

AT LEFT. *Schofield 1875 and Cattleman 1873 Single Action revolvers*

all his Westerns, "period correct" or not. Only shooters and firearms fanciers knew the difference. The old '92 is so deeply imbedded in our minds because we watched so many movies and television programs wherein it figured so prominently, even in films set in the 1870s. Only fairly recently have moviemakers bothered with realism and authenticity. Perhaps more Cowboy/Western Action Shooters will eventually follow suit.

Replica Model '92s can be acquired from American Western Arms, EMF, Navy Arms and U.S. Repeating Arms. AWA offers slick, beautifully finished Model 1892s in the classic rifle, carbine and short rifle formats, all available in the classic cowboy calibers: .357/.38, .44-40 and .45 Colt. EMF offers three versions built by Armi San Marco with 24-inch octagon barrels. The Standard model is blued throughout, except for its color case lever and forearm tip. The deluxe model has a color case lever, receiver and forearm tip, while the Premier model has select grade walnut stocks, buckhorn rear sight, and color case hardened receiver. All are .45 Colt caliber.

Navy Arms provides shooters with six variations of the venerable Winchester Model 1892. The two most likely to be found around the ranch in the 1890s were equipped with blued 24-inch, octagon barrels (the carbine had round barrels). Both are available in .357 Magnum, .44-40 or .45 Colt. The same pair can be ordered in stainless steel (not period accurate) in the same calibers, as can that Southwestern favorite, the Short Rifle. It features a color case hardened receiver and forearm tip. Like the carbine, the so-called "Texas Special" octagon barrels are 20 inches long. Navy Arms '92s are made specially for it by Rossi and are the pride of the firm's founder, Val Forgett.

From U.S. Repeating Arms, cowboy riflemen can acquire a reproduced Model '92 that says "Winchester" on the barrel. Following its rebirth in 1997 in response to the demand from cowboy shootists, the new Winchester Model '92s come replete with a tang-mounted, sliding shotgun-type safety. While this is some better than those ugly, redundant and period incorrect crossbolt things found on some modern lever guns it was never used on an original '92. Lever action rifles—especially Models '92 and '94—are fast and easy to chamber, and safe in an empty chamber, not a button or a switch.

The Winchester Model 1894, America's deer rifle in 30-30, was also the 20th century Cowboy's prized saddle gun. The new Winchester *Trails End* '94 model, despite its disfiguring cross bolt mechanism, is also an excellent Cowboy Action carbine in .357 Magnum, .44 Remington Magnum and .45 Colt. Its capacity (11 rounds) is sufficient for matches, as are its driftable front ramp and buckhorn rear sights. The rifle version, called the *Legacy*, has a 24-inch barrel and holds 12 rounds of the same calibers. It carries the same sights but sports a cut-checkered pistol grip and forend.

MARLIN: THE "OTHER LEVER ACTION"

Those cowboy competitors who do not choose Winchester replicas for their post-1890 smokeless powder persona are probably shooting Marlins, whose Models I (.45 Colt) and II (.357/.38 Special or .44 Magnum/.44 Special) have won many a Cowboy match. Always in the shadow of Winchester (except in the eyes of Marlin shooters, of course) these fine rifles and carbines have been shooting a niche for themselves since 1870. Marlin shooters especially like the smooth action and side ejection feature. Both models have 10-round magazine tubes and 24-inch octagonal barrels, are blued and have ramp-type buckhorn sights, same as the originals. The Cowboy Models have deep-cut, six-groove Ballard-type rifling and traditional straight stocks of checkered, straight-grained walnut. The Marlin Model 1894S is four inches shorter, its round-barreled carbine holding 10 rounds of .44 Magnum/.44 Special. All Marlins now come equipped with politically (but not period) correct cross bolt safeties.

The other lever action option for Cowboy-style shooters fortunate enough to find an original is the Browning Model 1892, which is virtually identical to the Winchester and equally desirable. Browning re-introduced these fine rifles in 1979, but only in .44 Magnum/Special. and .357 magnum/.38 Special. Marlin quit making them for some reason, but shooters can still hunt them up at gun shops and shows. Paired with .38 or .44 Special six-guns, they make great cowboy rifles.

Side Match Single Shots

While single shot rifles are rarely required in main match Cowboy Action stages, side matches afford the opportunity to shoot some of the most historic and romantic rifles of the Old West. Long Range or Precision Rifle side matches are usually shot with falling block designs, such as the 1874 Sharps and 1885 Winchester High Wall, or Remington Rolling Block or 1873 Trapdoor Springfield rifles. These rifles, all in .45-70 caliber, are the *Buffalo* guns, the artillery used to clear the Great Plains of those pesky, migratory giants and the people who depended upon them. Custer took his first Grizzly with an engraved, tang-sighted Remington Creedmore Rolling Block, only to have it captured by one of the victors at Last Stand Hill. It hasn't been seen since. Billy Dixon's lucky long shot at Adobe Walls put the fear of Sharps into the Commanches, and Sharps shooter Matthew Quigley of movie fame quickly caused the quietus of those miserable miscreants down under, one round at a time.

Cowboy contestants like to shoot replicas of these big guns in the *Buffalo Single Shot* category, booming forth .45-70 rounds amid clouds of white blackpowder smoke from heavy barrels resting on "buffalo sticks." Other SASS categories allow lever action rifles using rifle and pistol calibers. But for serious 1870s and '80s lovers, the Buffalo Single Shot is the right rifle choice.

As our sport-filled lifestyle grows, more shooters are shooting more replicas of more Old West guns. The aforementioned buffalo guns are all available through Cowboy/Western Action suppliers, and all are quality rifles at reasonable prices. Cimarron offers three Sharps models, the differences largely those of furniture. The *Silueta* is a basic Sharps .45-70 with a 32-inch medium-weight octagonal barrel, a ladder rear sight, and a pistol grip on a walnut shotgun-style stock. The 1874 Sporting Rifle sports the same barrel, but with the addition of premium checkered walnut stock, German silver forend cap, and a Creedmore Vernier tang sight. But for sheer eye appeal, it's the *Quigley* Model, in either .45-70 or .45-120, that stands out. All three are accurate, competitive rifles, with double set triggers, but the Quigley carries all the qualities of the Sporting Rifle, plus an old-time color case patch box inlaid in a grain-rich walnut stock.

Dixie Gun Works also offers three Sharps models. The Sharps Number One Sporting Rifle has a 30-inch, matte blued and tapered octagon barrel. Its case hardened receiver is mated to a satin, oil-finished walnut stock with smooth pistol grip. The rear sight is a flip-up ladder or elevator, marked to 800 yards. Triggers are double-set, double phase. The Sporting rifle is available in both .45-70 and .40-65 blackpowder cartridge calibers. Dixie's Sharps No.3 Sporter (blackpowder .45-70) has a 32-inch octagon barrel and case hardened receiver mounted on a straight, oil-

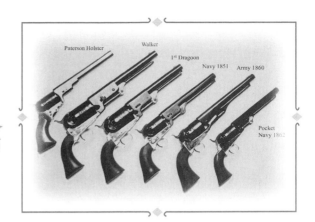

AT RIGHT. *A pictorial history of Colt's percussion revolvers, all replicated by Uberti. Note the size and mass of the Walker Model compared to later models, especially the graceful 1862 Navy Pocket.*

ABOVE. *The Marlin 1894 Cowboy Rifle (in .45 Colt, .38/.357 and .44 Mag/Spl.)is a classic cowboy competition lever rifle with an octagon 24-inch barrel, a 10-round magazine, ramp and buckhorn iron rear sight and Marble front sight.*

finished walnut stock. Sights and triggers are the same as on the No. 1 A "business" rifle, as they called 'em on the Plains. Dixie's engraved *Silueta* Model is a full-dress No.1 Sporting Rifle with engraved receiver left in the white. With stock and forend of select oiled walnut, it makes a handsome piece indeed.

EMF markets Sharps replicas made by the Davide Pedersoli Italian arms factory. Aficionados of the Buffalo rifle can choose the standard "business rifle" with its blued, medium-weight 32-inch octagonal barrel, case hardened receiver and open sights. It's in .45-70 caliber, but there's also a shorter carbine chambered for .54 caliber. The Premier

EMF Pedersoli Sharps is a richly finished Sporting Rifle in .45-70 Government and featuring a pistol grip walnut stock, German silver forend cap and flip-up ladder rear sight. All but the carbines have double set triggers.

Navy Arms offers six Sharps configurations, all built by Pedersoli. Three of these models are of special interest, both historically and competitively. The first is the 1874 Sharps Buffalo Rifle, as fine a friend as a Plainsman could ever know. With its heavy, but handy 28-inch barrel, flip-up rear sight, double set triggers and figured walnut stock, this here is a real buffler gun. It throws .45-70 or .45-90, whatever the shoulder can stand, but the

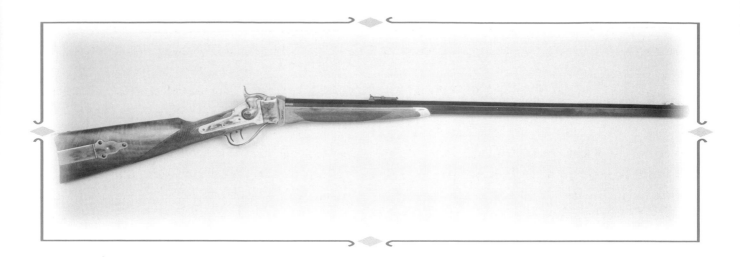

ABOVE. The Quigley Model 1874 Sharps (made famous by Tom Selleck in the film Quigley Down Under) is a favorite among cowboy sharpshooters, with its distinctive forend cap, double set triggers and patchbox.

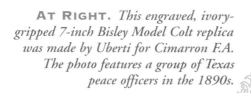 

AT RIGHT. This engraved, ivory-gripped 7-inch Bisley Model Colt replica was made by Uberti for Cimarron F.A. The photo features a group of Texas peace officers in the 1890s.

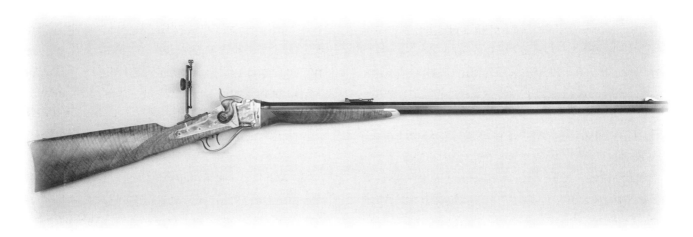

ABOVE. The Billy Dixon 1874 Sharps Model (made for Cimarron by Uberti) commemorates the famous 1,538-yard-long shot Dixon made at the Battle of Adobe Walls. Note the octagon barrel, silver forend cap, finely figured and checkered stock, double set triggers and tang-mounted Vernier rear sight.

twelve pounds the gun weighs helps some. Add the optional Pedersoli tang Vernier sight and all that's lacking is ammo and practice.

Another infrequently seen, but historically important Sharps is the 1874 Cavalry Carbine in .45-70, which was issued to some of Col. Custer's feckless troops, among others. A 22-inch barrel kept weight down to less than eight pounds, making it handy in the saddle as well. Geronimo is sometimes pictured with one. It's a good choice for students of the Indian Wars. So too is the Sharps Infantry Rifle in .45-70. With its three-banded, full-length walnut stock, sling swivels and patchbox, it resembles the muskets of its ancestry. One almost expects a ramrod beneath its 30-inch barrel. Double set triggers and tang sight are options that help make this unique Sharps such a sharpshooter.

Taylor's & Company's own fine 1874 Sharps replicas are made in Italy by Armi Sport in several styles considered ideal for Cowboy/Western Action single shot shooting. The company's '74 Sporting rifle is available with 30-inch and 32-inch octagon barrels and with single or double set triggers, a ladder rear sight and walnut stock. All these goodies are optional. Shooters may choose case hardened or white receivers, a patchbox and a Hartford pewter forend cap. Add Creedmore sights, select a checkered or an Infantry Model stock—or even an old Berdan one-piece stock—and enjoy the Sharps model of your dreams. All Taylor's & Co. Sharps are .45-70 caliber.

THE REMINGTONS

Important as Sharps rifles were on the Great Plains of Western history, they weren't out there alone. The Remington Rolling Block rifle of the same period had its subscribers, most of whom worked them with great success on buffalo and other large animals. Like the Sharps, the Remington was favored by the marksmen and women of the day as well as buffalo hunters and frontiersmen who required long range, large caliber rifles. Cowboy shootists who know the joys of thumping lead into a reactive target way off yonder, using a rifle from the 1870s, frequently choose the Rolling Block for its in-line hammer and/or the rolling action of its breechblock. Historically, the Remington is a good option for Long Range Single Shot matches and those folks whose alter egos roamed the prairies of the 1870s.

Dixie Gun Works sells only one Remington Rolling Block model, but it's the rifle that was custom-made for the 1874 Creedmore matches on Long Island. It comes ready for the rifle range with a blued, 30-inch, tapered octagon barrel and case hardened receiver. Also featured are buckhorn and Vernier tang rear sights, a hooded front sight, and a satin-smooth walnut shotgun style stock with a checkered pistol grip. This fine blackpowder cartridge rifle is available in .45-70 or .40-65. EMF carries one Remington, too: the .45-70 Carbine with blued barrel and color case receiver. A good Indian Wars period choice, it has a brass barrel ring, trigger guard and buttplate, all decorated nicely with optional brass nailheads.

Navy Arms' three Rolling Blocks—all made by Pedersoli—include a business-like buffalo gun with a half-round, half octagon 26-inch or 30-inch blued barrel. The same rifle can be had with a heavy, full octagon barrel. The No.2 Creedmore target Model, with a 30-inch octagon blued barrel and case hardened receiver, is fitted with a Pedersoli Vernier tang sight and hooded front sight. The wood is select grade walnut with a finely checkered pistol grip. All are drilled and tapped for tang sights, making them highly competitive as Buffalo Single Shot match rifles.

THE 1873 SPRINGFIELD

Military history students know that during the Indian Wars the cavalryman's primary weapon was his saber. His pistol was the second weapon of choice, useful as a defensive weapon primarily. But when his adversary was upon him and his revolver was shot dry, it was time to draw the saber. The carbine became the first weapon of engagement.

The carbines and rifles of the U.S. Army were mostly 1873 Trapdoor Springfields, in the then new and powerful .45-70 caliber. Built by the government's Springfield Armory and shipped immediately to troops in the field, these rifles became the standard of the army, and some were used in the Spanish-American War. Springfields used by Colonel Custer's troopers were two years old when they "surprised" the Sioux and Cheyenne in June of 1876. The carbines and their Trapdoor bolts performed well, so well that the ejector frequently tore off the weak copper cartridge heads, leaving the rest of the casings stuck firmly in the breech. Sitting on the ground, digging out the stuck empties with their knives, the soldiers were easy targets for arrows, bullets and tomahawks. The change to brass cartridges took the government another 12 years.

The 1873 Trapdoor was built in cavalry carbine and infantry rifle models and both have been accurately replicated for the cowboy actioneers. It's a great choice for shooters in cavalry uniforms as well as plain old cowboys. Many '73s were pressed into service on the buffalo grass and then carried home to the ranch. Dixie Gun Works has 1873 Trapdoor Springfields in three configurations. The popular Cavalry Carbine has a round, 22-inch blued barrel and receiver, an oiled walnut full stock and a non-authentic (but useful) 400-yard ladder rear sight. The Infantry Rifle, with its 32-inch blued barrel, has an oil finish, a full-length walnut full stock. There are also blued barrel rings, sling swivels, steel cleaning rod and a 500-yard ladder rear sight.

Dixie's top-of-the-line '73 Trapdoor is the Officer's Model. Only 477 of the originals were made (as hunting rifles for army officers) between 1875 and 1885. It has a deeply blued barrel and furniture, plus a color case hardened receiver and breechblock. The gun is mounted on a satin finish, oiled halfstock containing a wooden pewter-tipped cleaning rod to match the forend cap. Rank does have its privileges, after all. These beautiful Dixie Springfields made by Pedersoli are stamped with the U.S. and eagle markings of the originals, and all are in .45-70 caliber.

Navy Arms' Springfields (also made by Pedersoli) are faithful to the originals as well. In .45-70 caliber, the carbine and rifle both feature blued lockplate, barrels, buttplate and barrel ring and a case hardened breechblock on walnut stocks. The Cavalry Carbine has a saddle bar and ring for carrying the over-the-shoulder carbine harness.

THE 1885 WINCHESTER SINGLE SHOT

The Winchester Model 1885, John Browning's 1879 falling block design, came late to the buffalo slaughter, but served the passing frontier and the early 20th century well as an excellent big game and target rifle. Nicknamed "High Wall" or "Low Wall" after its receiver designs, the 1885 Winchester served shooting stars like Pawnee Bill as well as ordinary cowboys and game-fed farmers. Nowadays, it is the Long Range rifle of choice for many Cowboy/Western Action shooters.

Cimarron Firearms stocks the '85 Winchester by Uberti in .45-70, .45-90, .40-65 and .38-55 calibers. With blued 30-inch octagon barrel, color case hardened receiver and lever action trigger guard, this High Wall model is supplied with a brass sectional cleaning rod tucked into its walnut stock via a trap door in the blued butt plate. The front sight is a driftable blade and the rear a ramp and buckhorn, same as in the originals. A hand-checkered pistol grip and double set triggers are optional.

Navy Arms '85 High Wall is by Pedersoli and comes in two styles, both accurately replicated in .45-70. One features a 30-inch medium weight, blued octagon barrel, with a rifle-style crescent

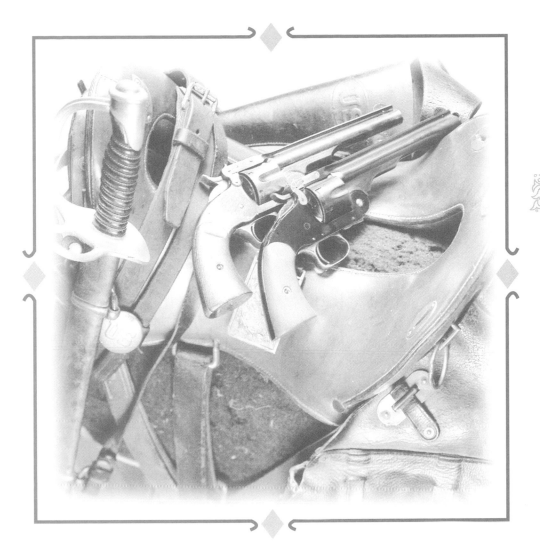

butt plate. The other has a 28-inch barrel and a shotgun-style butt. Both have open sights, but Winchester-style tang and globe front sights are optional.

And then there are the Brownings. The company has reproduced its Low and High Wall models (see above) in response to the growing interest in Cowboy Action Shooting and Long Range Precision and Plainsman events. Beautifully blued and precise in fit, finish and function, the Brownings deemed most appropriate for cowboy Long Range and Silueta shooters are the 1885 High Wall Black Powder Cartridge Rifle (BPCR)

in .40-65 and .45-70 calibers, the Browning High Wall Traditional Hunter in .38-55 and .45-70, and the Low Wall Traditional Hunter in .38/357 Magnum, .44 Magnum and .45 Colt. The BPCR has a 30-inch half octagon, half round barrel and is equipped with a hooded spirit-level front sight with eight inserts and a tang-mounted Vernier rear sight with three aperture sizes. The receiver on this very serious Long Range rifle is color case hardened and the stock is figured walnut (shotgun style) with checkered pistol grip.

Browning's High Wall Traditional Hunter has a 28-inch octagonal barrel, ramp buckhorn and tang

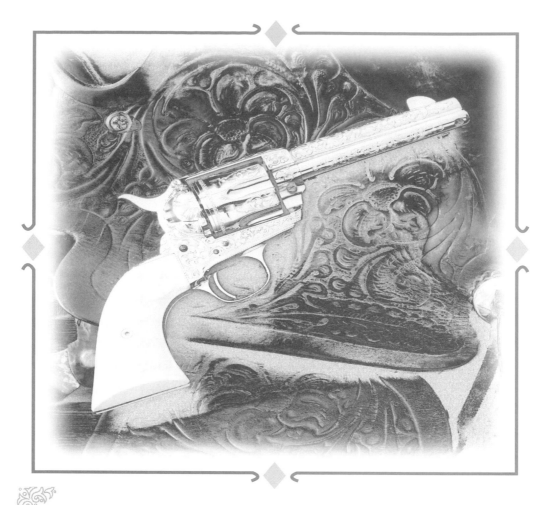

peep rear sight, all on a straight butt walnut stock. The receiver and barrel are both deeply blued. The company's Low Wall version has a 24-inch half-and-half blued barrel in a case hardened receiver. The sights and walnut stocks are the same, along with sling swivel lugs and Schnabel forends. The Traditional Hunters are both smokeless and black powder rifles. The BPCR is black powder only when firing the .40-65 caliber. Regardless, cowboy competitors who demand authenticity should remember that in 1885 smokeless powder was yet to come. Moreover, SASS rules limit the Buffalo Single Shot category to black powder. For period accuracy and shootin' fun, it's the right thing to do.

COWBOY SHOTGUNS

If you could ask an average frontiersman or woman what they'd choose if they could have but one gun, chances are they'd pick a double-barreled shotgun, between 10 and 20 gauge. Shotguns defended the ranch, the covered wagons and stagecoaches of the Old West and brought down fowl for the famished. British Greeners were so popular that shotguns were referred to in general as "Greeners," whether they were or not. Far too many brands existed to list here, but the big names in American arms makers had to include Ithaca, Parker, Remington and Winchester.

Shotguns were central to life on the frontier, and they play an important role in cowboy competition. Many match stages include knock-down shotgun targets. Ironically, both originals and replicas of these commonly used shotguns of the Old West have become increasingly difficult to come by. This is why the Single Action Shooting Society allows internal hammer double guns in competition. SASS also allows Winchester Model 1887 lever action shotguns, assuming originals can be found. The legendary Winchester 1897 Pump model is also a favorite with shooters not choosing the side-by-side. The lever action Winchester 1887 in 12 gauge would be a great gun if replicated. Those who would shoot a period correct double with exposed side mount hammers face a minimal selection. Recognizing the demand for mule-eared Coach Guns and shotguns, Uberti plans a 20-inch 12-gauge shotgun with "period correct" exposed hammers and lockwork by Beretta on period walnut stocks. The Cowboy community anxiously awaits such a realistic replica.

The EMF Stagecoach in 12 gauge would look more authentic with a straight stock, but old-time shotguns did have pistol grips frequently; otherwise, the gun is a genuine Mule Ear with exposed, side-mounted hammers and a side-push barrel release mounted on top of the receiver. Many an old-timer shotgun had bottom action levers that curled up around the receiver, making it handy for the shooter's thumb. To break the gun open, the lever had to be depressed, the empties withdrawn and the gun reloaded. The barrel was then closed, the hammers drawn to full cock, and the gun was ready to shoot.

Built in Italy, the EMF Stagecoach has blued 20-inch "Coach Gun" barrels and lock, checkered walnut stocks and double triggers. The hammers are nicely done side mounts in that curvy, percus-sion style that lends the old-time look so sought after by cowboy types. The same gun is available with 26-inch barrels for cowboy actioneers who also happen to be bird hunters. Not all shotguns in the Old West were coach guns, either. Folks along the frontier were far more likely to own a full-length fowling piece that they hung over the cabin door than a Wells Fargo coach gun. Either EMF gun is ideal for cowboy work, but ought rightly be charged with black powder.

Among cowboy competitors the 12-gauge IGA shotgun with internal hammer from Stoeger is popular in either the 20-inch Coach Gun or 26-inch Uplander model. Stoeger calls them "workhorses" and indeed they are with their strong, tight locks and extractors. They also feature an automatic tang-mounted safety and chrome-moly, micro-polished bores. With or without a laser-engraved stagecoach scene on their hardwood stock, they make a practical and affordable choice for the cowboy shootist.

With a manufacturing life dating from 1897 and lasting until 1957, the Winchester Model '97 Slide Action shotgun is hardly a period Old West firearm. This, the first Winchester shotgun chambered for 2 3/4 inch smokeless powder shells, has become, nonetheless, a legal shotgun in the eyes of SASS and a cowboy favorite. The originals are rapidly disappearing into the gun carts of cowboy competitors, though, probably never to be sold again. They are fast and accurate, evoking images of a fading frontier. More than a million of the Winchester shotguns were produced, however, so fanciers of the old '97 model still have a chance.

Given the few choices open to cowboy shotgunners, replicators would do well by offering Cowboy Action shooters sturdy reproductions of shotguns similar to the 1882 Remington and the 1886 Winchester in 12 and 20 gauge. Cowboy shotgun is fun. Blackpowder shogunning is a blast. 🔔

CHAPTER FOUR

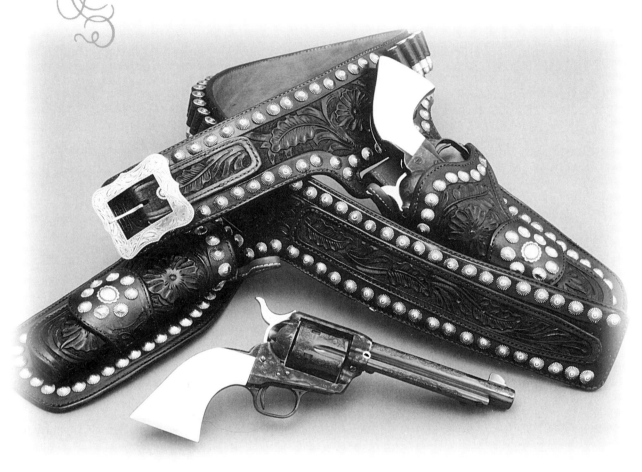

ABOVE. *A treasure in gunleather by the holster patron himself, John Bianchi.*

AT RIGHT. *A carved and stamped holster (made by Rick Bachman) features the deeply recurved throat of later model California Patterns.*

Gunleather & Gun Carts

According to Richard C. Rattenbury, author of Packing Iron, the oldest surviving examples of leather containers used for carrying firearms on horseback were the pommel holsters of the early 19th century Dragoons. As Rattenbury explains, pommel holsters were leather boxes with "pipes" extending beneath them and a flap over the top. Until Samuel Colt invented the Paterson revolver, these pommel holsters were used to carry a single shot flintlock or percussion pistol. Since Dragoons were expected to work with sabers in their right hands, the Army decreed the offside (right) holster to be a box.... "containing a horse shoe, nails, currycomb and brush, etc.." A Dragoon needed his horse more than a single shot pistol, which was kept in the near side (left) holster. Once that one ball was gone, it was war to the knife.

THE CALIFORNIA PATTERN

With the advent of Colt's six-shooters, holster design changed slowly, and one of each pair of pommel holsters was still configured for horse equipment. Not until the adoption of the 1851 Colt Navy, or Belt Model, did military holsters evolve into a softer, more revolver-shaped scabbard. With and without flaps, these were pressed into service by civilians and their patterns were copied and modified as holster design followed firearm form.

Horse soldiers usually had time to unflap their holsters and draw their Colt Dragoons before the ball was opened. But cowboys, lawmen and others soon found that faster access to their sidearms could be the advantage that made the difference. In the ante bellum West, the flapped Army holsters served well, but the need for faster, more practical

holsters were soon met by frontier saddlers and bootmakers. Their early efforts simply copied the form-fitting design of the military holsters, but without the flap. The result was the so-called "California" pattern or "Slim Jim" holster, the first civilian gunleather commonly carried on the Frontier.

Since the period recreated by Cowboy and Western Action Shooting really begins with the end of the War Between the States, it is with this early holster that we begin our look at the options available to cowboy actioneers, whether their goal is historic authenticity or Hollywood fantasy.

California Pattern holsters apparently originated in the shops of northern California saddle and harness makers like Main & Winchester and the L.D. Stone Company. California gold fields were not for the fainthearted or the unarmed, hence these first "Slim Jims" were made to pack the prevailing Colt Dragoons and '51 Navy Models. These first belt holsters were usually form-fitted to the only revolver for which they were intended and were occasionally decorated with floral or other designs. Some originals were carved, stamped, fringed and embroidered, frequently with bullion thread. Caps of silver, gold and nickel silver, carried over from the pommel holsters, sometimes finished the toe of the pipe. Otherwise, the toes were either sewn closed, left open or fitted with a sewn-in toe plug.

The earliest, and perhaps most attractive and practical California holster, had no re-curved cut-out to expose the trigger to the trigger finger; instead, it had an arched convex throat that allowed only the grip to protrude for drawing the pistol. This feature protected the pistol somewhat against brush, bramble and weather, while providing a measure of insurance against accidental discharge in the holster. The most common originals as well as most reproductions have a recurved throat, or top opening, allowing the trigger finger within the trigger guard, even as the pistol is pulled.

California holsters were held to the belt by simple straps or loops sewn and/or riveted to the back. They were broad enough for the wide belts that carried the weight of the pistol, a pouch or

ABOVE. *An elegant California pattern holster and cartridge belt (by Garret Roberts of Kicking Mule Outfitters in Camp Verde, Arizona) display a traditional southwestern look.*

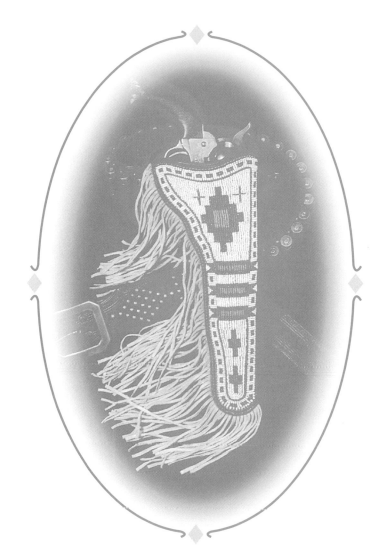

The California Pattern holster and early gunbelt feature: A precise plains beadwork and buckskin fringe by Wild Bill Cleaver *(left)*; another California Pattern holster *(above)* by Wild Bill Cleaver with seed bead Plains decoration and a semi-recurved throat halfway between the full recurve and the rare round top design and three beaded plains holsters *(below)*, courtesy of Wild Bill's Originals.

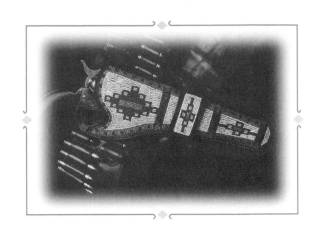

AT RIGHT.
A heavily beaded single loop Mexican holster holds a 7-inch Cavalry Model, with a wide money belt bearing .45 Colt and .45-70 rifle rounds (both by Wild Bill Cleaver).

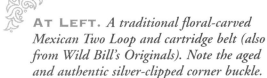

AT LEFT. *A traditional floral-carved Mexican Two Loop and cartridge belt (also from Wild Bill's Originals). Note the aged and authentic silver-clipped corner buckle.*

AT RIGHT.
A re-creation of the Old West is given an antiqued look by Wild Bill's Originals (Vashon Island, WA).

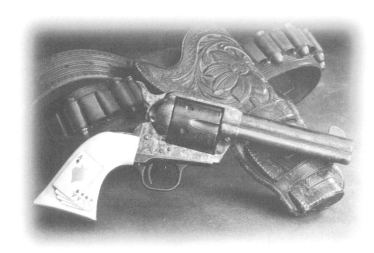

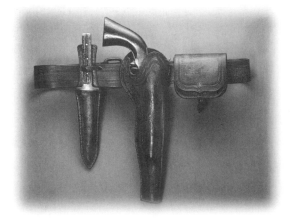

AT LEFT. *Worthy of a museum display, this period outfit by Wild Bill Cleaver includes a California Pattern holster for an 1860 Colt Army Conversion, a cartridge pouch and a Bowie knife sheath, all on a plain, roller buckle belt.*

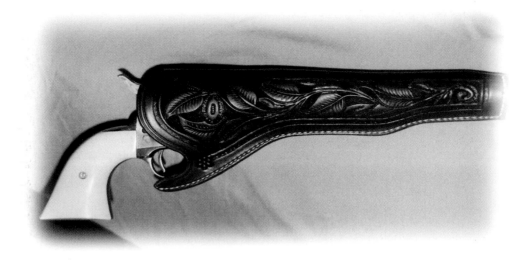

ABOVE. *Made for a 7-inch SAA, this California holster by Dave Rowland (Rio Verde Saddlery) is embellished with a leaf pattern against a stamped background.*

two for ball and caps and the ubiquitous Bowie-type knife that was deployed more often than the gun. This minimalist strap arrangement remains the only negative aspect of these graceful California scabbards. Cartridge belts are simply too thick to slide through the narrow belt loop, which in turn allows the pistol too much lateral movement, especially when riding the quicker gaits or trotting off on foot for another shooting position.

When equipped with an adequate belt loop, California holsters remained handsome and period appropriate right up through the 1890s. Folks used them then and the cowboy actioneers use them now. They are especially well suited for those 1851 Navy and 1860 Army Colt replicas favored by cowboy percussionists, not to mention the slender Colt Conversion models, such as the 1872 Open Top.

THE MEXICAN LOOP PATTERN

The next major development in frontier holster design was the Mexican loop holster. If any holster contributed to "winning the West," it was the Mexican Loop. Certainly it was the most popular Colt pouch used on the frontier and is still the preferred design of the many cowboy Colt

carriers. Like much of the language, equipage and tack used by cowboys then and now, the Mexican Loop was invented "South of the Border," appearing in the West shortly after the Civil War. By the early 1870s, Texas drovers, lawdogs and outlaws had spread the word about the practicality and handiness of this design. As a result, saddlers all over the West began making holsters with belts that held the new cartridge ammunition, along with a cowboy's cash.

It was probably those metallic cartridges that inspired the Mexican Loop holster. Gunbelts now had loops sewn to them for holding anywhere from 6 to 30 or more rounds. Most would not pass through the belt billet of the California-style holster. The innovation that created the Mexican Loop is so simple one wonders why the U.S. Army quartermasters didn't think of it. Instead, it took some poor Mexican *silladero* (saddle maker) to bend the flap of a covered military holster over backwards, cut slits in it, and then push the pipe of the holster through the slits. The progression after that first experiment must have been rapid. For carry on cartridge belts, a better design has yet to be conceived.

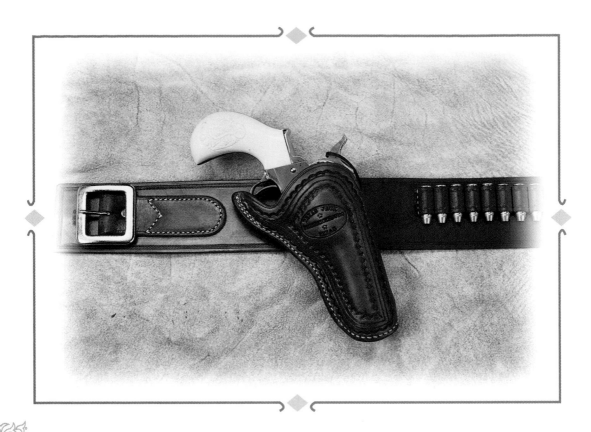

ABOVE. *A Texas Jack crossdraw holster for Cimarron's Thunderer. Note the proper angle for a crossdraw.*

Saddlemakers soon developed the Mexican Loop into an ideal pistol pouch, as well as an example of the leathercrafter's art. Names like F.A. Meanea and J.S. Collins (Cheyenne, WY) made gunleather that today rests in private collections or public museums. To the collector of Western memorabilia or the devout cowboy actioneer, leathermakers like Gallatin, H.H. Heiser, Main & Winchester, the Moran Brothers (Miles City, MT) and El Paso's S.D. Meyers constitute the pantheon of original frontier gunleather. These men and others like Al Furstnow in Montana and R.T. Frazier in Pueblo, Colorado, have perfected their individualized patterns and made commissioned variations for ranch hands and cowboys. Maker's designs and decorations became recognizable and regional peculiarities were fashionable in some locales: the "Texas Jock Strap" comes to mind. Cowboys in their bunkhouses,

too far removed from a saddlery to select a pistol rig off the peg, copied the originals themselves. Because Mexican Loop holsters are normally cut from one piece of leather and require minimal sewing, these "Bunkhouse Specials" served cowboys all over the West, showing up now in fine picture books, captioned "maker unknown".

Interestingly, research obtained through the growing number of books, papers and articles on early Western gunleather reveals few cross-draw holsters and little evidence of studs, conchos, beadwork or fringe. While Mexican examples are frequently embroidered, the first masters of Western gunleather and their customers seemed satisfied with minimal embellishments. The elaborate decorations so typical of gun rigs seen in movies and on television arrived much later, well after the turn of the century. Unless

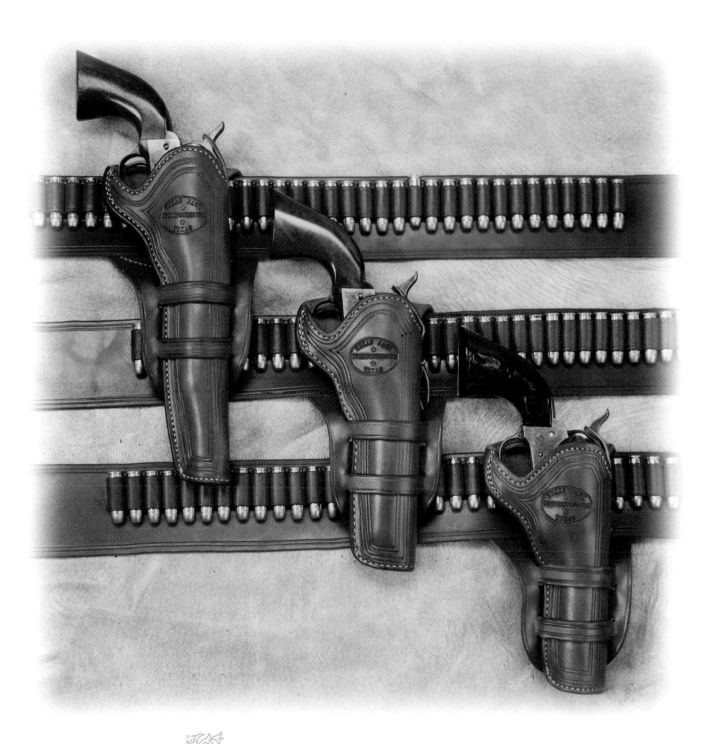

✦ **ABOVE.** *Shown are Mexican Loop rigs for 4 ³/₄, 5 ¹/₂ and 7 ¹/₂ inch Peacemakers featuring fine gunleather by Texas Jack.*

AT LEFT.
A deluxe three-piece Cowboy Action outfit, hand-tooled with a Lone Star motif and handsomely studded by Tombstone Outfitters.

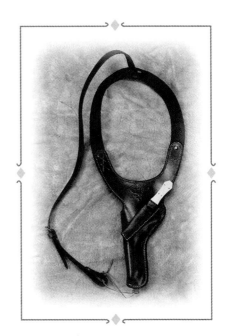

AT RIGHT. *A hideaway shoulder holster (by Texas Jack) modeled after one used by Doc Holiday in "Tombstone" (ivory-handled knife is not included).*

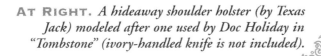

AT LEFT.
A Remington rides in an elegant old-style Mexican Loop with three-piece set (Tombstone Outfitters, Marietta, GA).

ABOVE. *A beautiful, rarely seen interpretation of an early Mexican Loop holster and cartridge belt by Mario Hanel (Hanel's Antiqued Leather Goods). Note the graduated stud motif continued in the sterling silver, hand-engraved buckle (by master engraver Peter Kretzmann).*

cowboy/western shootists are portraying characters from old westerns, they would do well to stick with the designs and decorations of the original makers. They could do no better.

GUN BELTS

Of the gun belts preferred by cowboy shootists, the simple cartridge and money/cartridge belt reproductions are easily the most popular. That's largely because the gun rig full of .45 ammo and a Colt six-shooter is such an indelible and stirring image, a symbol of our emerging frontier culture and independent American spirit. It's also because these modern gunbelts are comfortable, practical and historically accurate. It's what those old-time buckaroos wore, and they needed them. With several reloads of pistol (or rifle) ammunition on his belt, his trusty shooter safely tucked into his Mexican Two Loop, and his all-purpose Bowie knife, the American cowboy was equipped for

the worst, on horse or a-foot. If his cartridge belt was also a money belt, he might even have a silver dollar or two.

Most cowboy actioneers are likely to keep their cash in a wallet, but many still prefer the "money belt" simply because it's more comfortable. While well-made cartridge belts are usually crafted of oak-tanned saddle skirting (for strength and shape retention), money belts are more supple because of their *chaparero* sides or similar flexible leather. Folded and stitched to create a flat, hollow tube, the belt was left open at the buckle for accepting silver money, greenbacks and paperwork. Billets and buckles were sewn on, and there was an opening cut through both layers of leather through which the belt was buckled. This secured the cowboy's net worth—his pistol, knife, ammunition and treasury—all worn around his waist. Everything else of value was on his horse.

(continued on p. 137)

ABOVE. *A "period perfect" Mexican Two Loop and matching money belt from the COWS Packing Iron collection.*

AT RIGHT.
A studded Mexican Three Loop holster (by Kicking Mule Outfitters) clearly indicates the transition from California Pattern to Mexican Loop.

AT LEFT.
This Cheyenne-style Mexican Two Loop and Money Belt combo (Rick Bachman's Old West Reproductions) duplicates the original exactly.

ABOVE. *A dressy rig (from John Bianchi's Frontier Gunleather) shows off the Mexican Two Loop holster, featuring a squared, open toe. The cartridge belt allows interchangeable buckles.*

ABOVE. *Gunleather fit for The King of the The Cowboys. Presented to Roy Rogers by John Bianchi in 1996, it can be seen at the Roy Rogers Museum in Victorville, CA.*

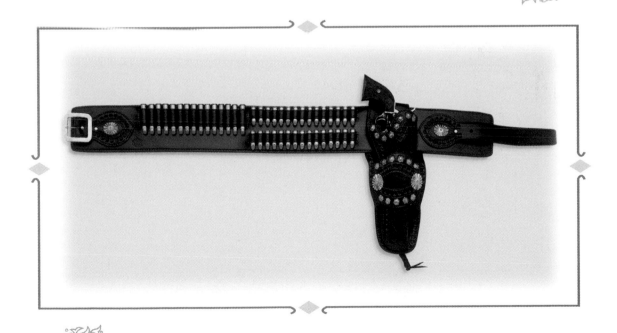

ABOVE. *The Arizona Ranger (Galco International) reproduces a favorite gun rig of the Old Southwest. The wide cartridge belt holds ammunition for both revolver and rifle. The Mexican Loop holster and belt are decorated with jeweler's bronze conchos.*

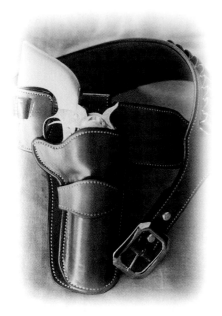

AT LEFT. *A late period outfit is a half-breed rig from John Bianchi's Frontier Gunleather. Note the cut-away in the belt, allowing the holster to ride lower than normal while staying in the same place on the cartridge belt.*

AT RIGHT. *The basic replicated Mexican Two Loop (from Classic Old West Styles, El Paso, TX).*

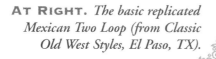

AT LEFT. *A sampling of the many authentic reproductions from Stan Dolega's shop indicates quality and historical accuracy throughout.*

THE PRAIRIE BELT

The U.S. military, meantime, had discovered the value of canvas as gunbelt material. Brass or copper cartridges left in leather belt loops produced a chemical reaction that forms a gummy, crusty coating of *verdigris* on the cartridge brass. This fouling makes removal of rounds from leather cartridge loops difficult; but worse, it can cause failure to chamber or extract. This could prove embarrassing during a shooting affray or cowboy match. Canvas solves the problem.

By the 1870s, canvas cartridge belts were all over the West, particularly on the buffalo ranges of the Southwest. Hide hunters wore canvas "Prairie Belts" full of buffalo rifle rounds—sometimes two at a time—draped over their shoulders like bandoleers. Cowboys found canvas "Mills Pattern" belts with pistol caliber loops an inexpensive alternative to fine russet leather. Big game hunters occasionally wore canvas belts full of rifle rounds above a leather pistol belt. Canvas gun belts are

being reproduced now by many leathercrafters who are making interesting additions to the cowboy actioneer's gun gear. Many cowboy shootists are using canvas shotgun belts worn above their pistol belts. This places the row of shells close to the open breach of a shotgun when reloading, possibly shaving hundredths of a second. The alternative chosen by most shooters is a shotgun slide, a leather or canvas device usually holding six or eight shotgun rounds. The device slides or snaps over a pistol belt at the stomach, ready for reloading.

BUSCADERO RIGS

Cowboy Action shooters who portray the heroes of the silver screen or television may elect to haul their pistols and ammo in a *Buscadero* rig. A corruption of the Spanish *Buscador* (hunter), the word has come to mean the gunleather made famous by Hollywood costumers in the 1940s and '50s.

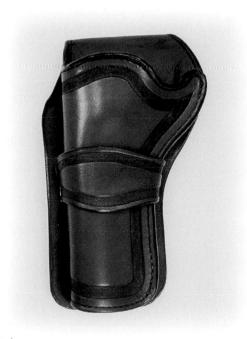

AT LEFT. *This Ranger Model Mexican Loop holster (from Aspen Leather, Basalt, CO) is as rugged and sturdy as it looks.*

AT RIGHT. *The basic gun cart carries long guns and ammo (the shooter's revolver is wornaround his waist).*

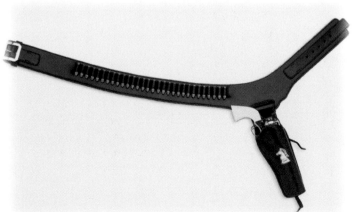

AT LEFT. *Galco recalls Richard Boone and the glory days of Paladin and other black and white TV westerns. This classy Buscadero rig is indeed formal gunleather.*

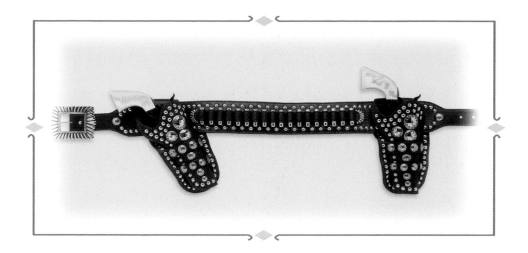

ABOVE. *This glittering gun fighter's gunleather (by Galco) features a crossdraw second gun and enough silver studs and conchos to satisfy Johnny Ringo himself.*

AT RIGHT.
Judge Roy Bean's personal gun rig (by JAX Leather Co.) is an elegant outfit with a handy matching belt pouch.

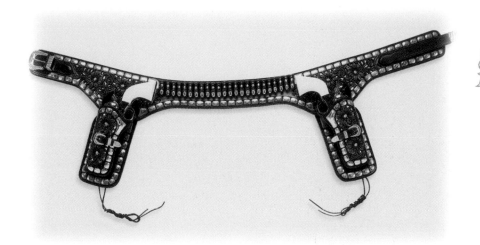

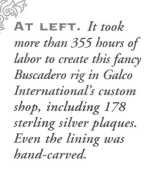

AT LEFT. *It took more than 355 hours of labor to create this fancy Buscadero rig in Galco International's custom shop, including 178 sterling silver plaques. Even the lining was hand-carved.*

These are the gun rigs that hang a pistol well down the thigh, tied down to the leg and close to the hand, ready for a fast draw. They are the stuff of movies and not of history, but some shooters do pay homage to those imaginary cowboys; hence, Buscadero outfits are legal according to SASS rules. The National Congress of Old West Shootists, however, proscribes these modern concoctions in the interest of authenticity. Mounted shooters, re-enactors and adventure riders eschew them as absolutely impractical for a horseman and they'd be a durned nuisance for the working cowboy.

Percussion shooters have their own gunbelt requirements. They have no need of cartridge loops but they do need someplace to carry powder, ball, patches and caps. These ammunition components are best arranged in boxes and pouches on the front of the plain, wide leather belt typical of the period. Reproduction U.S. Army gun belts are common, as are custom and bunkhouse rigs. Cap n' Ball cowboys usually carry a belt or shoulder "possibles" bag to accommodate some of the tools and paraphernalia required for their arcane and antique art. Everything else of value is on the gun cart.

AT LEFT. *Gun carts with large, wide wheels are easier to haul around cowboy matches, no matter what the weather or ground conditions.*

GUN CARTS

Because Cowboy and Western Action shooters need at least two revolvers, a rifle and a shotgun, plus hundreds of rounds needed for a typical ten-stage match (and perhaps a side match or two), cowboy shootists have developed a vehicle peculiar to their sport: a gun cart. No more individual a contraption was ever invented, and no two are ever exactly alike. Made of almost anything wooden and Western, they are usually two-wheeled, L-shaped boxes that haul whatever is required for a day on the range.

Some, powered by pedaling or batteries, can actually be ridden. Most are pulled, pushed and cussed at from one stage to the next. Shooters pack them with lunch, thermos bottles, camera gear, canteens, gunsmith tools, spare guns, gun cleaning stuff, rainwear, rags, plunder purchased from peddlers, and lots of personal "possibles." Anything goes, with concepts ranging from the sublime to the ridiculous. One is a live burro, and a patient SASS member with an alias and badge number.

Major Cowboy matches generally have a "Best Gun Cart" contest, featuring entries that are always interesting and innovative. Gun cart gridlock occurs at every major match, and they sure weren't around in the 19th century, but until they let us ride our horses to the line, or use real wagons or carriages, we're stuck with 'em. Actually, they're handier than a shirt pocket. With an umbrella, they become a chair in the shade for a visit with amigos, or studying stage instructions while waiting to shoot. We couldn't get along without them.

(continued on p. 146)

ABOVE.
Gun carts are as individual as the cowboys and cowgirls who ride them. This one—a U.S. Army late model McClellan—even has a saddle.

ABOVE. *Ellsworth T. Kincaid (right) built this well-upholstered cabinetry for his Lady Stetson and their plunder.*

ABOVE. *The shooter may stand in the sun, but his long guns and ammo rest in the shade of a Conestoga gun cart.*

AT RIGHT. *Dusty Boots proves cowboys in the Old West made do with the basics, complete with boots, duckins britches, homespun shirt, wild rag and vest. Gunleather to gun cart, he's period correct and equipped for a day's shooting at Ruger's WinerRange.*

AT LEFT. *Everybody's favorite gun cart is also a registered SASS member, with badge and number. It's a family membership, of course.*

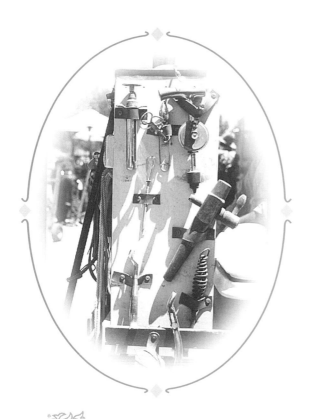

ABOVE. *Various "surgical" instruments like these (above) are not normally seen on the backs of gun carts. But Doc Peabody's cart (right), like the Doc himself, is not normal.*

ABOVE. *Some gun carts are eminently sensible (left), while others offer all the comforts of home (right).*

REPRODUCTION GUNLEATHER

Cowboy Actioneers fortunate enough to own original 19th century gunleather are unlikely to use it in competition. As with original firearms, such relics are too valuable or too fragile. The Old West had its master makers of saddlery and gunleather, and the New West has its masters of reproduction. Today's names of note include R.M Bachman (Florence, MT), John Bianchi (Rancho Mirage, CA), Wild Bill Cleaver (Burton, WA) and Mario Hanel (Sisters, OR). Like the makers of old, they are known by the cartouche stamped on their products.

Among the first to perfect the re-creation of genuine cowboy gunleather was Rick Bachman, who began as a collector. His treasury of original Western leather artifacts has grown to over 3,000 items during 40 years of serious gathering. Every piece in his collection was made before 1900, and some date as far back as the 1840s. His private museum provided the inspiration for his career. Well before the advent of Cowboy/Western Action Shooting, he began copying the originals in his vast reliquary of frontier leathercraft. "I had to," he says, "'cause I couldn't play with the originals." It's difficult to tell Bachman's reproductions from the real thing. His works are favorites among those who insist on absolute authenticity and Hermann Oak Tanned leather. The California and Mexican Loop designs of the old masters do indeed live on in the exacting work of Rick Bachman's gunleather and gear.

John Bianchi has been called the world's premier holster maker. His 40-year career produced some 40 million gun rigs for private, police and military users, including such notables as John Wayne, Paul Newman and the U.S. armed forces. Founder of Bianchi International, he is also author of *Blue Steel and Gunleather*, a major reference text on the history and use of gun-

leather. Holder of 200 patents, trademarks and copyrights, he is the founder of the famed Bianchi Cup pistol competition. His collection of Old West artifacts helped form the nucleus of the Gene Autry Western Heritage Museum in Los Angeles. Now "retired," Bianchi's time is spent building only Western gunleather, by hand and by himself. His signed and certified creations are highly regarded by discriminating shooters who want re-creations of gunleather used by the movie stars and rangeland heroes.

Another well-known name to collectors and readers of slick Western lifestyle magazines is Wild Bill Cleaver. His exquisite creations, which originate from Wild Bill's Originals (Vashon Island, WA), may not all be absolutely authentic, but they certainly look as if they were made on the Plains 130 years ago. Both the accurate reproductions and the artistic interpretations they inspire make Wild Bill's work museum-quality.

Cleaver, who favors the older designs of western gunleather, has a bent for breathtaking beadwork. Those holsters not encrusted with precision seed-bead tribal art may instead be carefully carved California Patterns and Mexican Loop designs, all so artfully antiqued they could pass for originals. But Wild Bill Cleaver is no low-down "artifaker." He happily makes gunleather for cowboy action-eers who fully intend wearing and using his products on the range, along with those who display his work as home or office decor. His masterful creations represent the high end of the gunleather market, for there is little like it available anywhere.

A former logger in the north woods, Mario Hanel (Hanel's Antiqued Leather Goods) is a relative greenhorn as a replica leathercrafter. He has only been at it nine years, but his intuitive feel for the hide goods of the Wild West, as with his mastery of the tools of the trade, combine to

ABOVE. *The stagecoach is not only a symbol of the Old West, it makes a decent gun cart. This one took a detour to Ruger's Winter Range, the National Championships of Cowboy Action Shooting.*

AT RIGHT.
Evil Roy and Colonel Shep demonstrate the proper use of a Cowboy Action gun cart between stages at SASS End of Trail.

ABOVE. *This impeccably replicated scale model tandem outfit won first prize at an End of Trail competition.*

produce saddles and gunleather that can stand with the best. Hanel has concocted a process for making his brand-new products look just like the originals displayed in museums. Like all good leathersmiths, he reminds his clients that when the cowboy leather of the Old West was new, it looked new. That antique patina so beloved today was earned each day on the trail. But many cowboy actioneers don't want to wait that long, says Hanel, so he applies antiqueing alchemy to whatever degree his customers desire.

Garret Roberts is a leathersmith whose face is seen in public as often as his gunleather. He's an

actor, with screen credits that include *Tombstone, Gettysburg, Hard Bounty,* among others, as well as TV commercials. A student of U.S. militaria and technical advisor to movies and museums, it follows that his quality gunleather finds its way into films and into the hands of Cowboy Action shooters. From his Kicking Mule Outfitters shop deep in the heart of Camp Verde, Arizona, Roberts sends his work around the world, to the delight of shooters, re-enactors and film producers.

Dave Rowland comes by his love of Old West gunleather naturally: He was born to a pioneer family whose members had lived on the bullet-riddled Kansas-Missouri border since the end of the Civil War. Having been exposed to his grandfather's memories and to the old gunleather still extant in that historic district, Dave developed a taste for authenticity. Upon graduation from a saddlemaking program at Spokane Falls College, he began researching Old West saddlery and gunleather. Rowland's work, which he runs from his Rio Verde Saddlery (Camp Verde, AZ), is not only highly prized by cowboy mounted shooters, it frequently is the First Place prize in CMSA World Point competitions around the world.

Texas Jack is the gunleather line from Cimarron Fire Arms, of Fredericksburg, Texas. Texas Jack is, of course, Cimarron trail boss Mike Harvey, who insists on period accuracy and fine oak tanned leather. The line includes black US Cavalry holsters, belts and belt plates, as well as California "Slim Jims", the various versions of the Mexican Loop and, of course, a Texas Jock Strap.

The "Texican Brand" Mexican Loop is especially interesting. Of natural saddle leather, it lacks the usual deep trigger finger recurve of most Cheyenne style holsters and has instead a gently sloping dip in the throat, just enough to keep itchy trigger finers out of mischief. Plain and solid, the Texican and matching lined cartridge belt are good selections for one whose persona is an early Texas drover/working cowboy.

In Laramie, Wyoming, Stan Dolega re-creates gunleather from the time of the Indian Wars, the last days of the Plains and its buffalo. Dolegas' Wolf Ears Equipment is an accurate and meticulously made line of leather and canvas reproductions, exactly like the originals from the 1870-1890 period so dear to our hearts. Dolegas uses only Hermann or Wickett & Craig oak tanned leather and the finest tenting canvas for his period correct holsters and Prairie Belts.

The Wolf Ears catalogue is an education in itself. Dolega fell in love with Western history as a cowkid and like so many of us, has made it his life's study. His specialties are Cheyenne style Mexican Loop, California Pattern and US Army holsters, both Regulation and Mexican Loop. These and his superb leather money and cartridge belts are well photographed, described and historically explained in his catalogue, as is his line of authentic canvas cartridge belts, the most complete offered anywhere. Wolf Ears belts are made for all cowboy cartridges and many obsolete period rounds that only buffalo rifle crazies like Dolega ever heard of.

Long Range, Silueta and Buffalo Rifle shooters will find Wolf Ears equipment absolutely authentic and penultimately practical. Shootists can select from several models of meanea, Collins Bros. and Gallatin holsters, appropriate canvas or leather belts and even the 1874 Dyer Cap Pouch and McKeever Cartridge Box. All this from a sculptor, veteran Buckskinner and leathersmith with a Master's in Fine Art.

Not all excellent Cowboy gunleather emanates from individual craftsmen, of course. Cowboy gunleather from Galco International is highly prized by shooters insisting on quality. Chief among Galco's Cowboy line are the Trail Boss rig, consisting of a Mexican Two Loop or two on a matching Money Belt and the Gallatin, an accurate reproduction of the Cheyenne-style outfits of the old masters.

Those more excited by the Hollywood West might choose Galco's Texas Ranger, a rig John Wayne would have liked. The Galco Arizona Ranger is an elegant, dark brown Mexican Loop holster, festooned with jeweler's bronz studs and conchos and mated to a matching double row cartridge belt for both rifle and pistol rounds. Buscadero and Fast Draw rigs are also available, built with the same high Galco quality.

The Jax Leather Company of Madera, California, uses only Hermann oak-tanned leather to build custom commissions by cowboy customers. Its gunbelts, for instance, frequently have only five or ten cartridge loops, supplying one or, at the most, two revolver reloads required in a match stage and reduces the extra weight carried. Jax holsters are formed and made for the pistols they'll carry, providing the fit that holds a revolver properly. The company's line of Jax Leather goods includes canvas cowboy accessories, such as Prairie Belts and shotgun belts, along with pack saddles and outfitter equipment.

Classic Old West Styles (COWS) is a fairly recent entry into the exploding Cowboy gunleather and clothing market, but their products boast both the best of workmanship, materials and accuracy of reproduction. The COWS basic holster line includes Mexican one- and two-loop styles and two California pattern replicas made for Colts and copies in all popular barrel lengths. Sparely decorated but period perfect, these holsters are about half the price of COWS' *Packing Iron* collection. This more expensive and elaborate line features replicas pulled from the pages of *Packing Iron,* as illustrated by photographer William Manns. Largely F.A. Meanea copies, these holsters and cartridge belts are not only finely stamped and carved, but made for virtually every pistol a cowboy actioneer is apt to use, including the Walker Colt, 1872 Open Tops, Schofields and even the rarely seen Merwin & Hulbert. COWS has also exactly copied the infamous gunleather of both Jesse James and Pat Garrett. Perhaps they could be persuaded to have the beautiful embroidery embellished belts and holsters of the *vaqueros, charros* and *Californios* reproduced. Mexican and Californio gun gear is hard to find and originals are too fragile for hard use. Many shooters and collectors would welcome a source of such colorfully historic reproductions.

THE WEARING, CARING AND FEEDING OF GUNLEATHER

While many Cowboy/Western Action Shooters come to the sport/lifestyle with a history of recreational shooting activities, many others strap on their first gunbelt for the initial stage of their first match. There are a few things these folks should know about packin' iron the cowboy way. Few cowboys in the Old West carried two six-shooters. When they did, it was in anticipation of terrible, if temporary, trouble. One has but to carry two guns and at least one loaded cartridge belt for a three-day Cowboy match to appreciate this. Add a second loaded and crisscrossed cartridge belt and the sacroiliac soon suffers the consequences. Most cowboy match stages require two pistols and a soft, wide folded Money Belt is probably a competitor's most comfortable type belt for one or two holsters. Percussion shooters don't need loops, but a broad, thick belt hauls these smokewagons better than a narrow, thin one in either case.

Successful competitors, whether on ground or mounted, wear their gunbelts high and snug, usually just below the trouser belt, at the waist. The holster(s) must hold the revolver securely, stay put when a pistol is drawn, and be where it's supposed to be when the shooter returns his gun to the holster. Gunbelts worn hanging down on the hips are troublesome at best and too sloppy for any self-respectin' cowboy. Mounted shooters know that Buscadero and other low-slung gun rigs are anathema a-horse and they're never seen on veteran riders. "Snug and secure" beats "floppy," every time. More to the point, a dropped or fallen gun is a dropped stage, and a dropped stage is a lost match, on the ground or in the saddle.

THE CONTROVERSIAL CROSSDRAW

The primary concern of all Cowboy/Western Action Shooting organizations and participants is **safety**. And central to the safety of everyone on or near the firing line of any course of fire is the

170-degree plane constituting the invisible barrier between the downrange field of fire and the safe zone behind the shooter. Any action which allows the muzzle of a shooter's firearm to point through or "break" that 170-degree plane is dangerous and grounds for a "DQ" (disqualification) for that stage. A repeat offense earns a DQ for the entire match.

Since a pistol in a crossdraw holster is already pointing through that safety plane as the shooter faces the targets ready to draw and fire, the shooter must pivot and swivel his or her body enough to allow the crossdrawn gun to be pointed well downrange before it is drawn. All too often, shooters fail to twist enough before drawing and breaking the safety plane, thus "covering" fellow posse members and/or Range Officials. The growing number of crossdraw DQs has caused crossdraw holsters to come under closer scrutiny. Many cowboy shootists are reconsidering the minimal advantage, if any, of this dubiously authentic holster style.

Research yields little historic justification for crossdraws, although some cowboys wore their right-hand holster on the left side to facilitate

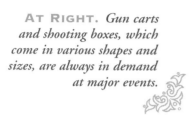

AT RIGHT. *Gun carts and shooting boxes, which come in various shapes and sizes, are always in demand at major events.*

ABOVE. *This highly creative gun cart was a winner at End of Trail.*

roping with their right hands. These were not the severely canted cross draw holsters used today, however, but simply a right side, upright holster worn for temperary convenience on the left side, out of the way of the coils of rope. It takes less than a second to draw with the "weak" hand and transfer the gun to the "strong" hand, but it takes about the same time to twist and turn sufficiently to avoid a devastating safety penalty. These crossdraw gyrations, properly done, require watching what you're doing, instead of concentrating on the target. Crossdraw holsters are counter-productive for shooting gunfighter style, a pistol in each hand.

While they're still legal, crossdraw remains a shooter's option and veteran shooters are unlikely to have trouble. New shooters, however, do well to begin with the upright right and left holsters worn butt to the rear and drawn with right and left hands. Those who insist on crossdrawing should choose holsters with very little slant to the rear. A lost match is a lot to gamble in exchange for a sliver of a second.

GUN GEAR MAINTENANCE

A survey of master leathercrafters reveals both divergency of opinion and universal agreement regarding proper care of gunleather. Assuming high grade leather, thread and workmanship, there are some rules of thumb that will keep gunleather healthy and handsome. As with firearms, the greatest threats are moisture and dirt. Desiccation, on the other hand, is as damaging as mildew. Leather is an amazing material, at once tough and fragile, resilient and susceptible. It was once an organ of a living animal. When made into cowboy equipment, it requires occasional replenishment of the nourishment it had when alive. Many fine namebrand soaps clean gunleather effectively and most work equally well. Most leathersmiths suggest a glycerin saddle soap and clean water to remove normal cowboy dirt like dust, blackpowder residue, horse sweat and such. But leather also needs lubrication to retain its suppleness and flexibility, and to maintain a proper balance between too much and too little moisture.

The choices among traditional and newfangled oils, creams, emulsions and emollients can be confusing, but three products are safe to suggest. Olive oil and Neatsfoot oil are both traditional, natural and effective lubricants for gunleather, but they must be the purest forms available. If olive oil is chosen, it must be Extra Virgin; and if it's Neatsfoot, it must be absolutely pure. Many master leathercrafters endorse lanolin as a food and preservative for gunleather, and most products feature one or more of these ingredients. Neatsfoot oil in particlar will stain clothing, even in its purest form, if not allowed to thoroughly penetrate the leather and dry out somewhat. Lexol is another effective leather lubricant and softener favored for gunleather. Its principle ingredient, lanolin, is prepared in an easily applied liquid form. Gunleather that is subjected to rain and snow is well protected and fed with SnoSeal, a waterproofing compound and leather lubricant.

Oiling to excess, conversely, is the wrong thing for holsters. A good holster is made for a particular revolver and the fit must be snug. Too much oil will eventually allow the leather to stretch and the fit to loosen. Most of these preparations, generic or brand name, will darken leather and are not to be used on suede or buckskin belts or holster linings. Gunleather drenched in a storm or while fording the Sweetwater at flood stage should be towel-dried, saddle-soaped, wiped clear of soap residue and allowed to dry slowly at room temperature. When completely dry, the leather can be fed from the above menu of nutrients. Detergents and petroleum by-products are to be avoided. When in doubt, consult the maker. He should know what's best for his own creations. 🤠

Chapter Five

ABOVE. *Winchester's smokeless Cowboy Action ammo: .38 Spl., 44-40 Winchester, .44 Spl. And .45 colt, is sold in diestinctive cowboy boxes.*

AT RIGHT. *Black Hills Ammunition makes a complete line of cowboy calibers designed for the guns of the Old West.*

Cowboy Action Ammunition

The age we celebrate and re-create with our old-time guns, gear and clothing was of a time when firearms and ammunition, like all things technical, were transformed by the Industrial Revolution. For those of us nostalgic for our beloved frontier, the feeling is deepest for those early years before the buffalo were gone, before the railroads and barbed wire. Those were the days when most six-shooters were still "cap n' ball" and keeping your powder dry was critical. In those halcyon days prior to planned obsolescence, folks hung onto their possessions, using them as long as they functioned before passing them on to the next generation. Our pioneers were particularly parsimonious. If their percussion pistol still served, why waste good money on these newfangled guns and cartridges? Percussion revolvers abounded throughout the last half of the 19th century and are thus period appropriate for almost any Cowboy/Western Action persona. They afford more opportunities to shoot, too. Cowboy percussionists may shoot the Plainsman and similar side matches, along with main match stages, and then finish up shooting in a cartridge category. Plus, they get to spend considerably more time cleaning guns.

Beyond authenticity, cowboy actioneers shoot cap and ball for perhaps the same reasons people fish with fly tackle, hunt with muzzleloaders or reload cartridge ammunition: they enjoy doing it their way. For those unfamiliar with, but curious about percussion firearms, a short introduction is in order. Those seriously interested in pursuing these arcane arms are referred to John Taffin's books: Action Shooting Cowboy Style and Big Bore Sixguns. These fine books are compendiums of ammunition information and test-firing results represent the life's work of a confessed single action and blackpowder addict.

LOADIN' UP

Loading cap and ball revolvers consists of building rounds of ammunition inside the cylinders of a pistol, the chambers acting as cartridge cases. There are four basic steps:

1. The hammer is placed on half-cock, allowing the cylinder to rotate freely. A revolver loading stand is a big help. A carefully measured amount of blackpowder or blackpowder substitute, such as Pyrodex is poured into the chamber. Always use a powder measure. Never pour loose powder directly into the firearm without measuring. Powder measures are inexpensive: get one that has a funnel.

2. A lubricated wad is placed over the powder charge and pressed into place. A short length of dowel rod is helpful. The wad is a primary protection against chain-firing, a catastrophe in which more

than one chamber fires when the hammer drops. A dollop of grease, such as Crisco, placed over the chambers after loading is further insurance.

3. A slightly over-sized round lead ball is placed into the chamber. The cylinder is turned so that the charged chamber is directly under the loading lever, which is then rammed down, compressing powder, wad and ball snugly and completely into the cylinder chamber. Extending the tiniest portion of the ball beyond the mouth of the chamber will prevent the cylinder from turning freely. A properly seated ball will shave off a small ring of lead to fall from the mouth of the chamber.

4. When all chambers are loaded—and not until then—percussion caps are snapped onto the nipples at the rear of the cylinders.

CAPPING IT OFF

Note that the caps are the last step in the loading process and are never pressed onto the nipples until all chambers are loaded. Charging the chambers requires that the pistol be tilted muzzle up. Only with the cylinder charged and the revolver facing safely down range are the nipples capped. In Cowboy Action Shooting, the shooter may load all six chambers, but may only cap five; the hammer is rested on the uncapped chamber. One round loads are accomplished by capping the last chamber under the clock, a process requiring about the same time as reloading a cartridge six-gun.

If there's a shortcoming intrinsic to percussion pistols, it is the caps. Tiny, hard to handle and easy to drop (a revolver capper is a must), they can be problematic unless they fit the nipple snugly, enough to stay on after being deformed by firing. They must be pressed on, usually with a tool like that nifty antler gadget from your possibles bag.

Loose caps will invariably fall into the works of a gun, frequently locking up the action like a bank vault. As with powder charges, caps require some experimentation, starting always with the manufacturers' recommendations and/or the advice of a learned mentor. Today's caps from makers like CCI, Speer and Remington are unlikely to misfire, so nipple fit is the primary concern. Most replica percussion revolvers use #10 or #11 caps, depending on make and model.

Black Powder

Black powder is a mixture of sulphur, saltpeter (potassium nitrate) and charcoal. Black powder and modern replicas, like Pyrodex, Clean Shot and Clear Shot, must always be stored in their original containers, clearly marked and tightly sealed. A blackish color does not always indicate black powder. All gunpowder can be dangerous. When a firearm barrel is stamped "Black Powder Only," they're not kidding. Smokeless powder must never be used in black powder firearms, period. To do so invites disaster.

Black powder is measured by grains weight. The letters used to describe black powder indicate granulation, the size of the powder grains. Grain size controls the rate of speed at which the powder burns; the coarser the granulation, the slower the powder burns. 1F or Fg is coarse and slow burning; 4F or FFFFg is the fastest. 1F, for instance, is the powder used in cannons, muskets and 10 gauge muzzleloading shotguns. 2F (FFg) is used for shotguns of 12 through 20 gauge and percussion *pistoleros* of the pioneer persuasion use 3F (FFFg),

PERCUSSION COLT LOADS

1847 Colt Walker Model	.454 round ball	.44 revolver wad	25 gr. FFFg	#11 caps
Colt 1st Model Dragoon	.454 round ball	.44 revolver wad	22 gr. FFFg	#11 caps
Colt 2nd Model Dragoon	.454 round ball	.44 revolver wad	22 gr. FFFg	#11 caps
Cole 3rd Model Dragoon	.454 round ball	.44 revolver wad	22 gr. FFFg	#11 caps
Colt 1849 Pocket Model	.321 round ball	.31 revolver wad	12 gr. FFFg	#11 caps
Colt 1851 Navy Model	.376 round ball	.36 revolver wad	18 gr. FFFg	#11 caps
Colt 1860 Army Model	.454 round ball	.44revolver wad	22 gr, FFFg	#11 caps
Colt 1861 Navy Model	.376 round ball	.36 revolver wad	18 gr. FFFg	#11 caps

REMINGTON PERCUSSION LOADS

Remington 1863 New Model Army	.454 round ball	.44 Revolver wad	22 gr. FFFg	#11 caps
Remington 1863 Navy Model	.376 Round ball	.36 revolver wad	18 gr. FFFg	#11 caps

RUGER PERCUSSION LOAD

Ruger Old Army Model	.457 round ball	.45 revolver wad	25 gr. FFFg	#10 caps

AT RIGHT.
*Replica black powder
cartridges from
Cor-Bon (Sturgis,
SD) are packaged
96 to the box. That's
19.2 cylinders of
cowboy shootin' fun.*

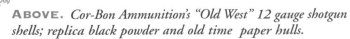

ABOVE. *Cor-Bon Ammunition's "Old West" 12 gauge shotgun
shells; replica black powder and old time paper hulls.*

the ideal black powder for Colt and Remington cap and ball revolvers. 4F (FFFFg) is extremely fast-burning and is intended for use in the priming pans of flintlock firearms. Some percussion shooters prime the hole of the nipple with 4F (FFFFg) for more certain ignition but 4F must *never* be used as a main charge. Such use is seriously dangerous to both shooter and firearm.

Please note: Pyrodex Replica Black Powder is measured not by grains weight, but by volume. Those who choose Pyrodex should consult Hodgdon literature regarding proper Pyrodex loads for certain firearms. That said, the chart shown on p.157 are manufacturer-recommended black powder loads for Uberti replicas and other revolvers commonly used by Cowboy/ Western Action Shooters. They are suggested starting points from which to experiment to arrive at the least recoil and most accurate loads for the firearms used. Again, greenhorn percussion shooters are advised to consult experienced black powder *pistoleros* and appropriate publications before experimenting.

Black Powder Substitutes

For years, the only viable alternative to black powder as offered by brands like Elephant and Goex, was Hodgdon's Pyrodex, which is made in three grades corresponding to the granulations of black powder:

Pyrodex P is formulated for pistols and small caliber rifles up to .45 caliber. Pyrodex P compares to FFFg black powder on a particle size basis.

Pyrodex RS is commonly used in percussion muzzleloading rifles and shotguns and is perhaps the most versatile of the Pyrodex powders. The RS compares to FFg black powder.

Pyrodex Select replaces the old cartridge designation and is the most consistent of the Pyrodex loose propellants. It's ideal for loading black powder cartridges. All Pyrodex formulas burn cleaner and foul less than plain black powder.

The growing popularity of Cowboy-Western Action Shooting, Muzzleloading, Re-enacting and Living History performances has hastened development of other black powder replicas providing the authenticity of black powder without the fouling and constant cleaning. These substitutes are safe and appropriate for use in muzzleloaders and cap and ball revolvers, as well as in shotgun shells. The use of replica powders may be argued by purists, but their advantages cannot. The newest and most promising replica propellants are *Goex Clear Shot* and a similar product with a similar name: *Clean Shot.*

Clean Shot powder is described as "a pyrotechnic composition replica black powder." Classified by the government as a "flammable solid," it can be shipped in limited quantities by common carrier. Clean Shot is intended for percussion and black powder cartridge arms, yielding the wonderful billows of smoke and the deep booms that resonate so pleasurably among cowboy actioneers.

Used on a volume-to-volume basis with black powder, shooters can expect much the same velocities and pressures. Since it contains no sulfur—and therefore no malodorous sulphur smell—shooters are deprived of one of black powder's more familiar frontier characteristics. But no sulphur also means no sulphur fouling or corrosion. Firearms still require a thorough cleaning with soap and water or solvent, but after the match, not after each stage. Clean Shot Powder ballistics curves are similar to black powder. Overloading is strictly proscribed, however; the manufacturer's recommendations must *never* be exceeded. Clean Shot advises a hard pack when seating balls or bullets, suggesting that tight compression increases velocities.

Goex Clear Shot is that company's replica propellant that burns cleaner than black powder and has no residue build-up from shot to shot.

Goex Clear Shot contains no perchloric acid salts and will not corrode barrels. Keeping your powder dry is easier with Clear Shot, which is non-hygroscopic; i.e., it won't attract moisture, even in humid regions. Goex boasts that its Clear Shot product has an indefinite shelf life, with consistent velocities and low pressures. It's designed to behave like black powder with its low standard deviations but without the fouling and corrosion. Clear Shot ships like smokeless powder and cleans up with water.

REPLICA BLACK POWDER PELLETS

Black powder replica pellets are the newest alternative to genuine black powder. Of particular interest to percussion revolver shooters are the pelletized powder charges of Pyrodex and Clean Shot. These newfangled solid plugs of powder come caliber-sized, ready to be dropped into a barrel or cylinder chamber without the use of horn, flask or measure. There's no powder to spill, no worry about supplying exact loads from chamber to chamber. Time spent reloading is considerably shorter, but normal loading sequences—powder pellet, wad, ball and cap—are the same and both makers recommend compressing the ball firmly against the charge. Pyrodex Pistol pellets are 30 grain volume equivalent pre-formed charges of Pyrodex designed for us in .44 and .45 caliber modern replica cap and ball revolvers. Pyrodex cautions that the maximum load of one (1) revolver pellet must *never* be exceeded.

Clean Shot pelletizes its product into Quick Shot Pellets, pre-measured 30 and 50 grain velocity equivalent charges of Clean Shot Powder. The 30 grain pellets are for .44 and .45 caliber percussion pistols; the 50 grain pellets are for rifles and percussion pistols of .50 caliber and up. Again, the manufacturer makes it clear that the projectile must be seated firmly onto the Quick Shot charge.

With pelletized propellants, crushing the pellet while firmly seating a ball does no harm and nothing is lost in the way of velocity and accuracy. Quick Shot Pellets, like Clean Shot Powder, cleans up with water. Complete cleaning and oiling after matches, however, is always recommended.

Products like these make shooting and cleaning cap and ball revolvers easy to do. With the most common objections to percussion pistol shooting removed or negated, and with more ammunition makers building black powder replica cartridges, perhaps more shooters will take up the arms of that romantic early era when the American frontier was still open and new.

BLACK POWDER CARTRIDGES

While an exhaustive exegesis of cartridge ammunition is beyond the purview of this book, a look at the most popular cowboy cartridge ammunition, both black powder and smokeless, is in order. Several premier ammunition companies are now making smokeless rounds in cowboy calibers, but black powder cartridges used by cowboy shootists are hand-loaded either by the shooter or a custom munitions maker. Components are more readily available than black powder cartridges.

This is historically ironic. Most frontiersmen and women during most of the period we aspouse had only black powder ammunition. Only a few, mostly buffalo hunters, had any reloading skill and equipment. Cowboy actioneers who don't roll their own must do what most frontiersmen did: forage up a dependable supply of reliable store-bought ammunition. Those who pine for powder kegs of pistol provender and a garage full of reloading paraphernalia can learn from books (see our bibliography) and the volumes of information published by propellant purveyors and reloading retailers listed in the appendices to this book.

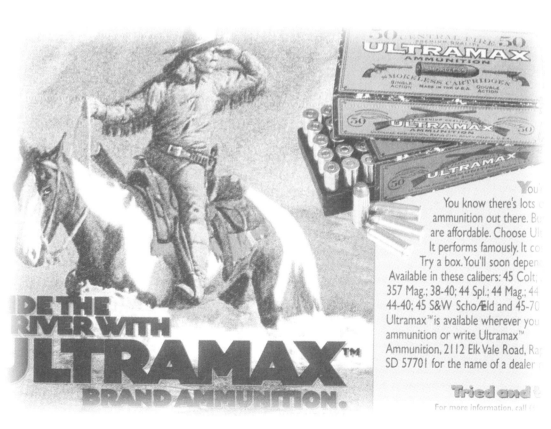
ABOVE. *Ultramax Ammunition makes a full line of Cowboy Action ammunition for both rifles and revolvers.*

TEN-X AMMUNITION

Cowboy/Western Action shooters today are luckier than their ancestors. Ready-made replica black powder cartridge ammunition is available from Ken McKenzie" Ten-X Ammunition, one of only a few manufacturers of black powder cowboy cartridges. A 35-year veteran ammunitions maker, McKenzie makes both black powder and smokeless cartridges for cowboy shootists; and while he doesn't sell reloaded ammunition, he does offer custom reloading service—replica black powder or smokeless—using a shooter's brass.

Ten-X black powder cartridges are Starline brass with Federal primers loaded with Clean Shot and Red Line #2 hard cast lead bullets. This combination reduces fouling by powder residue and leading up, which translates in turn to less cleaning and better accuracy. McKenzie claims he can fire 50 rounds in each pistol before any cleaning is required, thanks to a simple 50-50 water-vinegar mixture. This gets a shooter through a day's match stages, or a decent pistol practice, before having to spend a fun evening of gun cleaning with the family. Ten-X replica black powder cartridge ammunition comes in all popular Cowboy Action calibers that were generally available over the counter in the Old West. Shotgun ammunition is 12 gauge 2³/₄-inch #7¹/₂ shot only, charged with 60 grains of Clean Shot in Winchester AA hulls. Ten-X doesn't reload shotgun shells; it does, however, reload or custom-make replica black powder Long Range and Buffalo Rifle rounds in .45-70, .45-90 and .45-120.

Cor-Bon, made by Sturgis in South Dakota, calls its new cowboy line "U.S. Cavalry Black Powder Ammunition." Cor-Bon loads the line with a non-carbon-based replica black powder and flat-point lead. Only four revolver rounds are currently offered, but they're biggies: 250 grain .45 Colt; 158 grain .38 Spl.; 200 grain .44 WCF; and a 230 grain .45 Schofield. Cor-Bon also builds replica black powder shot shells in 12 gauge 2-inch old-time paper hulls loaded with 1.5 ounces of soft lead #8 shot. This stagecoach-guardin' scattergun feed comes in Old West style boxes to complete the historical illusion. If only they made round point black powder replica 405 grain .45-70 government ammunition and more Old West pistol calibers, this line would be complete. Old West Scrounger (Montague, CA) offers two black powder .45-70 cartridges, with 405 and 500 grain round nose bullets. These are good rounds for Buffalo Gun shooters.

Thanks to the miracle of modern munitions science, cowboy shootists have access to the authentic smoke and boom of black powder and the convenience of cartridges, with minimal fouling and clean-up. As more cowboy actioneers shoot more "black powder," more manufacturers are sure to make replica black powder ammunition. Consequently, more shooters will look authentic as they volley through the floating smoke so reminiscent of our fading frontier.

SMOKELESS POWDER CARTRIDGES

Smokeless cartridge ammunition remains the most convenient, readily available firearms fodder fed by Cowboy/Western Action shooters. Of the major manufacturers, Winchester was first with the calibers of the Old West, developed in cooperation with SASS. So far, Winchester offers the four cowboy calibers most used in competition: .38 Spl., .44-40 Winchester, .44 Spl. and .45 Colt. All fire flat-nosed lead bullets of 158, 225, 240 and 250 grains, respectively. When the demand prevails, Winchester may commence production of more cowboy calibers.

Winchester's 12 gauge Super Featherlite is ideal cowboy shotgun ammo. The 2³/₄-inch shell fires #8 shot at 980 feet per second. That's slow for 12 gauge but plenty fast for cowboy work—and with far less

recoil and noise. This minimizes the flinching inspired by more powerful shotgun rounds, but it still knocks down those pesky pepper-popper targets. The vicuna in Winchester cowboy line is a round-nosed lead .45-70 rifle round for Single Shot Long Range and Buffalo Gun matches. Winchester's 300 grain, jacketed hollow point .45-70 Gov. is unusable in matches. SASS, NCOWS and OWSA all forbid the use of jacketed and/or hollow points, primarily for range safety reasons. But a company making 510 grain .458 Winchester Magnum Cape Buffalo medicine can surely build lead .45-70 rounds for Sharps, Winchester High Wall, Rolling Block and Springfield shooters with real Buffalo rifles.

Black Hills Ammunition (Rapid City, SD) makes a complete line of Cowboy Action ammunition, including rounds that were, until recently, considered ammunition esoterica. These include authentic calibers—the .32-20, .38-40, .45 Schofield—and a 405 grain .45-70. All Black Hills cowboy calibers are made using flat-nosed lead bullets of the preferred weights and loaded to SASS match velocities. This broad caliber spread accounts for some of Black Hills Ammunition's popularity with cowboy actioneers. As the demand increases, perhaps Black Hills will expand into replica black powder cartridges. Owners Jeff and Kristi Hoffman follow Cowboy/Western Action Shooting closely and are aware of the growing interest in black powder replica cartridge shooting.

South Dakota, home of Ultramax, must be a hotbed of munitions manufacture. The company makes nine pistol calibers with bullet weights and velocities for Cowboy Action Shooting. They're all

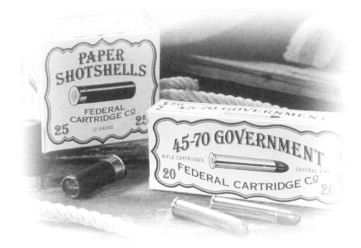

flat point, for use in both pistols and tube magazine lever action rifles. At this writing, no .45-70 or shotgun ammunition is available—except for the Federal Cartridge Company, which builds a 405 grain .45-70 Government round specifically for Cowboy/Western Action Shooting. Loaded to original velocity specifications, Federal's .45-70 features reduced recoil, a benefit sure to please Long Range Single Shot shooters. Federal also makes an authentic paper-hulled Cowboy Action shotgun shell. The 2³/₄-inch shell throws 7/8-oz. of #8 shot with lower velocity and recoil for cowboy competition.

With the incredible growth of the sport, and with shooters enjoying an ever-widening range of Cowboy Action, ammo manufacturers have proliferated. Black powder or smokeless, it's shooter's choice, but for the sake of authenticity, the pick should be black powder or a modern replica. The deep boom and thick smoke (even if it doesn't smell bad) is a palpable remnant of the frontier. Unless a shooter's character lived this side of 1890, he could not have shot smokeless ammunition. Nor did everyone shoot smokeless even after it became available. Fact is, black powder is the real Cowboy/Western Action Shooting ammunition. With the ready availability of today's replica black powder and cartridges, there's no real reason not to shoot like they did on the frontier.

CLEANIN' UP

Cleaning a gun is part of the fun. Black powder residue is corrosive, and percussion and black powder cartridge arms—those fired with traditional black powder and replica powders must be cleaned as soon as possible after being fired. This is especially important after a match involving 100 or more rounds. Canny competitors who use genuine black powder clean their firearms between stages, at least by running patches soaked in Windex or a black powder solvent through the barrel and cylinder chambers. For quick cleaning to avoid serious fouling of the moving parts, Windex (with ammonia and/or vinegar) can cut fouling like a knife. It's handy for use on the range, but it's no substitute for thorough cleaning and oiling on a daily basis.

Complete cleaning involves soap, water and a little time. It gets a mite tedious, what with toothbrush and Q-tip and alcohol to dispel water. And every few matches or practices, revolvers must be disassembled and their internal organs cleaned and oiled. But them old frontiersmen had to do it, by fire or lantern light, usually with water hauled from a stream, and lye soap. Gun cleaning is indeed part of this great game, yet another way to taste the heady flavor of the Old West.

AT RIGHT. *Clear Shot offers its black powder replacement product in both powder and pelletized forms. Pellets are the latest and handles charges for cowboy cap-and-ball shooters*

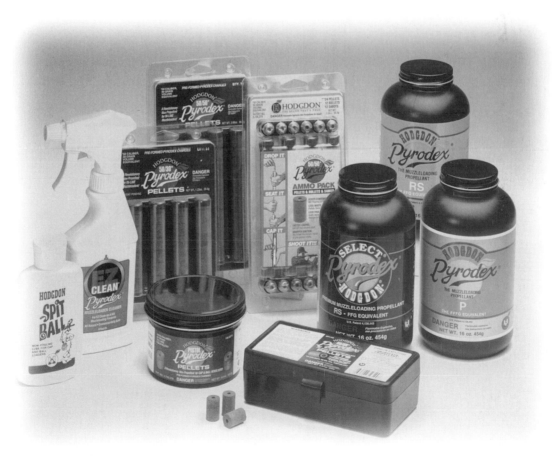

ABOVE. *Hodgdon Pyrodex, the traditional replica black powder, now comes in pellet form along with three grades of powder for revolvers, rifles and shotguns.*

CHAPTER SIX

We See by Our Outfits That We Are All Cowpersons

The period about which Cowboy/Western Action shooters study and fantasize is generally considered to begin with the end of the Civil War. Historically, the frontier had moved west of the Mississippi by 1840. These were the days of Manifest Destiny, the Oregon and Santa Fe Trails and the flowering of Westward Expansion. In terms of dress and cultural influences, our Cowboy Period" is also the Victorian Age (1837-1901). When Victoria was crowned Queen of England, we had been independent for 57 years, but still emulated them in clothing, architecture and manners. The 1840s were the nascent decade of the Industrial Revolution. Sam Colt had invented the revolver, his pistols had helped defeat Santa Ana and Mexican mavericks roamed the southwest. The day of the Western Frontier—and the cowboy —was dawning.

CLOTHES MAKE THE COWBOY AND COWGIRL

It was also the age of the photograph. With the advent of the daguerreotype in 1839, folks fell for photography. As the art form developed, everyone wanted to be a photographer or be photographed. People posed in black and white or sepia cabinet photos, stern of visage and dressed to the nines in their best black. It was from these crepuscular images that we know our ancestors and their fashions. But few daguerreotypists rode the cattle trails or rattled along in emigrant wagons. It wasn't until the Civil War and Matthew Brady's work that candid photographs of plain people —emigrants, tradespeople and cowboys—were recorded. What we know of the daily wear of the westerners on the early frontier owes as much to artists like Karl Bodmer and George Catlin as to photographers.

The earliest era usually portrayed by Cowboy/Western Action shooters is that first decade of the revolver, the 1850s. Ladies fashions then and on into the '60s fill volumes with pictures of huge hoop skirts and multi-tiered sleeves requiring yards and yards of fabric. Except for the odd figure of a working man in homespun wool or cotton, gentlemen were depicted in black wool suits and frock coats with white shirts, black silk ties or neckclothes and waistcoats. Vests were a man's only garment of self-expression and were sometimes of silk or brocade in a contrasting color. Cowboys, in them days, were in the southwest and were mostly *Californios* or Mexican *Vaqueros*. Their outfits reflected a Spanish heritage and were often curious

(continued on pg. 172)

ABOVE. *Leggings like these were used by the vaqueros of Mexico and the Southwest.*

ABOVE. *Mounted shooter Darn It Darr displays one of her marvelous Wild West Show outfits. Such turnouts add color and spectator appeal to the sport. Note the handy competition arrangement of pistols.*

ABOVE. *Many Cowboy Actioneers sew their own clothing. Buckaroo Bobbins provides patterns for carefully researched period pieces. Shooters can then choose colors, cloth and fit.*

AT LEFT. *Victorian era clothing had a style and presence unmatched by today's slovenly dress standards. This elegant couple lends an Old West ambiance to cowboy matches.*

AT RIGHT. *Actor Lance Hendrickson at SASS End of Trail. Celebrities are well treated by shooters and events.*

mixtures of embroidered short jackets, flat, wide-brimmed sombreros and buckskins. These useful frontier garments were worn long after the Taos trappers switched to guiding and scouting for a living.

As it did in everything, the 1860s brought changes in fashions. The Civil War lent a certain military look, even to ladies dresses. At war's end, soldiers from both armies pressed uniforms and parts thereof into everyday service and went West to start all over. By the 1870s, westerners were developing a style of their own, and it is with the dress and equipment of the 30-year period from 1870 to 1900 that cowboy actioneers are most familiar. Except for those who choose their characters from western movies and television (perfectly acceptable for SASS and OWSA members, but unacceptable in NCOWS), cowboys and girls have a plethora of publications and photographs from which to select outfits for their personas. Readers who look into the books cited in the bibliography will become, perforce, knowledgeable about frontier clothing and gear. Readers should consult the appendix as well. Catalogs from the purveyors of pioneer paraphernalia will provide a short-cut of sorts to proper outfitting. For Cowboy Action clothing worn by frontier folk of both genders changed little over the years we re-enact and folks wore clothes 'til they were plumb used up. Articles of dress and gear from the 1870s are, therefore, appropriate for a character from the 1880s or '90s, but the other way 'round doesn't play.

AT RIGHT.
A brace of beauties in traditional Navajo dress grace the streets of Ruger's Winter Range. Turquoise, blue velvet and silver are elegantly authentic.

ABOVE. *Charly "Judge" Gullet poses in front of his gun cart, dressed in a proper outfit for the 1880s and 90s.*

AT RIGHT. *Outfits like these are ideal for ridin' and shootin', on the ground or in the saddle*

Lady's fashions, then as now, changed more frequently than mens', but for shooters with a penchant for historical accuracy the devil is in the details. These may include things like forgetting to remove your Rolex or wearing modern blue jeans or pointy-toed "cowboy boots" when you're supposed to be a Texas drover on the trail. Such shocking sartorial slips won't get you shot or thrown out of an SASS event, but some measure of authentic ambiance is necessary to complete the illusion on which our fantasies depend. The outfits we wear create much of our living history theater. Absent our outfits, our game would be just another target shoot. We owe it to each other and our life-style to appear as real as possible, whether we portray people from history or from Hollywood.

DRUMMERS, PEDDLERS & PURVEYORS

As with our firearms, gunleather and ammunition, businesses have blossomed to supply our ever-increasing demand for reproduction clothing and accouterments of the late 19th century. Space prohibits a complete accounting of manufacturers and stores, but a short list of some of the oldest and most respected vendors of Victorian Western Americana is helpful. The catalogs and brochures of leading suppliers are excellent research and resource material, as well as wonderful "wish books."

ABOVE. *Two vaquero outfits from Horsefly's Old West Clothing spell double trouble at End of Trail.*

Classic Old West styles (COWS in El Paso, Texas) sews a broad spectrum of Victorian designs and accessories, from basic range riding-and-shooting wear to formal "Sunday-go-to-meeting" dress for men and women. The author can vouch for the one piece of COWS apparel he owns: a canvas four-button frock coat that has served and survived several week-long trail rides on the Oregon and Outlaw trails and still looks good enough to wear out to dinner.

A comprehensive compendium of 19th century dry goods is published annually by Dixie Gun Works (Union City, TN). Since 1954 this company has provided buckskinners, cowboy actioneers and re-enactors with firearms, clothing and equipment. Their 720-page catalog—a gold mine of historical information—belongs on the shelf of anyone interested in the arms, costumes and implements of the American frontier. Another valuable reference text—and a source of authentic Cowboy/Western Action clothing and gear as well—is the 145-page River Junction Trade Company catalog. Founded in 1973 by its proprietor, Jim Boeke, River Junction (McGregor, Iowa) produces and purveys 19th century dry goods with a strong emphasis on the Old West. Because River Junction stocks much more than clothing, it ranks among the best outfitters dealing in dry goods of the

ABOVE.
It's the 1890s all over again for this young lady lounging in the shade at End of Trail 2000.

ABOVE. *This isn't Jason Robards and Lee Marvin, but Pat Garrett and Long Rider, lookin' plumb real at Ruger's Winter range.*

176 *All About Cowboy Action Shooting*

ABOVE. *These ladies wait to board the noon stage from Norco c. 1890. Their day dresses are correct to the last detail.*

AT LEFT. *Cimarron Sue as a soldada of the Revolution, totes a 71/2-inch Uberti Colt replica.*

AT RIGHT. *Cavalry re-enactors add greatly to the color at Cowboy/Western Action events.*

ABOVE. *El Escritor, the mysterious legend of the Old Southwest.*

ALLEN WAHOO WAH:
Creator Of Cowboy Clothing

Clothes may not make the man, but the Victorian era clothing worn by Cowboy/Western Action shooters plays a major role in this anachronistic shooting sport. That participants are so well turned out owes much to the foresight and talents of one Allen Wahoo Wah.

Wah's grandfather immigrated from China in 1884 so his pioneer spirit comes naturally. He learned to love tribal people and the Old West much the same way. Wah's father opened a general store in 1938 on the Yuma Reservation, and the young lad grew up in a place steeped in Western history. He earned his degree in industrial design at UCLA, but he minored in anthropology and native American studies.

Wah's career in clothing design took a Western turn in 1984 when he created his own line, called Native American Traditions, which became a perennially popular Southwestern look. Wah was researching frontier clothing in 1986 when a good friend, Jim Rodgers, introduced him to Cowboy Action Shooting. The rest is Western history.

Wah's clothing was designed to be worn out there on the frontier. From the saddle pants and Osnaburg shirts to high Victorian fashion, Allen Wah's work can be seen at matches, on adventure trail rides and Saturday night celebrations. It's worn in movies and many countries around the world, earning him accolades as the "Ralph Lauren of Western Wear." Cowboy actioneers don't think of Wah's work as fashion, but as outfits providing still another way to experience Western history. That's just the way Wah wants it.

western frontier. Many customers decorate their homes and businesses, along with themselves, from River Junction. Some items are genuine antiques, garnered from Jim Boeke's lifetime of collecting. Others are accurate re-creations sewn or manufactured to his rigid standards of Old West authenticity.

Wild West Mercantile (Phoenix, AZ), whose only business is outfitting cowboy actioneers with ready-made clothing and accessories, was founded in 1994 by Tom and Claudia Ingoglia (*C.S. Fly* and *Claudia Feather*). Their business has grown, thanks to Cowboy/Western Action Shooting, until it is now one of the world's largest retailers of Old West clothing. Tom Ingoglia is former president of Ruger's Winter Range and the Cowboy Action Nationals, while Claudia has won state, regional, national and world championships. Their company also sponsors cowboy events worldwide, promoting shooting sports and our western heritage.

Tombstone Outfitters has been part of Cowboy/Western Action Shooting from the start. John and Susan Corn run perhaps the largest store of its kind in Kingston, Georgia and still manage to pitch the Tombstone tent at major events around the country. Besides the basic 19th century clothing needed by all cowboy actioneers, Tombstone Outfitters stocks items rarely found elsewhere, including some vaquero designs and the only quality old-style sombreros and Spanish hats available. Their gunleather, knives and sheaths must be seen to be appreciated. The Tombstone Outfitters line includes leather by F.A. Meanea (Cheyenne, Wyoming) and Tombstone's own cartouche. Elegant and Old Southwest, the Tombstone look is one of distinctive quality.

One of the few other sources of accurate reproductions of vaquero and Californio clothing is Horsefly's Old West Clothing. Located in

ABOVE. *Lady L'Amour and 2 Step Sartain have won may a dance and costume contest along with dozens of shooting matches. Like most cowboy actioneers, they like to dress up.*

AT LEFT. *Boy meets girl on the streets of End of Trail, c. 1890s. The carbine is an 1892 .30-40 Krag-Jorgensen. Dress, hat, parasol and snood are all "period correct."*

AT RIGHT.
A cavalry officer and his lady promenade along End of Trail 2000; their costumes are authentic in every way.

AT LEFT. *This formal couple appear far less somber than their dress. Cutaway coats, top hats and muttonchops are unusual, even at End of Trail.*

AT RIGHT.
A lovely Victorian gown—and lady—with an overskirt and matching hat. Many lady shootists sew their own 19th century dresses.

ABOVE. *Paul Sherrill plays the role of Buffalo Bill dressed in a Metis-type buckskin coat made and decorated with "Quill Painting" by Sherri Heath.*

Henrietta, Texas, Horsefly's patterns are the most elaborate example of this colorful and historic garb, but his embroidered saddle pants and Mexican short jackets are only part of the line of Old West clothing sewn there. A long-time vendor and sponsor, Horsefly's tent is pitched at most large matches and events.

The above represents some of the major purveyors of "period proper" frontier provisions: the general stores of the lifestyle, if you will. Cowboy shootists are individualists who rarely limit themselves to one store or catalog. An alter ego is a special thing, and a Cowboy Action event is a community of alter egos, freed for a moment on the theatrical plains of a real and imagined history. Players outfit themselves as they imagine thcy would have, wherever they might have lived morc than a hundred years ago.

This frequently means sewing one's own clothes or having them tailored. Such folks look to a pattern publishing company like Buckaroo Bobbins (Chino Valley, AZ). An old-fashioned "Mom and Pop" operation, Buckaroo Bobbins is the creation of Roger and Geneva Eads, longtime friends of Cowboy Action Shooting. Shooters, re-enactors and living history docents have come to rely on their patterns for the proper cut, cloth and fit unavailable off the rack. Their catalog, published in an old-time newspaper format, is as

ABOVE. *All kinds turn up at Cowboy matches, even "saloon entertainers" and their admirers.*

ABOVE. *A borderlands cowboy keeps a wary eye on the daguerriotypist as he attempts to capture the loveliness of a lady in her 19th century finery.*

ABOVE. *Judge Roy Bean's hacendado suit may be the most elaborate example extant. The sombrero is equally ornate, and the rufflefront shirt lends an appropriate final touch.*

We See by Our Outfits That We Are All Cowpersons 187

AT LEFT. *Silks and satins don't slow down this lady as she sweeps across the plaza at End of Trail 2000. Note the high collar, cameo and muttonleg sleeves typical of the '90s.*

AT RIGHT.
This young brave lad is not to be trifled with. In addition to his bow and quiver of arrows, he wears a .45-70 '73 Trapdoor Springfield Carbine.

valuable for information and philosophical style as for its essential Old West styles. And Buckaroo Bobbins patterns for children are a boon to parents. Cowkids love to play dress-up durn near as much as Mom and Dad.

Cowboy actioneers need gear of leather and beaver felt and the artistic equipage of the characters they portray. Thus, they regularly require re-rigging from the artisans and craftsmen who re-create the boots, buckskins, beadwork and buckles they can't build in the bunkhouse. A short list of some of the best follows. Without peer are the tall Coffeyville boots and short *botinas* of custom bootmaker David Espinoza (Phoenix, AZ), who brings 30 years of experience, expertise and research to his reproductions of the original cowboy boots of the Old West. Made of the finest leathers, Espinoza boots are custom hand-made-to-order, as they were for the drovers out on the cattle trails. They're fully lined and have all the features of those early stovepipes; the smooth, one-piece front, working spur shelves and traditional heel and toe shapes.

Cowboy shootists with a taste for northern plains tribal clothing can do no better than Les Bois Brule Metis Trading Co. on the Crow reservation (Lodge Grass, Montana). The museum-quality buckskin, quill and beadwork is the product of Gary *Jean Baptiste* Johnson and Louella *Juneberries* Johnson. Gary is "a full-blooded half-breed," he says, and Louella is the granddaughter of famous Custer scout *White Man Runs Him*. Their work is seen in museums, magazine and movies, as well as on cowboy shootists, re-enactors and canny collectors. Tedious and time intensive, the authenticity and precision of reproductions from Les Bois Brule isn't cheap, but it's the best.

As are the exquisite Southern Plains recreations of Sherri and Bill Heath and their son

ABOVE. *"Sister Sarah"*
poses in her nun's costume

ABOVE. *Mounted shooters Wes Walton, Mickey Free and Phil Spangenberger palaver between stages. Mounted shooters have a special penchant for colorful clothing.*

AT RIGHT.
End of Trail, the World Championships of Cowboy Action Shooting, draws international competitors as well. This Canadian couple indicates that the Redcoats are still coming.

AT LEFT. *The boots worn by this lady were custom-made (by David Espinosa) for walking and riding. Dressy and sturdy, lace-ups like these are ideal for cowboy competition.*

AT RIGHT. *The basic boot of the Old West features a square toe, one-piece fronts, high Cuban (or underslung) heel, and a spur shelf.*

AT LEFT. *Boots like these customized Cavalry-style models a cowboy favorite on trail drives and in railhead towns during the 1870s and '90s.*

Diamond Jim, resplendent in his woolies of Icelandic sheep and Bianchi-made gunleather.

Blue. The Heath family owns Blue Skies Mercantile (Cherokee, TX) from whence they ship their uniquely decorated clothing and accessories to buckskin lovers around the world. Of highest quality deer, elk, moose and buffalo leather, Sherri Heath applies a decorating technique that date back to the 18th century Hidatsa, which she rediscovered on her own. Designs are burned into the leather and then delicately painted with the colors used by tribal artisans of long ago. The result looks enough like quillwork to fool even the astute without close examination. But quillwork is fragile and requires occasional repair, if used regularly. Heath's artistry becomes part of the piece and can't unravel or come loose. Blue Skies buckskins are wetted and stretched at least twice to minimize bagging and sagging. Sinews sewn and leather laced, Sherri Heath's art may be ancient, but it's meant to be worn and used by cowboy actioneers and buckskinners. "Quill Painting," as she calls it, is under copyright. There's really nothing else like it, anywhere.

If there is one article of apparel that clearly identifies the cowboy or girl, it is his or her hat. And if there's one hat that qualifies as the original cowboy hat, it's probably the John B. Stetson Boss of the Plains. Before Stetson designed his perfect cowboy cover, cowboys and drovers made do with leftovers from the eastern frontier and the Mexican and Civil wars. The so-called "ten gallon" hat is a product of the early years of the 20th century, inspired by the flamboyant styles of the Wild West shows and early western movies. Many hat blockings and creasings thought of today as "Cowboy" were unknown in the real Old West.

The first cowboy actioneers studied old photographs and late 19th century catalogs for images of the real thing, then modified their modern western hats by re-blocking and creasing them to resemble the hats of their chosen decade and range. Happily, this is no longer necessary. Thanks to the widespread growth of Cowboy/Western Action Shooting and the general re-awakening of interest in western history, major hat makers and custom hatters have been inspired to re-create the hats of both the historical and Hollywood West. Shootists depend on such great names among hatters as Bailey Hat Co., D Bar J Hat Co., O'Farrell's and, of course, Stetson. A cursory examination of *The Cowboy Chronicle*, the official SASS journal, will probably lead a cowboy actioneer to the sombrero of his or her dreams.

Between the boots and the hat, shooters have come to rely on a few makers who have invested heavily in and consistently support Cowboy/ Western Action Shooting and the Old West lifestyles. Principle among these stalwarts is

ABOVE. *Prairie Weet keeps cool in her 1890s sun suit while waiting to shoot at End of Trail. Her shotgun is a Stoeger 12 gauge Coach Gun, shown with the action open as required by SASS safety rules.*

AT LEFT. *Not all 19th-century men were cowboys. An Express Company guard from the late 1890s, armed with his 1897 Winchester 12 gauge, is ready for anything.*

AT RIGHT. *Armed with his 1873 Winchester rifle and 7.5-inch Colt, this early period vaquero is prepared to defend the wagon train from those quarrelsome Commanches.*

AT LEFT. *This Southern Lady of the frontier brightens a cloudy day at End of Trail. Many cowboy auctioneers sew their own carefully researched period clothing with charmingly authentic results.*

Scully Wah Maker, known for the most authentic attire we think of as Old West. Much of the clothing seen in these pages are Allen Wah designs, which are executed by Scully/Wah Maker Cowboy Clothing.

Scully Leather Company—founded by Dan Scully's grandfather in 1906—was a pioneer in western wear, becoming in time the ideal manufacturer for handling the growing demand for frontier and Victorian clothing. Allen Wah sold his designs and label to Scully, who sold them to shooters, re-enactors and motion picture companies. Much of the authentic clothing seen in recent western films was created by Scully Wah Maker, and most Old West retailers stock from the same line.

There's more between boot and hat than clothes. Boots need spurs and spurs need spurleather. Pants need belts and/or suspenders, and pockets need watches. A lady in her bustled daytime dress needs her *chatelaine*, while a cowboy dressed for work needs his sheath knife. Over time, actioneers sink deeper into their happy lifestyle, while more and more accessories and equipage are collected. After all, cowboy matches and events generally last three or four days, and most cowboy actioneers enjoy changing their outfits and showing off their plunder. In the end, boots and booty make up a good portion of the theatrical fun to be had in Cowboy/Western Action Shooting. Moreover, our outfits don't have to be put away between performances; many of us live in the duckins, collarless shirts and hats we shoot in at matches. Our boots, moccasins and vests are everyday wear. We carry pocket watches and Barlow knives and value our personal style over frumious foreign fashions. We recognize one another. And we see by our outfits that we are all cowboys. 🤠

CHAPTER SEVEN

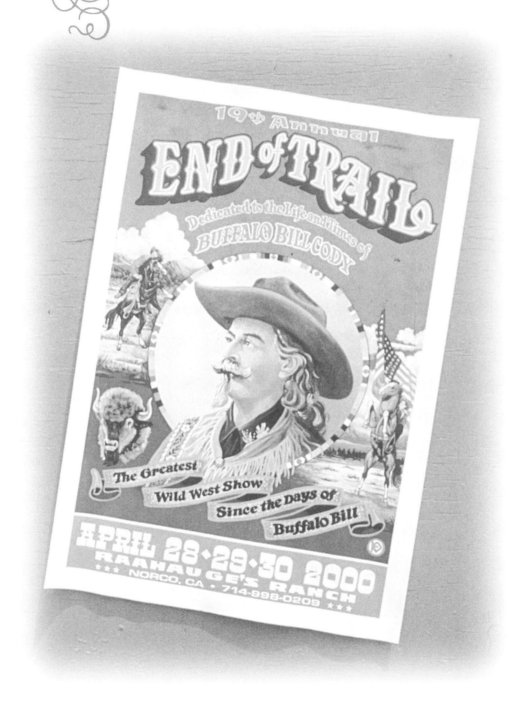

Fun & Festivities

Shooting sports are fun. Western Action Shooting is the most fun you can have with your guns on. But fond as we are of our smokewagons and long guns, cowboy actioneering is much more than shooting matches. The match is the foundation of our game, the event that puts the sport in our sport/hobby/lifestyle. Firearms are the backbone of re-enactment. Without guns, we'd still be the impotent subjects of the British Empire or some other crown. With our firearms fun, we celebrate both our western heritage and our freedom.

Cowboy Action matches are social events as well as they were on our western frontier. While local match shooters may content themselves with a Saturday night dinner or dance, a "Best Dress" contest or an awards ceremony, it's the major Regional, National and World Championships, along with the various frontier exhibitions and encampments that must be seen to be believed. Canvas tent cities spring up like "Brigadoon," stagecoaches rumble down the streets of vendor tents, and frontier music fills the air. Many shooters devote their precious vacation time to these multi-day events, each match a lifetime memory.

At End of Trail, there's so much to see and do that some shooters never see or do it all. At any given time during a major event, several opportunities for entertainment, enlightenment and enjoyment present themselves, often at opposite ends of the grounds and at the same time. Musicians like Sourdough Slim, Belinda Gale and a couple called Prickly Pear perform all day and into the night. Spontaneous dancing breaks out and cowboy poets like Larry Maurice and Nat Love fetch a tear or a laugh. A group of neophyte mounted shooters may be found sitting on hay bales listening to horse trainer and riding instructor Vince *Horse Dancer* Spiaggia, while another group learns about quilting and still another picks up valuable cooking skills for the chuck wagon. End of Trail even features a chuckwagon cooking contest so folks can sample the chuck those old drovers ate along the cattle trails. Grub goes down better in the shade of a Studebaker chuckwagon. If you're still hungry, line up at the chili cook-off or one of several vendor wagons and eat hearty. Cowboy events take energy.

(continued on pg. 203)

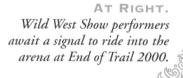

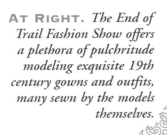

AT RIGHT. *The End of Trail Fashion Show offers a plethora of pulchritude modeling exquisite 19th century gowns and outfits, many sewn by the models themselves.*

AT LEFT. *Wes Walton is a born Wild West performer who pays homage to his tribal brothers in Plains dress (and he's good with those arrows, too).*

ABOVE. *The End of Trail Fashion Show models present plenty of pulchritude as they display exquisite 19th century gowns and outfits, many sewn by the models themselves.*

AT RIGHT.
*T.C. Thorstensen takes a
buckin' bareback ride at
SASS End of Trail.*

ABOVE. *The chuckwagon race at the End of Trail Wild West Show
is a dangerous and exciting event that rivets audience attention.*

AT LEFT. *It's best not to mess much with the Carridine Brothers. The show they put on at Cowboy Action events is better than some western movies.*

AT RIGHT. *A trick rider at the SASS End of Trail Wild West Show jumps a fence while standing on two horses at once.*

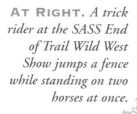

< a></>

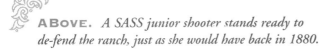
ABOVE. *A SASS junior shooter stands ready to de-fend the ranch, just as she would have back in 1880.*

These and other seminars are usually repeated during the event so that all shooters—the public included—get a chance to attend. Amateur and professional performers spin ropes or amaze their audiences like Joe Bowman does, with his astonishing gun-handling and firearms safety messages. One can learn the holy game of poker from *La Fitte*, Knight of the Green Cloth, Doctor of Faro and Practitioner of Practical Prestidigitation. Just don't play cards with him. If you're lucky, you might catch Jim Dunham's famous portrayal of Mark Twain or his unforgettable exhibition of fine and fancy pistol twistin'.

(continued on pg. 208)

JOEL DUTCH DORTCH
SASS 455

Dutch is SASS Director of Entertainment and producer of the "The Greatest Wild West Show since the days of Buffalo Bill." He is also Executive Director of the Happy Trails Children's Foundation and founder and Director of the annual "Roy Rogers and Dale Evans Western Film Festival," which benefits Happy Trails Foundation.

Dutch is as deeply involved with good works as with Cowboy Action Shooting. He's on the Board of the Roy Rogers and Dale Evans Museum, in Victorville, CA and is a Charter Member of SASS, the Coto Cowboys, the Gene Autry Museum of Western Heritage and the Double R Bar Regulators.

Born in Alabama a long time ago, Dutch and his wife Donna **Duchess** *Dortch, SASS 4500, reside in Riverside, CA.*

Trail bosses always warned their riders to stay out of the notorious Gem Saloon, but "Soiled Doves" like these make it difficult for the cowboys to pay attention.

ABOVE. *Ebb Tarr portrays Buffalo Bill for audiences throughout the country, but he attends SASS End of Trail for fun.*

ABOVE. *A happy cowboy, ready to ride, wins the Best Dressed contest at End of Trail.*

ABOVE. *Billy the Kid is arrested and brought in for trial. Shortly after, he escaped again.*

Fun & Festivities **207**

Fashion shows and "Best Dressed" contests cover history, Hollywood and idiosyncractic imagings. A parade of 19th century characters compete for praise, prizes and laughs. There are cowboys, of course, along with cavalry soldiers, bankers, law-men, "Soiled Doves" and respectable ladies. The whole spectrum of Old West society is modeled. Small children and teenagers dress up in their favorite categories and the effects of the 19th century outfits are absolutely charming. Indeed, Cowboy/Western Action kids probably learn as much American history from these experiences as they learn in school.

Dancing and dance contests are standard nighttime celebration, but don't expect the latest barroom dancing craze. Like the bumper sticker says, "Real cowboys don't line dance. A buckaroo won't even watch." Instead, we practice the Texas Two-Step, the Fox Trot and the Waltz. One wouldn't be surprised to see a Virginia Reel or Square Dance. It's amazing how much energy folks can exert dancing all night after a day of shootin', shoppin' and socializin'. And there's no place like a dance for showing off one's evening finery. The big tent on Saturday night is a veritable encyclopedia of 19th century dress in the American West, but the one thing everyone wears is a smile.

Re-enactors are encouraged to participate. Their presence, performances and displays help create the event ambiance. As the History Channel has discovered, re-enactors provide excellent sources of accurate historical information. Spend some time in a re-enactor camp and you're guaranteed to learn things the history books—especially the new, politically correct and revised editions—never mention. It's fun to be haggling with a peddler as a contingent of cavalry marches by, or to be confronted by a platoon of uppity Suffragettes from the Ladies Tea and Resting Room (a den of troublemakers if there ever was one).

The largest Cowboy event can hardly accommodate 500 or so Action shooters for their main and side matches without the event spreading over a week or more. But these celebrations are far too much fun to miss and thus are peopled with shooter's families, friends, re-enactors, waddies, vendors, performers, horses and frequently the public. Folks get gussied up to dance or carouse and gamble, usually with somewhat more restraint than in the original frontier towns. The result is Old West spectacle so compelling it draws press and media and causes books to be written. This here ain't no ordinary shootin' match.

(continued on pg. 216)

ABOVE.
Many gowns and outfits worn in the Best Dressed contest are sewn by hand, as this winner can attest.

ABOVE. *Street theater provides great entertainment at matches and events, often staged as a competition between troupes of actors.*

ABOVE. *A trio of temptresses, denizens of the demimonde, salute the beloved Soiled Doves of the frontier.*

ABOVE. *Little cowboy actioneers and actionettes pose in their Best Dressed contest best.*

ABOVE. *Lawless Linda and Rawhide Rawlins (Mrs. & Mrs. Phil Spangenberger) cavort on a Saturday night at the SASS World Championships.*

ABOVE. *Wait 'til Tex finds out Cat Ballou has taken up with this unarmed vaquero! He'll call him out, sure as shootin'.*

ABOVE. *La Dona Susana, or Cimarron Sue, dances a solo while El Escritor mans the camera at End of Trail.*

ABOVE. *Mr. & Mrs. U.S. Grant (Boyd and Mimi Davis) join in the festivities.*

ABOVE. *The internationally renowned Bob Munden, "The Fastest Gun in the World," puts on several shows at SASS End of Trail. He's so fast and accurate, his audiences can hardly believe what they see.*

For shooters in pursuit of that elusive Holy Grail of Cowboy Action—the World Championships —SASS End of Trail is indeed the end of the trail. The "Top Gun Shootoff" on Sunday morning finds the bleachers full of spectators. But the event that fills the stands and lines the rails is the End of Trail "Wild West" Show. The impresario of the show is Joel *Dutch* Dortch, a Wild Bunch Member and SASS Treasurer. Dutch is also Director of Entertainment for End of Trail, the man who turns shootin' matches into Wild West Jubilees. While he is far too deeply involved with cowboy actioneering to list his many positions of responsibility and involvements, it's enough to state that Dutch has, as a forefather of the movement, been shooting Cowboy Action matches since 1987.

A typical Dortch extravaganza might feature a trained buffalo named Harvey Wallbanger and his sidekick, T.C. Thorstensen, or an unbelievable performance by the "One-Armed Bandit" and his animal entourage. There is often a stagecoach hold-up, and surely the highwaymen will be caught and punished, although not without a fight. Wild Indians will abound, of course, along with wilder cowboys. There are chuckwagon races, marksmanship demonstrations and re-enactments. At SASS End of Trail 2000, Buffalo Bill himself showed up and speechified for a while, putting his stamp of approval on Dutch's presentation. Rain or shine, the Wild West Show goes on and the crowds roar.

When the shootin', shoppin' and show-goin' is done and the sun slips over the mountain, the guns come off and the dresses and suits go on. No firearms are allowed in town after five o'clock, but cowboys who feel naked without their gunbelts, or who are unable to resist shooting into the air as a form of applause, are invited to wear their cap pistols and have fun the way they did in the old Birdcage in Tombstone or the Longbranch in Dodge.

(continued on pg. 222)

ABOVE. *This lady's day dress and the flair with which she wears it brings down the house at the Fashion Show, an annual feature of End f Trail.*

ABOVE. *Street musicians perform on the streets of Cowboy Action events, just as they once did on the streets of frontier towns. Authentic period music is important to the Old West environment.*

Don't play cards with this man, often seen performing great feats of prestidigitation at Cowboy Action events around the West. He is the notorious LaFitte, Knight of the Green Cloth, Doctor of Faro and Prince of Poker. He's also an SASS shooter and a fair hand with his 1851 Navy Colts.

ABOVE. *These ladies may look innocent enough, as they repose in the Ladies Tea & Resting Room, but don't be fooled. No doubt they are Suffragettes making plans.*

AT RIGHT.
James A. Dunham, gunfighter and fashion plate fresh from the frontier, in a rare cabinet photo from the mid 80s. Note the short tie and sleeve garters.

AT RIGHT.
Shooters and the public can find their way around Cowboy Action matches with the aid of helpful signs like these.

BELOW. *Roy Rogers, Gene Autry and other legendary cowboy stars had lunch boxes made for cowboys and girls to carry back and forth to school. Colonel Shep's picture and Cowboy Code are sure to be worth big bucks someday.*

AT LEFT.
If there's a pot of chili or a camera around, 2-Step Sartain and Lady L'Amour will find them both.

After dinner, most folks line up at the main tent for dancing and socializing at Winter Range and End of Trail, it's off to the local saloon for gambling like they did on the frontier. Instead of using electronic "gaming" devices, they play Faro and poker, roulette, wheels of fortune and dice. At the Belle Union Saloon and Gambling Emporium, End of Trail's most popular nighttime attraction, gamblers (not "players") are treated to a background of clinking poker chips, the clicking of the roulette wheels and real frontier music from the tinkling piano of Dave Bourne. His renditions of Buffalo Gal, Goodbye Old Paint and all the other frontier songs greatly contribute to the illusion that this is what it was really like, all those yesteryears ago.

(continued on pg. 225)

AT RIGHT. *Frontier piano player Dave Bourn, the **Lobo Ranger** himself, tickles the ivories, mostly songs of the Old West in the saloons and gambling halls at Cowboy Action events.*

ABOVE. *"Chuckwagon Cookies" are up at first light to prepare for the Chuckwagon Cooking Contest. Correct rigging and utensils are an important part of the competition. Note this handy outfit's proper wagon fly, furled wagon cover and fire pit.*

AT LEFT. *The Studebaker (the real thing, not a reproduction) was a popular wagon long before the automobile was invented.*

AT RIGHT.
Chained and padlocked, this chuckwagon's Winchesters are ready for the long, dangerous trail.

ABOVE. *Real cowboys make real hemp rope in a real chuckwagon camp. Cowboy Actioneering is more than shooting matches; it's living history.*

The Belle Union features a genuine 19th century bar where saloon girls hover hopefully. No money changes hands; the big winners are awarded prizes for having garnered the most chips, but it's enormous fun and that's the game. Those who aren't asleep, in the main tent dancing or gambling, are probably sit-ting around a campfire with friends and loved ones. Jokes and stories will be carried home, data and information exchanged, news and absent amigos talked about. Then the fires are banked, Dave Bourne's piano falls silent and theres only starlight and the snuffle of horses. ⚜

CHAPTER EIGHT

ABOVE. *The National Rifle Association booth at Ruger's Winter Range 2000.*

AT RIGHT.
Ken The Chiseler Amorosano, SASS Public Relations, Media and Membership Director, discusses End of Trail with the crew of TNN's American Shooter program.

Vendors and Sponsors

At Cowboy/Western Action events, folks do as much shoppin' as they do shootin' and socializin'. Some of the Western Americana on display in the vendor booths is available only at the tent towns that spring up around the cowboy matches. Shooters and participants look forward to the bigger events, partly for the shopping they afford. Much of the socializin' takes place when shooters finish for the day and head into town. Like the streets of Tombstone and Dodge City, Santa Fe and Cheyenne, the vendor rows of Winter Range, End of Trail and other big matches teem with shoppers and visiting friends.

Some displays are in large, elaborate false-front tents, others are quaint marquee boxes or open, sweeping flys offering welcome shade. Some are teepees, or huge outfitter tents. The Arizona Stagecoach Clothing Company sells its wares straight from an authentic peddler's wagon. All present a charming Old West atmosphere that's easier to experience than describe.

A walk along Vendors Row is an educational experience. Here a saddlemaker sews leather on a horn cap, there a gunsmith repairs a shooter's six-gun. Through the palaver and laughter floats the metronomic beat of an engraver's hammer, carving art onto a Winchester Yellowboy receiver. Books, thankfully, are a big seller. Cowboy actioneers are readers, students of Western and other history. They watch the History Channel and have an insatiable appetite for Western films. Most are avid collectors of all things Old West. Vendors

Row at a major match is an irresistible mother lode of plunder and possibles.

Vendors and sponsors return again and again to the big cowboy matches and events. Western actioneers are a loyal breed. Once a brand or supplier becomes a favorite, shooters would rather fight than switch, even at a lower price. It's just another of our old-fashioned philosophies. Over time, the vendors, peddlers and drummers become more than storekeeps and proprietors. "Vendor's Row" is a mighty friendly place.

Where else can one find—for sale or trade —shotgun chaps from the 1870s, an 1880s day dress or a Damascus steel Spanish Belduque? Frontier pistols, rifles and shotguns stand at attention inviting inspection; bits and spurs glitter on tables in the sun and shoppers inhabit

(continued on pg. 241)

ABOVE. *When he's not out shooting in the match, Winchester Jim mans the booth for his namesake company at major Cowboy Action events.*

ABOVE. *The Ten-X Ammunition store at SASS End of Trail is filled as usual with black powder cartridge shooters lined up for re-supply.*

Vendors and Sponsors **229**

AT RIGHT. *Mike "Texas Jack" Harvey listens to "El Escritor" plead for a brace of Cimarron's 1872 Colt Open Top revolvers.*

AT LEFT. *Professor Jim Boeke serves customers in his tent store at events around the country.*

AT RIGHT.
Allen "Wahoo" Wah, Tom "C.S. Fly" Ingoglia and Ron "El Escritor" Harris pose with the Wah Wagon at Ruger's Winter Range.

ABOVE. *The River Junction Trade Company (Jim Boeke, Proprietor) is open for the day's business at a Wes-tern Action match.*

KEN "THE CHISELER" AMOROSANO SASS 392

Vendors, sponsors and the media who deal with SASS deal with The Chiseler, as he is affectionately known. To Amorosano falls the happy task of serving as SASS Public Relations and Marketing Director, as well as Managing Editor of The Cowboy Chronicle, the Journal of the Single Action Shooting Society. And he does more.

The Chiseler's duties include advertising, membership development and the SASS Mercantile catalog and sales. He designed and maintains the SASS Website and services vendors at End of Trail. He's a Mounted shooter, a Cowboy Action shooter, and an Adventure Trail rider. He and wife Doc Drillem shoot in Traditional category with Ken's home club, the Coto Cowboys.

After sixteen years in the entertainment PR and marketing business, Amorosano survives by enjoying Western History, Cowboy Actioneering and his activities as a voting member of the Academy of Country Music. He's proud to be a staunch supporter of the Second Amendment of our Bill of Rights.

ABOVE. *Interior of the River Junction Trade Co. store in McGregor, Iowa. It's good to know that such a complete 19th century dry goods store still exists.*

AT LEFT.
*Hank Clark tends his shop at
End of Trail. Argent Express is a
long-time vendor and supporter
of cowboy actioneering.*

AT RIGHT. *The original
perennial Victorian Traveler
herself show off her finely
made period carpetbags,
favorites of cowgirl actioneers.*

ABOVE. *Roger and Geneva Eads pose in front of their tent store full of patterns for sewing authentic frontier wear. "Save a day's wages," they suggest, "and sew it yourself."*

AT RIGHT.
Thunderbolt shows off his wares at Ruger's Winter Range. Vendors there fill three streets, with shooters traveling from around the world for the four-day National Championships held each year in Arizona.

Vendors and Sponsors **233**

ABOVE. *At larger matches, blacksmiths build made-to-order items as crowds gather to watch the men pursue the ancient alchemy of fire and steel.*

ABOVE. *A vendor street at SASS End of Trail is viewed from high atop a stagecoach carrying shoppers and sightseers around the frontier town.*

AT LEFT. *An early bird vendor sips his morning coffee waiting for the action to start (and the customers to arrive).*

AT RIGHT. *Tammy Loy explains to Cimarron Sue why ordering a new Uberti Spencer Carbine replica is the right thing to do.*

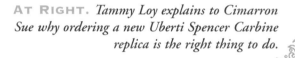

AT LEFT. *The infamous Bitterroot "Bit and Spur" spread at SASS End of Trail. Owners Frank and Vikki Schultz are known the world over for their authenticity and square dealing.*

AT RIGHT. *Coon Creek specializes in hard-to-find cavalry, cowboy and ladies Victorian wear and accessories.*

ABOVE. *The COWS tent store at the End of Trail is, as always, filled with frontier clothing, gunleather and eager shoppers.*

AT RIGHT. *An engraver at work on an 1866 Yellowboy at End of Trail. Engraved guns are as highly prized by today's shooters as they were in the Old West.*

AT LEFT. *It's time to get into line for Bill Johnson's Big Apple at Ruger's Winter Range and other events.*

ABOVE. *Bob Buckshot Roberts Rainwater's business, Alias Images, designs Western movie posters for shooters who pose at his event store.*

ABOVE. *Ruger is the signature sponsor of Winter Range; the famous Ruger Frontier Armory is always busy at Cowboy Action events.*

AT RIGHT.
The Wild West Mercantile tent at Ruger's Winter Range supplies much of the "Wah Maker" 19th century clothing worn by shooters and re-enactors.

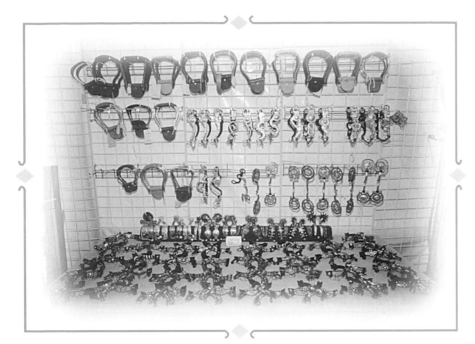

AT LEFT. *Bits, spurs and tack are popular items at Cowboy/Western Action events.*

ABOVE. *Ruger's General Manager Robert "The Major" Stutler shows off a Ruger Single Shot Anniversary rifle in the company's Frontier Armory at Winter Range.*

the haberdashers, feeling the fabric and fur. Saddles are sold and buckskins bought. New boots and hats abound. Ladies can select from a wealth of such diverse delectables as bustles and snoods.

Many vendors are also sponsors, that generous genus of businesses without which Cowboy/ Western Action Shooting could not exist—at least not on the scale we know. There can be no more symbiotic relationship than that between cowboy actioneers and their suppliers and sponsors. One could hardly exist without the other.

For ours is an amateur sport, kept safe from commercialism by sponsorship of the sport, not the sportsman, the matches and not the shooters. It's difficult to appear period correct and in character with logo patches sewn all over your clothes. When shooters affix a Winchester or Uberti decal to their gun cart, it's brand loyalty, not an advertising royalty that compels them. Our vendors and sponsors are also the same companies and organizations who are fighting hardest on political battlefields, trying against overwhelming odds to salvage what's left of our Constitutional rights. Patronizing vendors and sponsors is the cowboy way of saying, "Thank you."

CHAPTER NINE

Courtesy of Buck Taylor

 **ABOVE.** *The Chase.*

MOUNTED COWBOY ACTION SHOOTING

*T*he horse knew from the way his rider made him trot circles that something was up. The cowboy patted the horse's neck as he sized up the ten crooks blocking his way. Five bullies stood in a loose semi-circle a few yards away and five more were lined up down the center of the dirt street. It was a dangerous gauntlet, but it had to be ridden. His pistols held five pills apiece and he didn't intend to miss.

Let's get to it, he thought, and put his left leg hard on the horse. The horse leaped off on the right lead as the cowboy pulled his off-side six-gun and made for the middle of the miscreants. In seconds he put paid to them all and holstered his empty shooter as he swung his horse around a barrel at the end of the street. Galloping back up the street, he drew his other gun. Escape never entered his mind. At the end of the street, he suddenly wheeled his horse and ran down the final five felons, firing as he came. Standing his stirrups and bathed in billows of black powder smoke, the courageous cowboy coolly cocked and fired, as one by one the craven cowards crumbled before his unerring aim. With his last shot, he sat his horse and gently drew him down, patting him on the neck.

The above is not some passage from a poorly written 19th century dime novel, but an annoyingly alliterative account of a typical stage, or *course of fire*, in a Cowboy Mounted Shooting event. The dirt street could be an equestrian arena or some other suitable open ground. The "Bad Men" are ten-inch balloons atop four-foot flexible poles. A contestant's performance is timed to within one one-hundredth of a second and misses and/or unengaged targets pulling penalties of five seconds each. Procedural errors cost ten seconds apiece, and a dropped pistol while on the course earns a DQ (disqualification) for the stage. More difficult than it sounds, Cowboy Mounted

Shooting demands concentration, horsemanship and skillful gun handling, all under great pressure.

Part barrel race, part shootin' match and part Wild West Show, Mounted Shooting is about as safe as such a heart-and-hoof pounding sport can be. Match ammunition is either Cowboy Mounted Shooting Association, CMSA, or Single Action Shooting Society, SASS, .45 Colt Caliber blanks carefully regulated. No other ammunition of any kind is allowed anywhere near the arena. Not that railbirds are in any danger. Only 1.5 cc of FFg black powder propels .5 cc of soft corn cob media,

(continued on pg. 250)

ABOVE. *CMSA founder Jim Rodgers and his authentic half-seat, Staggs-rigged Great Plains saddle.*

ABOVE. *A fashion-conscious Mounted Shooting team. The author poses as an 1890s Regulator complete with: Espinosa boots, duckins britches, John Bianchi gunleather, plaque-front shirt, wild rag and slide and Boss-of-the-Plains Stetson. His horse Jack wears an 1890s Loop Seat Santa Barbara saddle by Gordon Davis.*

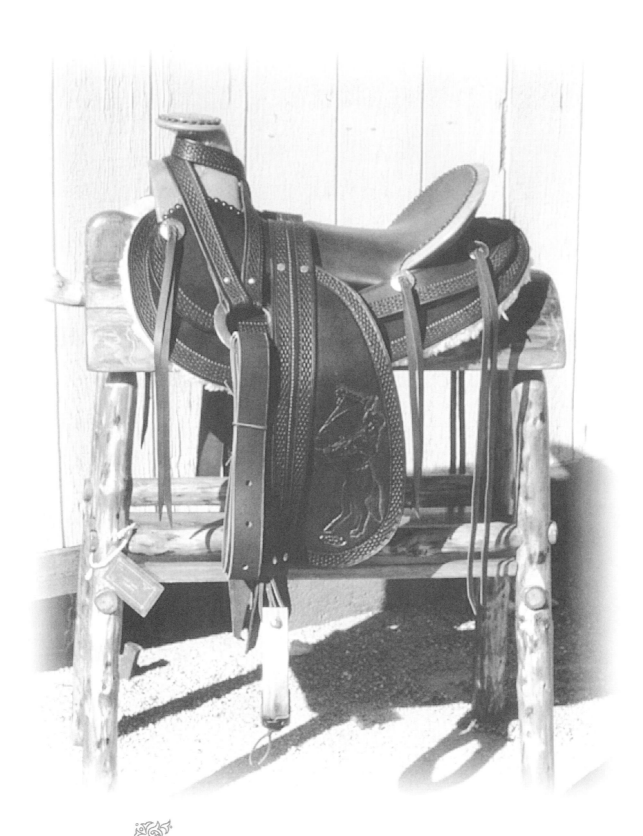

All About Cowboy Action Shooting

ABOVE. *The Texas Trail saddle is built on a Hope tree. Light and three-quarter-rigged, it's a great choice for mounted competition.*

ABOVE. *This full, double-rigged roping saddle was awarded to Bobbi Deschenes, the 1998 Women's World Point Champion.*

ABOVE. *La silla y brida del charro Fernando Vasquez. Hulls like this were the basis for Western stock saddles.*

ABOVE. *A Staggs-rigged Cheyenne-style half-seat saddle built and completely tooled by Mario Hanel. The Angora saddle bags are authentic and period-correct.*

the range at which blanks will burst a balloon is barely 10 or 12 feet away, depending on the wind direction. Even so, all firearms are loaded and unloaded by the official match armorer, and nobody is allowed to leave the arena with a loaded gun.

Revolvers must be period correct, and while Colt replicas are most popular with mounted competitors, as with "ground" shooters, Remingtons and Schofields are appropriate and equally effective. Riders have individual theories on barrel length, with 4³/₄-inch probably most desirable for its cone of dispersal and ease of handling in the saddle. Gunleather is perhaps a more important consideration. Drawing and holstering is done at speed while maneuvering

through the course of fire and setting up for the next target. Pistols and holsters must be secure and quickly accessible.

The rider's apparel and gear must also be accurate for the period, as must each contestant's tack. Only leather saddles and bridles are allowed, and these ought to be the types used prior to 1900. Half-seat Great Plains, Texas Trail and Hope (Santa Fe) saddles are much ridden by competitors, as are Mexican Charro and the later Loop Seat stock saddles. McClellan Cavalry saddles and early period Mochila or Mother Hubbards are also used, reproduced by savvy saddlemakers. But while authentically recreated saddles, bridles, clothing and gunleather may be readily available,

Above. *Dan Doc Bones Howard is the ramrod of SASS Mounted Shooting. Seen here at End of Trail, he prefers to go lightly armed.*

riding ability and pistolcraft come only with hard work and practice. Gunhandling and marksmanship can be acquired rather quickly, but horsemanship is another matter.

"Ours is an equestrian sport", says CMSA founder and six-time CMSA National Champion Jim *Wm. Bruce* Rodgers. "The guns and balloons create an exciting horse competition. Like roping, it gives you something challenging to do with your hands." Rodgers is a real estate broker from Scottsdale, AZ who started the CMSA organization in 1994 with co-founders John *Bronc* Peel (first CMSA World Champion) and noted gun writer and Wild West performer Phil Spangenberger. When the first official CMSA

match was held at Winter Range in February of 1994, the hell-for-leather, horse-and-gun game thrilled both riders and spectators. As with Cowboy Action Shooting, the number of members and events continues to grow daily.

Once mounted shooting was added to the World Championships, that event grew dramatically, requiring two arenas and three full days to accommodate the ballooning number of contestants. Many competitors also perform in the Wild West Show, another popular annual attraction at End of Trail. Trail boss for the SASS Mounted program is Dan *Doc Bones* Howard, who views Mounted Shooting as a natural extension of Cowboy Action, leading to the completion of the

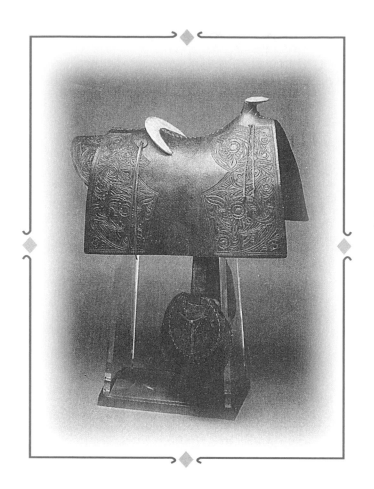

AT LEFT. *A beautiful and historically accurate Californio saddle was created by noted reproduction saddlemaker Frank Costanza (Stevensville, Montana). Note the tooled mochila, the early stirrups and tapaderos and the anquera extending behind the cantle.*

AT RIGHT. *F.A. Meanea's famous #2 saddle, Taylor tree, 3/4 Sam Stagg rigged, half-seat with plain border stamping. A perfectly authentic working stock saddle from the 1870s on.*

ABOVE. *Tools of the mounted shooter's trade: A brace of .45 Colt Peacemakers, balloons, stopwatch and plenty of blanks.*

AT RIGHT. *The Fathers of the Cowboy Mounted Shooting Association include (left to right): First World Champion John Peel, six-time World Champion Jim Rodgers and noted Wild West performer, gun writer and historian Phil Spangenberger.*

Above. *A group of CMSA riders arrive at a match at Tombstone, Arizona, in typical mounted shooter style.*

AT LEFT.
At only 24 lbs., the author's Santa Fe-style saddle is ideal for both Mounted Shooting and trail riding. Built by Gino D'Ambrose on a Hope tree, it features engraved silver conchos by Frank Schultz (Bitteroot Bit and Spur).

AT RIGHT.
A match armorer unloads a rider's 4 1/2-inch Peacemakers following a stage event.

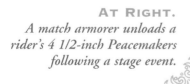

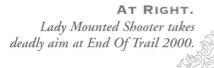 **ABOVE.** *Billy "Concho" Lang performs on the desert course at Winter Range in Phoenix, AZ. The balloon is deforming before it explodes.*

AT RIGHT.
Lady Mounted Shooter takes deadly aim at End Of Trail 2000.

The author has lost one pistol even before starting to shoot the stage—but he doesn't know it yet. His mount, Albert, knows but doesn't care. Holsters must hold the pistol securely under all conditions.

ABOVE. *Jerry "James Butler" Tarantino get his reward for winning the Mounted Event at SASS End of Trail. The traditional ceremony is called "Chappin," here joyfully administered by Cassie Redwine.*

ABOVE. *When practical and safe, Mounted Shooting matches are held in natural settings, like this arroyo near Tombstone.*

triad of cowboy, horse and six-gun. "The SASS Mounted Shooting program is intended to help fulfill the fantasies so many folks have of the Old West during the cowboy era," says Howard. "While we enjoy the competition, the real intent is to enjoy the horses, the traditional 19th century dress and tack, and the Spirit of the Game." Howard's hope is that SASS Mounted Shooting, like Cowboy Action, will remain an amateur sport, existing without the corrupting influences of money prizes and sponsored competitors.

Both CMSA and SASS play the game pretty much the same way, emphasizing safety, horsemanship and pistol proficiency. Both hold authenticity of garb, gear and guns central to the game.

And both require a safe level of riding ability and manageable. Like roping and polo, it's one-handed work demanding an independent seat wherein the rider is secure at all gaits, in balance with his horse and free to do other things with his hands and attention. It's the ability to ride and rope or shoot with or without stirrups, reins or hanging on the horn of the saddle. It is keeping your heels down, your mind in the middle and your legs on the horse, no matter what. If you can't sit a trot, or find yourself grabbing the horn to stay in the saddle, or if you have to use rubber bands to keep from loosing stirrups, you need more instruction and saddle time prior to competing.

(continued on pg. 264)

AT RIGHT.
*Jim Rodgers and Chappo
reach the moment of truth
at End of Trail.*

AT LEFT.
*The author and Joker at End of
Trail. A Palomino Paint gelding,
the horse's pedigree is distinctive
(he's out of Utah, by Trailer).*

ABOVE. *Patty Motley leans in for a close-up shot at a balloon.*

ABOVE. *Shakey Jake looks every inch the 1880s cowboy as he rounds a barrel in a Mounted match. Note how he looks where he's going, his pistol pointed safely upwards.*

AT LEFT. *A woman-on-woman stage at End of Trail involves Darn It Darr vs. Lawless Linda in a battle down to the wire.*

AT RIGHT. *A vaquero nonchalantly rubs out his last balloon at End of Trail.*

AT LEFT. *Actor/Entertainer Peter Sharayko on the Mounted Shooting course at End of Trail. Sharayko played Texas Jack in the movie Tombstone.*

The rest is up to the horse. Jim Rodgers is correct in describing the horse as a "running, shooting platform who delivers his rider to the target as fast and as close as possible." As in roping and barrel racing, the horse's athletic ability is paramount. Mounted Shooting involves intricate patterns executed while aiming at ten-inch targets, changing both guns and leads at least twice and sometimes simultaneously. Riders need that "independent seat" and the horse must remain in hand while digging around barrels and stretching out for top speed. "The horse has to come into the bridle when asked," Rodgers adds, "to position itself at targets and bend around your leg at the barrels. These horses have to be flexible and light on the forehand. They have to sprint and then come right back to you." Rogers calls it continuity of movement. Such horses result only from patient training.

Quarter horses and quarter types prevail, although Arabians and mules do well. The CMSA and SASS are "all-breed" organizations. A horse's ability to tolerate gunfire is more important than his papers. Ear plugs may help in special cases, but the only correct approach is patient training. The consensus among successful mounted shooters is that the horse should be started with a cap gun, shotgun primer, or a percussion pistol cap, in a round pen or other appropriate enclosure. The horse should be shown

ABOVE. *Cowboy photographer Robert Dawson displays what good mounted shooting form is all about: deep seat, arm extended at 45 degree angle, and eyes on the target.*

ABOVE. *Charro Fernando Vasquez at End of Trail. Note the pommel holsters on his charro saddle, leg wraps and over-reach bell boots.*

ABOVE. *At SASS End of Trail 2000, Cody Walton proves he can hit balloons with his eyes closed and without reins.*

AT RIGHT.
Horse trainer/riding instructor Vincent Horse Dancer Spiaggia and his mount, Little Big Horse, storm down the course at End of Trail.

ABOVE. *Mounted Shooting is full of surprises. It pays to keep your legs on the horse.*

ABOVE. *This top hand from Wyoming fan-cocked every round, kept his heels down, and never touched the reins nor missed a balloon!*

the gun, allowed to smell it and, as Jim Rodgers says, be "sacked out" with the pistol: Rubbed and gently touched with it until he senses no threat. The animal should also be introduced to balloons separately, so it doesn't associate the balloons with gunfire. He'll do that soon enough. Eight to twelve inch balloons aren't that hard to hit from four or five feet away, if standing still on the ground. Galloping by on a fast horse, 10 balloons go by like pickets in a fence, especially when they must be engaged in a particular order, with barrels and other obstacles skillfully negotiated exactly. Such skills aren't learned from books, but must be mastered before entering that first Mounted Shooting match.

A rider's seat can only be acquired by riding and with qualified instruction. Gun handling and shooting skills are a matter of instruction and practice. Both the CMSA and SASS offer clinics and private instruction in both spheres is readily available. Most Cowboy Mounted shooters were horsemen and women before strapping on six-guns and Mounted Shooting is a great weekend horse game that doesn't require cows or stock pens. It does require gunleather that's appropriate for horseback use. This means secure period-correct holster and a gunbelt worn high and snug. Some of the sport's "gamesmen" wear both holsters on their stomachs, obliquely canted toward their strong hand. Perhaps

ABOVE. *Jerry Tarantino cleans a stage at End of Trail 2000 in his usual high style, with 7-inch Colts.*

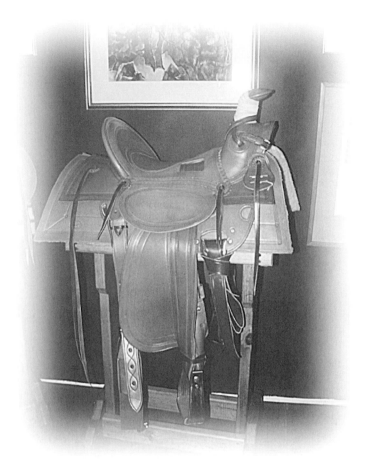

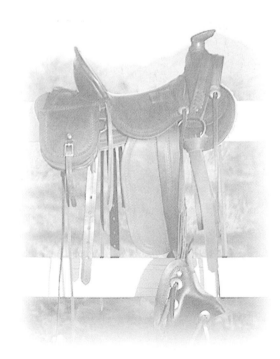

AT LEFT. *A Loop Seat Meanea roper with modern rigging (F.A. Meanea Co., Cheyenne, Wyoming). Saddles like these are as practical today as they were in the 1890s.*

AT RIGHT.
The author's Loop Seat Santa Barbara-style saddle (by Gordon Davis) with tapaderos and saddle bags. Rounded and cutaway skirts allow closer contact with the horse.

Courtesy of Buck Taylor

ABOVE. *The Chase*

they hope to gain a hundredth of a second, drawing or holstering by this affectation. Others use pommel holsters for the same reason. It's doubtful that either of these less than authentic measures provide the shooter with any real competitive edge. Period photographs fail to reveal such uses among the real cowboys in the Old West.

Crossdraw, on the other hand, may be a good idea for some mounted shooters. With short range blanks, they aren't the same safety consideration as with Cowboy Action shooters. Severely canted crossdraws, though, can lose a pistol on the course if they're not snug enough to retain it through the rough-and-tumble of a stage. A gun in the dirt is a "stage DQ." Nor should neophyte mounted shooters be deterred by the prowess of the sport's Top Hands. Both the CMSA and SASS classify riders by experience and skill levels, awarding points and prizes accordingly. These divisions level the arena, because nobody starts at the top. Those who yearn for the thrill of galloping around blazing away with six-guns like they've always wanted to, have but to train themselves and an equine teammate, and then join SASS and the CMSA. Cowboy Action Shooting, a-horse or a-foot, evokes the fantasies that re-create the Old West in our heart and minds.

CHAPTER TEN

AT LEFT.
"She Fights By His Side". An Alias Images movie poster stars El Escritor & Cimarron Sue.

Up The Trail

That the gentle reader has read this far indicates more than a passing interest in Cowboy and/or Western Action Shooting. The difference, remember, is simply one of trademarks and copyrights names, along with logos distinguishing these two approaches to the shooter sports. The term "Cowboy Actioneer" was coined by the author as a term for those who engage in shooting and myriad other activities ancillary to the life-style. It also avoids the awful misnomer "Cowboy Shooter." We don't shoot cowboys, even when we sometimes ought to.

Interest abiding this far deserves a leg getting started. First, join the organization(s) of your choice before investing a dime. Unless you have an extensive history of three-weapon shooting sports and action shooting competition, and are well versed in Western American history and folklore, much can be learned from the journals of SASS, NCOWS, and the CMSA. A shooter's first few matches are far more fun and considerably less anxious after reading these informative publications and visiting with local members. The same is true of the web sites of these august but neighborly clubs. Their membership packets contain copies of each club's publication and the all-important rule book. These are the instructions covering the assembly of your new shooting career and must be read cover-to-cover. "Them's the rules" every shooter is expected to know and obey.

Armed with this newly acquired knowledge, attend a match as a spectator. Confess to being a greenhorn and ask questions. You'll be welcomed and assisted in every way. Cowboy types love little better than dispensing opinion and advice, some of which may even be genuinely helpful. Watch the shooters closely as each stage is shot, from loading table to unloading table. Observe the Range Officers and posse members who assist in running the stages. You'll be expected to do the same recording time, counting misses and re-setting knock-down targets. Study stage scenarios and procedures and watch how different shooters attack different problems. Watch the best shooters very closely.

Observe too the dress and gunleather, especially of top shooters. They will probably have on outfits that are fairly simple and practical. Champion shooters are rarely fashion plates:

(continued on pg. 282)

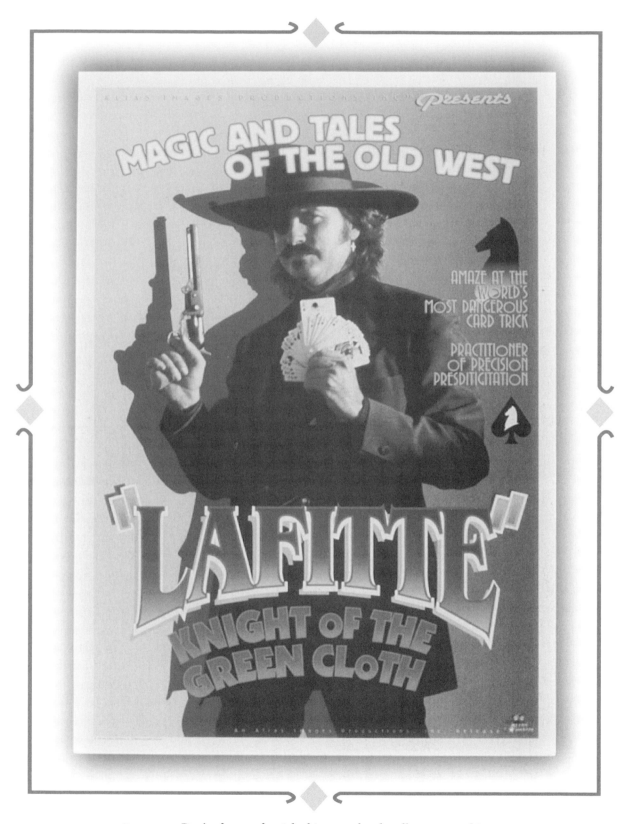

ABOVE. *Don't play cards with this man, but by all means see his*
act in Las Vegas or Ruger's Winter Range and SASS End of Trail.

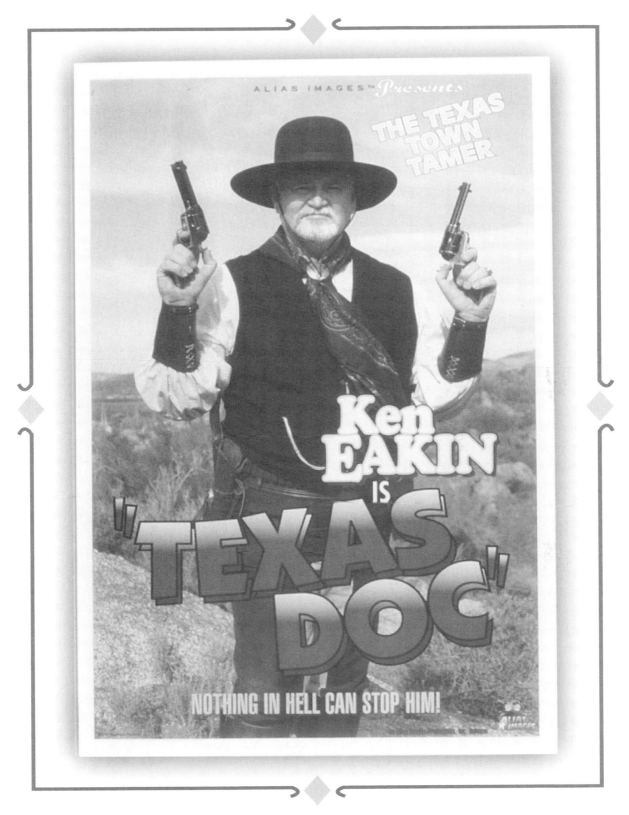

ABOVE. *Alias Images cast members frequently pay real homage to ancestors. Texas Doc's grandfather was a physician on the Texas frontier.*

AT RIGHT. *Pearl Magee, an expert on 19th century fashion, sewed this and other period dresses herself.*

 AT LEFT. *Corporal Cho is an Apache Scout at an SASS match, but he also teaches school in Colorado.*

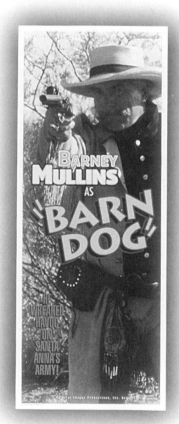

AT RIGHT. *Barn Dog's character lived throughout the frontier during and after the Mexican War.*

ABOVE. *Some cowboy actioneers, Enrique Salmon among them, are also buck-skinners who re-enact characters from the American Revolution and early frontier.*

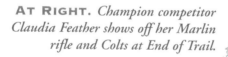

AT LEFT. *Field artillery is not SASS legal for competition, but it does add considerable smoke and boom to the ambiance at SASS End of Trail.*

AT RIGHT. *Champion competitor Claudia Feather shows off her Marlin rifle and Colts at End of Trail.*

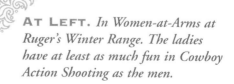

AT LEFT. *In Women-at-Arms at Ruger's Winter Range. The ladies have at least as much fun in Cowboy Action Shooting as the men.*

AT LEFT. *Robert The Major Stutler is Ruger's General Manager and an avid cowboy actioneer. Note his full double gun rig with a pair of 7-inch Rugers.*

AT RIGHT.
Metis artisan Gary "Jean Baptiste" Johnson stands ready to start the day at Ruger's Winter Range. Teepees are a typical choice of those who camp in the primitive camping area of Ben Avery Shooting Facility (Phoenix, AZ).

ABOVE. *These Wild Bunch members, past and present, made the Single Action Shooting Society what it is today: the fastest growing shooting sport in the world.*

Spurs, chaps, full double gun rigs, suspenders, vest and watch chains, huge wild rags and long, fancy wind strings are all quite authentic and photogenic, but become potential impediments when the shootin' starts.

Those who move quickest, travel lightest. Unless you can really shake a leg wearing all that cowboy kit, start with the basic period clothes and wear them 'till you feel at home in them and you won't look so "punchy" when it's time to shoot in them. This applies to ladies in particular. Save your bustled 1880s gown for dinner and dancing or the Best Dressed Contest. Don't handicap yourself

under 50 yards of fabric. Eschew anything that could cause you to fall or drop a gun.

Those unfamiliar with single action revolvers, lever action rifles, slide action shotguns or double barreled shotguns, have but to ask and all manner of frontier firearms will be proffered for test firing. Cowboys and girls are a helpful bunch. Many large gun stores have ranges where the test-firing of guns is allowed. Just remember, the gun store selection you make will doubtless be out-of-the-box new, whereas the firearms loaned by shooters may well have been blessed by a world class gunsmith. There's a *(continued on pg. 288)*

ABOVE. *Jerky Jarr, a Junior SASS shooter, poses at End of Trail. Note his eye and ear protection, and the shotgun belt secured above his gun belt. Juniors are the future of shooting sports.*

ABOVE. *Charros Don Fernando and Don Ricardo are on their way to ride and shoot in the SASS End of Trail Mounted event.*

AT LEFT. *Watching small children in their 19th century garb adds authenticity to Cowboy/Western Action events.*

AT RIGHT.
Three generations of Rogers: Roy Rogers, The King of the Cowboys, with his son Roy Jr. and grandson Dustin. End of Trail 1998 was Roy Rogers' last public appearance.

AT LEFT. *Roy Dusty Rogers, Jr. Longtime cowboy actioneer, shooter and entertainer at SASS End of Trail.*

AT RIGHT.
T.R. Roosevelt attends many Cowboy Action events, inspiring shooters with rousing speeches.

AT LEFT. *The Chiseler, The Judge and The General talk things over at SASS End of Trail. Wild Bunch members must hustle to keep things running smoothly at the World Championships.*

AT RIGHT. *Kareem Abdul Jabbar, alias Trinidad Slim, shoots the guns of the Old West as well as he did basketballs.*

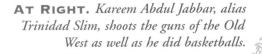

AT LEFT. *Television star Eric CHIPS Estrada loads a Winchester '73 under the supervision of End of Trail Match Director Brad Hipshot Meyers.*

ABOVE. *The Three Actioneers—Randy Travis, Roy Rogers and Roy Rogers, Jr.—exemplify a love of Western history and the guns of the Old West as they are passed from one generation to the next.*

day and night difference. The actual selection of fire-arms for personal use—including calibers, match ammunition and gunleather—is so subjective we leave to the new shooters and their trusted advisors in the hope that this book (and those listed in the bibliography) have helped. That said, some suggestions:

Select your first revolvers as a matched pair. One should feel just like the other in your hands. Ideally, they'll be tuned by a competent gunsmith and zeroed to point of aim at Cowboy Action range roughly 50 feet or so, with about a two-pound trigger. Your selection will largely determine the categories in which you shoot. Consider the period

espoused and the character you portray. Authenticity is its own reward.

Practice before entering a match. Many new shooters do not, but invariably wish they had. Handled your six-guns and long guns (cleared and empty, of course) and practice their operation until your fingers and hands know the drill. Then head for the range and practice with the ammunition you intend to use in the match. When you finish, clean your guns and enter a Cowboy match. Make a check list and bring everything you need, including gunsmith screwdrivers *(continued on pg. 296)*

AT LEFT. *This watch was presented to lawman Pat Garrett, who shot Billy the Kid in 1886. Such artifacts are treasured by cowboy actioneers.*

AT RIGHT. *This Metis/Crow quirt, with its handle of antler, was reproduced by Les Bois Brule, of Lodge Grass, Montana. Such artifacts are sometimes found on vendor's row at Cowboy Action events.*

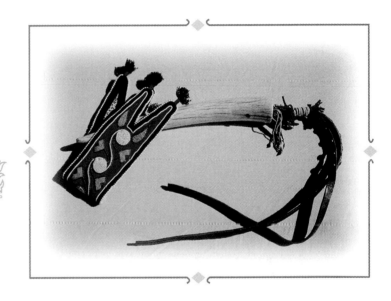

AT LEFT. *This early Waltham pocket watch was carried by a shooter with a penchant for authenticity and punctuality.*

AT LEFT. *Some shooters prefer a shoulder holster to a regular cross draw second gun holster.*

AT RIGHT. *Belt bags—whether plain or artistic—are a practical shooter's accessory. This quill painted bag was created by Sherri Heath (Blue Skies Mercantile, Cherokee, Texas).*

AT LEFT. *Watch chains can be quite simple or as elaborate as this antique Sterling chain. It belongs to LaFitte, magician and Knight of the Green Cloth.*

AT RIGHT.
*This 7-inch Colt and matching buckle
were hand-engraved by Peter Kretzmann
(Flagstaff, AZ). Holster and money belt
are by Mario Hanel.*

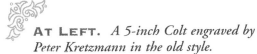

AT LEFT. *A 5-inch Colt engraved by
Peter Kretzmann in the old style.*

AT RIGHT.
*Lever action rifles and six-guns engraved by
Peter Kretzmann (Flagstaff, AZ).*

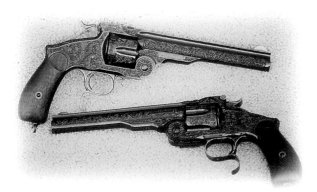

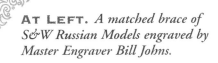

AT LEFT. *A matched brace of
S&W Russian Models engraved by
Master Engraver Bill Johns.*

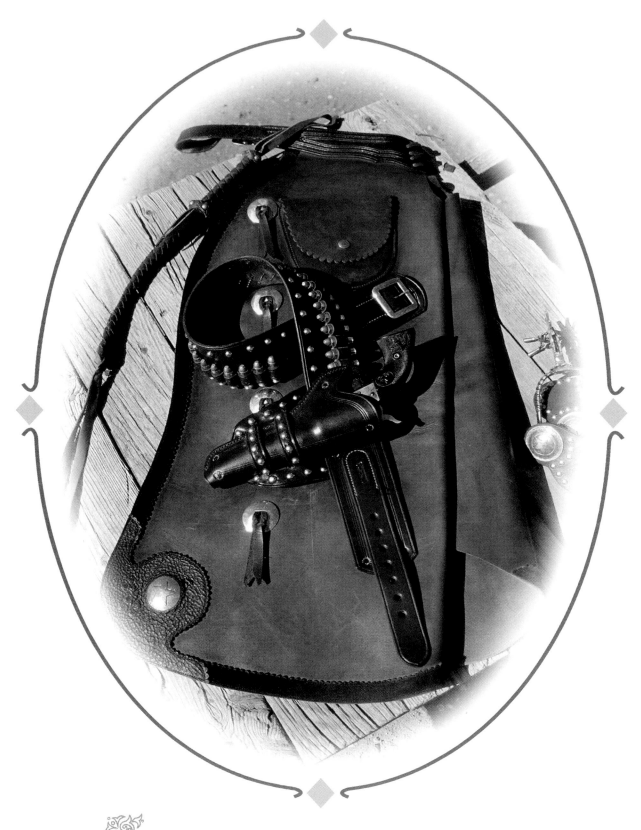

ABOVE. *These cathedral-stitched Coffeeville boots by David Espinoza are worn by the author. Garcia spurs with spur leathers and sterling concho by Frank Schultz (Bitterroot Bit & Spur).*

Up The Trail **293**

ABOVE. *Exact copies of early Spanish Colonial spurs were hand-forged by Joe De La Ronde (Glorieta, NM). Shown on old-style Bird Wing leathers.*

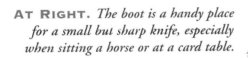

AT LEFT. *A replica of the famous Searles Bowie knife from the Alamo Museum, as reproduced for Dixie Gun Works by Davide Pedersoli.*

AT RIGHT. *The boot is a handy place for a small but sharp knife, especially when sitting a horse or at a card table.*

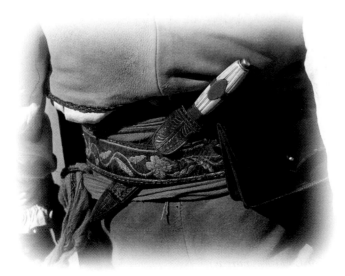

AT LEFT. *Old and elegant, this caballero's dagger is replete with ivory grip, fancy curved quillion and carved sheath. It is worn here correctly, under an embroidered bullion belt.*

and cleaning tools. Be on time for the initial shooter's meeting and pay attention. Obey all safety rules and follow the Range Officer's instructions immediately and explicitly. Try to remember how much fun you're having.

The feeling when you've shot your first Cowboy or Western Action match is difficult to describe, but the word "catharsis" comes close. It is at once empowering and relaxing and an excellent tonic for self-confidence. It can even be a life-changing experience and certainly does become a life style for ten of thousands of otherwise sane sensible people. Cowboy actioneering has this somewhat magical effect because it touches us on so many cultural and personal levels.

The growth of Cowboy Action Shooting and its influence has developed into a sort of movement that attracts those with a certain philosophy that bonds us together. We call it The Cowboy Way, The Spirit of the Game, The Code of the West. It's an attitude, a belief system and an ethical stance. It's a philosophy embodied in The Virginian and all our cowboy heroes of that heroic era we cannot recall, but so vividly imagine.

Cowboy Actioneers have been called frustrated actors in our own home movies. But if our game is largely extemporaneous theater, it's also a truly American shooting sport, a family activity and a kind of Living History presentation.

(continued on pg. 309)

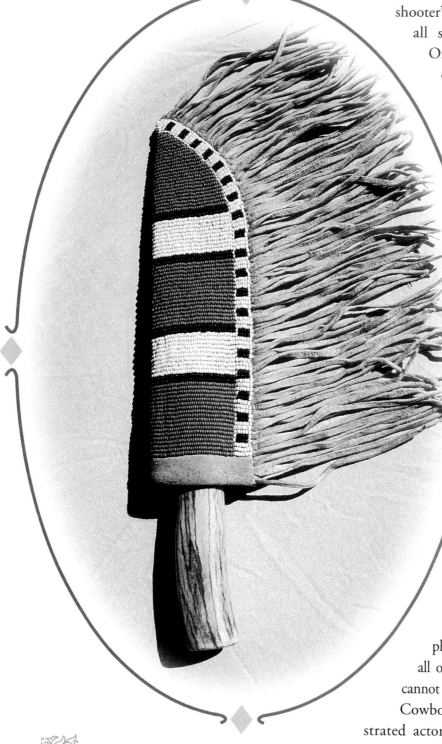

ABOVE. *An old antler-gripped Crow knife in a museum-quality beaded and fringed buckskin sheath (by Metis artisan Gary Jean Baptiste Johnson).*

ABOVE. *A knife is always loaded. Judge Roy Bean's Mexican bone-handled Bowie knife is worn handy, much the same as his ivory-gripped nickel Colts.*

AT LEFT. *Out of the way yet easy to draw, this is a handy way to wear a knife. The antler-gripped knife rests in a "Texas Jock Strap sheath."*

AT RIGHT.
This old Crow knife decorated with men's quillwork by Gary Johnson belongs in a museum.

AT LEFT. *Three handmade reproductions of the original Spanish Belduque by Joe DeLaRande. The middle knife blade is made of Damascus steel, an ancient—and difficult—blade-making process.*

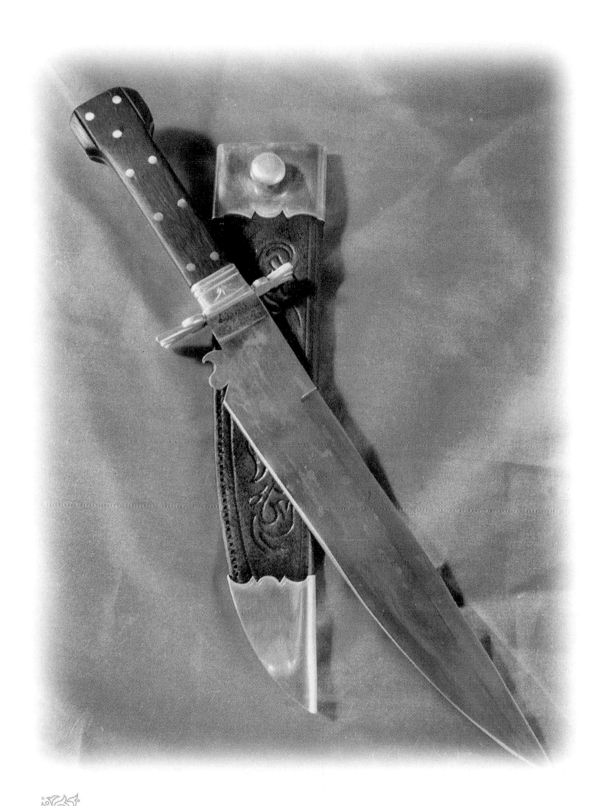

ABOVE. *A Spanish Belduque with Dog Bone handle and fancy quillion (guard). Note the decorative filework at the blade's ricasso, a mysterious touch peculiar to old Spanish blades. The sheath is tooled and silver-mounted. A masterpiece by Joe DeLaRonde, of Glorieta, NM.*

STREET SCENES AT COWBOY ACTION EVENTS

AT LEFT.
Cowboy Action Shooters are an unashamedly patriotic breed.

AT RIGHT.
A young colt tethered to the wagon at End Of Trail. Probably ought to shorten that lead shank.

AT RIGHT.
El Commandante, Zorro and Faithful Servant, Bernardo walk the streets of End of Trail 2000.

ABOVE. *General U.S. Grant, SASS President, is liveried in style to the End of Trail Wild West Show.*

ABOVE. *A blacksmith enjoys his morning coffee at Ruger's Winter Range,*
the National Championships at Ben Avery Range (near Phoenix, AZ).

AT RIGHT.
The best way to get around a large Cowboy match is with a Stagecoach and four-in-hand.

AT LEFT. *Some folks even get married at major events like the World Championships at End of Trail. So far, no divorces—and hangings are rare.*

AT RIGHT.
The famous "Wah Maker" wagon is a fixture at big Cowboy/Western matches.

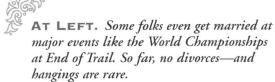

AT LEFT. *The Ladies Tea & Resting Room at SASS End of Trail—a known haunt of Suffragettes and other troublesome women.*

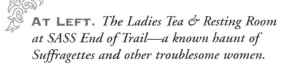

AT RIGHT.
Cowboy Action Shooting is a lifestyle that teaches family values straight out of the American frontier.

ABOVE. *The Buffalo Hump Saloon is no place for an honest cowboy just off the trail.*

AT RIGHT.
Cowboy Mounted Shooters start young. This cowkid is well on his way to a championship.

AT LEFT. *A trucker and his wife take their love of the Old West and Cowboy Action Shooting on the road.*

AT RIGHT.
Frank Schultz, of Bitterroot Bit & Spur, does some slick pistol handling for his audience of one at SASS End Of Trail.

ABOVE. *Rawhide Rawlins and Lawless Linda, (Mr. & Mrs. Phil Spangenberger) gussied up for a posh Saturday night party at End of Trail.*

306 *All About Cowboy Action Shooting*

ABOVE. *Not a gun cart, exactly, but a fine way to get around a Cowboy match—and it's period correct as well.*

ABOVE. *That's right, Pilgrim, it's him, photographed on the street at SASS End of Trail.*

ABOVE. *The Posse.*

That Cowboy and Western Action shooting events are sweeping the country should come as no surprise. After all, our foundation philosophy is the same as the nation's: We are the guardians of our own freedom and responsible for our own behavior. Proficiency at arms is a moral American trait. Our independence was won by armed American citizens, and only the same force keeps tyranny and crime at bay.

At a time when so many are willing to barter away rights and freedom for any sense of security, however false, organizations like the Single Action Shooting Society, the National Congress of Old West Shootists and the Cowboy Mounted Shooting Association are fostering a return to ideals long fallen into dusty desuetude. Cowboy actioneering is rekindling a love of our frontier history. That history, and the heritage it bequeathed, is the future of Cowboy Action Shooting and all firearms recreation in our country. We keep our beloved Western history alive by re-living it. We help preserve our constitutional right to keep and bear arms by using them; our determination is symbolized by the white smoke of our black powder. Cowboy Action Shooting is match competition and much more, so join up and join in. Stuff your war bag with your possibles and come a-shootin'! 🤠

ABOVE. *The end of a day at SASS End of Trail.*

Appendix

A complete compendium of Manufacturers, Retailers, Ammunition, Firearms & Other Purveyors of Cowboy Action Paraphernalia

AMMUNITION

A-Zoom Ammunition
4 Chrysler
Irvine, CA 92618
800/617-3239
www.a-zoom.com

Black Hills Ammunition Inc.
PO Box 3090
Rapid City, SD 57709
605/348-5150
800/568-6625
605/348-9827 Fax

Bull-X, Inc
520 North Main Street
Farmer City, IL 61842
309/928-2560 Inquires
800/248-3845 Orders
309/928-2130 Fax
bull-x@bull-x.com
www.bull-x.com

Cor-bon Bullet Co.
1311 Industry Road
Sturgis, SD 57785
800/626-7266
www.corbon.com

Dillan Precision Products
8009 East Dillon's Way
Scottsdale, AZ 85260
800/223-4570
602/998-2786

Double A Limited
315 N. Bridge Street
Henrietta, TX 76365
940/538-4108
doubleA3220.aol.com
www.doubleabullet.com

Federal Cartridge Co.
900 Ehlen Drive
Anoka, MN 55303
612/323-2300

Hornady Mfg. Co.
Box 1848
Grand Island, NE 68802-1848
800/338-3220
webmaster@hornady.com
www.hornady.com

Hunter Supply, Inc. (Ammunition)
PO Box 313
Tioga, TX 76271
800/868-6612

Kleen Bore
16 Industrial Parkway
Easthampton, MA 01027
800/445-0301

Lightening Bullets, Inc.
PO Box 11336
Columbia, SC 29211
877/424-2226
www.lighteningbullets.com

Lyman Products Company
475 Smith Street
Middletown, CT 06457
800/225-9626
860/632-1699
www.lymanproducts.com

Magma Engineering Company
PO Box 161
Queen Creek, AZ 85242
480/987-9008
480/987-0148
rclausen@ix.netcom.com
www.magmaengr.com

Meister Bullets, Inc.
PO Box 63232
Phoenix, AZ 85082
602/470-1880

National Bullet Company
1585 East 361 Street
Eastlake, Ohio 44095
440/951-1854
440/951-7761 Fax
www.nationalbullet.com

Oregon Trail Bullet Co.
PO Box 529
Baker City, OR 97814
800/811-0548
541/523-4697
541/523-1803 Fax
www.laser-cast.com

PMC Ammunition
Eldorado Cartridge Corp.
12801 US 95 South
PO Box 62508
Boulder City, NV 89006-2508
702/294-0025
702/294-0121 Fax

Redding Reloading Equipment
1089 Starr Road
Cortland, NY 13045
607/753-3331
607/756-8445 Fax

3-D Ammunition
PO Box 433
Doniphan, NE 68832
402/845-2285
402/845-6546 Fax

Starline Brass
1300 West Henry Street
PO Box 833
Sedalia, MO 65301
800/280-6660
660/827-6640
660/827-6650 Fax
www.starlinebrass.com

Ten-x Ammunition
201 S. Wineville #E
Ontario, CA 91761
909/605-1617
909/605-2844 Fax
www.ten-x.com

The Old Western Scrounger, Inc.
12924 Highway A-12
Montague, CA 96064
530/459-5445
530/459-3944 Fax

Winchester/Olin
427 North Shamrock Street, C4080
East Alton, IL 62024
618/258-2204
618/258-2427 Fax
www.winchester.com

UltraMax Ammunition
2112 Elk Vale Road
Rapid City, SD 57701
605/342-4141
605/342-8727 Fax

BLACK POWDER/POWDERS

Accurate (Powders)
5891 Highway. 230 West
McEwen, TN 37101
800/416-3006
www.accuratepowder.com

Clean Shot Powder
21218 St. Andrews Blvd.
Boca Raton, FL 33433
888/866-2532
561/477-7039
cleanshot@usa.com
cleanshot@aol.com
www.cleanshot.com

Goex Black Rifle Powder
PO Box 659
Doyline, LA 71023-0659
318/382-9300
318/382-9303 Fax
www.goexpowder.com

Hodgdon Powder
6231 Robinson Street
Shawnee Mission, Kansas 66202
913/362-9455
913/362-1307
help@hodgdon.com
www.hodgdon.com

Ramshot Powders
PO Box 158
Miles City, Montana 59301
800/497-1007

VihtaVuori Smokeless Powder
1241 Ellis Street
Bensenville, IL 60106
800/683-0464

Charities and Scholarships
Roy Rogers and Dale Evans Happy Trails
Children Foundation
10755 Apple Valley Road
Apple Valley, CA 92308
PO Box 1647
Apple Valley, CA 92307
760/240-3330
760/240-1458 Fax

SASS Scholarship Foundation
Angel and Badman Project
23255-A La Palma Avenue
Yorba Linda, CA 92887
714/694-1800
714/694-1815 Fax
sasseot@aol.com
www.sassnet.com

CLOTHING

Arizona Stagecoach Clothing Co.
21441 N. 3rd Avenue
Phoenix, AZ 85027
623/582-8989
623/582-8224 Fax
sass3367@mindspring.com

Blue Skies Mercantile
Bill and Sherri Heath
PO Box 340
301 Hwy. 16 N.
Cherokee, TX 76832
915/622-4428
915/622-4454
bluesky@centex.net

Bailey Hat Co.
PO Box 162375
Ft. Worth, TX 76161-2375
www.baileyhats.com

Buckaroo Bobbins
PO Box 1168
Chino Valley, AZ 86323-1168
520/636-1885

Buckworth Western Wear
3500 Sisk Road
Modesto, CA 95356
209/545-5553

Buffalo Runner Boots
107 South Bridge Street
PO Box 242
Henrietta, TX 76365
940/538-5301
817/538-4400
800/995-5301

Clark's Victorian Mercantile
19th Century Custom Clothing and
Firearms
PO Box 291417
Phelan, CA 92329-1417
760/949-7449
760/949-1455 Fax
clarksvm@calnet.net

Colorado Mountain Hat Co.
PO Box 1482
Fairplay, CO 80440
719/836-1411
719/836-0884 Fax
info@cmhats.com
www.cmhats.com

Classic Old West Styles
American Western Firearms
1060 Donniphan Park Circle, Suite C
El Paso, TX 79922
800/595-2697
915/587-0684
info@cows.com
www.cows.com

Cowboy Corral
219 N. Highway 89A
Sedona, AZ 86336
520/282-2040
800/457-2279
520/287-7007 Fax
info@cowboycorral.com
www.cowboycorral.com

Colonel Carter's Mercantile
141 Center Street
Grayslake, IL 60030
847/548-9315
847/223-1273 Fax

Cowboy's General Store
1174 West Eads Parkway
Lawrenceburg, Indiana 47025
812/537-3030

D-J Hat Company
3873 Springs Mountain Road
Las Vegas, Nevada 89102
702/ 362-4287

Durango Hat Company
O'Farrell of Durango
208 A Parker Avenue
Durango, CO 81301
970/259-4714
970/385-1970 Fax
ofarrelhat@aol.com

Espinoza Bootmaker
6042 North 16th Street
Phoenix, AZ 85016
602/263-8164

Micheal Malone
Handmade Cowboy Hats and Trappings
2201 Western Avenue
Ft. Worth, TX 76107
817/737-3481

Montana Boot Company
PO Box 77
Livingston, Montana 59047
406/222-7721

Mountain People Footwear
1703 Acacia Drive
Colorado Springs, CO 80907
719/598-0436

The Old Frontier Clothing Co.
7412 Fulton Avenue, Suite 1
North Hollywood, CA 91605
818/764-7787
818/982-2940 Fax

Recollections by Cactus Starr
3010 W. Echo Lane
Phoenix, AZ 85051
602/930-0949

Red River Trading Co.
Horsefly's Old West Clothing
107 South Bridge
Henrietta, TX 76365
800/995-5301
940/538-4400

River Junction Trade Co.
No. 312 Main Street
McGregor, Iowa 52157
319/873-2387
riverjct@mhtc.net

Running Iron Outfitters
46 Palomino Trail
PO Box 205
Sonoita, AZ 855637
520/455-5858

Stetson/Resistol
601 Marion Drive
Garland, TX 75042
214/631-2214
800/3255-2662

Texas Jacks Outfitters
117 North Adams Street
Fredericksburg, TX 78624
800/839-5225
830/997-6074
Realtime@www.texasjacks.com

Tombstone Outfitters
24 Railroad St.
PO Box 667
Kingston, GA 30145
770/336-9100
770/336-9101 Fax
tombstoneoutfit@mindspring.com
www.tombstoneoutfitters.com

Tonto Rim Trading Co.
5028 North Highway 31
Seymour, IN 47274
800/242-4287
821/522-7978

Victorian Traveler (Bags)
PO Box 305
Norco, CA 91760
909/361-3421
909/360-3566 Fax
victravelr@aol.com

Scully/Wah Maker-Cowboy Clothing
1701 Pacific Avenue
Oxnard, CA 93033
805/483-6339

Walker '47 (Outfitter)
1238 S. Beach Blvd., # G
Anaheim, CA 92804-4828
714/821-6655
714/821-9115
walkr47@ix.netcom.com

Wild West Mercantile
5637 North 19th Avenue
Phoenix, AZ 85015
800/596-0444
602/246-6078
800/528-5487
www.wildwestmercantile.com

EAR PROTECTION

E.S.P.
Electronic Shooters Protection, Inc.
11997 W. 85th Place
Arvada, CO 80005
Esp@usa.net
www.espamerica.com

ENGRAVING

Jim Downing
PO Box 4224
Springfield, MO 65808
417/865-5953
www.thegunengraver.com

Bill Falk Engraving
E. 10210 Laurel Road
Chattaroy, Washington 99003
509/292-8552

Jeff Flannery Engraving
11034 Riddles Run Road
Union, KY 41091
606/384-3127
606/384-2222 Fax

Bill Johns Master Engraver
PO Box 2332
Cody, WY 82414
307/587-5090

Peter-Michael Kretzmann
7825 Cowboy Way
Flagstaff, AZ 86004
520/526-6970

Clint Orms
Engravers and Silversmiths
9208 Rasmus #13
Houston, TX 77063
713/977-2105
713/785-4934 Fax

ENTERTAINMENT

Joe Bowman
PO Box 571024
Houston, Texas 77257-1024
713/785-2121
joebowman@webtv.net

James Dunham
4335 Briar Ridge Lane
Cummings, GA 30040
770/886-7809

LAFITTE (Entertainer)
Doctor of Faro
Magic and Tales of the Old West
drlafitte@aol.com
www.lafitte.cc

Lobo Rangers (Entertainment)
Dave Bourne
30645 Mainmast Drive
Agoura, CA 91301
818/991-2479

Bob Munden
Munden Enterprises
1621 Sampson
Butte, MT 59701
406/494-2833
406/494-6810 Fax
munden@montana.com
www.bob-munden.com

Dusty Rogers, Jr. and The Highriders
Happy Trails Children's Foundation
10755 Apple Valley Road
Apple Valley, CA 92308
760/240-3330

FIREARMS

American Derringer
127 N. Lacy Drive
Waco, TX 76705
254/799-9111
254/799-7935 Fax
amderr@iamerica.net
www.amderringer.com
www.ladyderringer.com

American Antiques Sporting Arms
245 Bloomfield Avenue
Bloomfield, NJ 07003
732/892-7272

Ballistol USA (Lubricant)
1 Cypress Knee Trail
Kitty Hawk, NC 27949
800/253-2460
www.ballistol.com

Beauchamp & Sons, Inc.
Flintlocks, etc.
PO Box 181
160 Rossiter Rd.
Richmond, MA 01254
413/698-3822
413/698-3866 Fax
flintetc@vgernet.net

Bond Arms, Inc.
PO Box 1296
204 Alpha Lane
Granbury, TX 76048
817/573-4445
817/573-5636
www.bondarms.com

Buffalo Arms Company
99 Raven Ridge
Sandpoint, ID 83864
208/263-6953

Cimarron FA. Company
PO Box 906
105 Winding Oak
Fredericksberg, TX 78624-0906
830/997-9090
830/997-0802 Fax
cimarron@fbg.net
www.cimarron-firearms.com

Centerfire Systems (Coach Gun)
102 Field View Dr.
Versailles, KY 40383
800/950-1231
859/873-2352 Inquires
859/873-1842 Fax

Clark's Victorian Mercantile
19th Century Custom Clothing and
Firearms
PO Box 291417
Phelan, CA 92329-1417
760/949-7449
760/949-1455 Fax
clarksvm@calnet.net

Colt's Manufacturing Co., Inc.
PO Box 1868
Hartford, CT 06144
860/236-6311
860/244-1442 Fax
Colt's Customer Service Dept.
800/962-2685
860/244-1449 Fax
www.colt.com

Dixie Gun Works
PO Box 130, Highway 51 S.
Union City, TN 38261
901/885-0561
901/885-0440 Fax

EMF Company
1900 East Warner Avenue 1-D
Santa Ana, CA 92705
714/261-6611
714/756-0133 Fax

European American Armory Corp.
PO Box 1299
Sharpes, FL 32959
407/639-4842
407/639-7006 Fax

Harrington & Richardson
60 Industrial Rowe
Gardner, MA 01440
978/632-9393
978/632-2300 Fax

IAR
International Antique Reproductions, Inc.
33171 Camino Capistrano
San Juan Capistrano, CA 92675
949/443-3642
949/443-3647 Fax
sales@iar-arms.com/
www.iar-arms.com

Lyman Products Company
475 Smith Street
Middletown, CT 06457
800/225-9626
860-632-1699
www.lymanproducts.com

Marlin Firearms
100 Kenna Drive
North Haven, CT 06473
203/239-5621
203/234-7991 Fax

Oglesby & Oglesby Gunmakers, Inc.
744 W. Andrew Road
Springfield, IL 62707
217/487-7100
217/487-7980
Orders 888/800-6440

Powder Custom, Inc.
29739 Highway J
Gravois Mills, MO 65037
573/372-5684
573/372-5799 Fax
rwpowers@laurie.net
www.powercustom.com

Navy Arms Company
689 Bergen Blvd.
Ridgefield, NJ 07657
201/945-2500
201/945-6859
info@navyarms.com
www.navyarms.com
Republic Arms, Inc.
15167 Sierra Bonita Lane
Chino, CA 91710
909/597-3873
909/597-2612 Fax

Remington Arms Co., Inc.
870 Remington Drive
PO Box 700
Madison, North Carolina 27025-0700
800/243-9700

Traditions Firearms
PO Box 776
1375 Boston Post Road
Old Saybrook, CT 06475
860/388-4656
860/388-4657
www.traditionsmuzzle.com

Shiloh Rifle Mfg.
PO Box 279
Big Timber, MT 59011
406/932-4454
406/932-5627 Fax

Smith & Wesson
2100 Roosevelt Avenue
Springfield, MA 01102
800/331-0852

Stoeger Industries
5 Mansard Court
Wayne, NJ 07470
800/631-0722
973/872-9500
973/872-2230 Fax

Sturm, Ruger and Company, Inc.
Lacey Place
Southport, CT 06490 USA
520/541-8820
www.ruger-firearms.com

Taylor's & Company
304 Lenoir Drive
Winchester, VA 22603
540/722-2017
540/722-2018 Fax
infor@taylorsfirearms.com
www.taylorsfirearms.com

Uberti USA, Inc.
362 Limerock Road
PO Box 509
Lime Rock, CT 06039

United States Fire-Arms Manufacturing Co., Inc.
The Historic East Armory
55 Van Dyke Avenue
Hartford, CT 06106
860/724—1152
860/724-6809 Fax

US Repeating Arms Company
(Winchester and Browning)
275 Winchester Avenue
Morgan, Utah 84050
801/876-3440
801/876-3331 Fax

Yaqui Arms
19 Port Monmouth Road
Keansburg, NJ 07734
732/787-1902

GRIPS

Ajax Custom Grips
PO Box 560129
Dallas, Texas 75356
214/630-8893
214/630-4942 Fax
www.AJAXGRIPS.com

Eagle Grips
460 Randy Road
Carol Stream, IL 60188
800/323-6144
630/260-0486 Fax
sales@eaglegrips.com
www.eaglegrips.com

Get a Grip Pistol Grips
PO Box 3227
Coeur d'Alene, Idaho 83816
208/765-6565
208/664-1854
getagrip@pistolgrips.com

Grip Maker
PO Box 511
Mt. Vernon, MO 65712
417/461-1123
info@gripmaker.com
www.gripmaker.com

Hogue Grips
PO Box 1138
Paso Robles, CA 93447
805/239-1440
805/239-2553 Fax
800/438-4747
support@hogueinc.com
www.getgrip.com

GUNCARTS

Cal-Graf Design (Guncarts)
PO Box 306
Big Timber, MT 59011
800/367-5203
406/932-6153 Fax
calgraf@mcn.net
www.mcn.net/~calgraf

E.M. Horton Wagon Co.
Roger Peterson Design
1464 East 29th Street
Long Beach, CA 90806
562/431-2400
562/988-777 Fax

Longhorn Leather & Carts
2 Hudson Street
Annapolis, MD 21401
410/573-1622
www.cartrightguncarts.com

Off the Wall Gun Carts
224 N. Howard Street
Greentown, IN 46936
765/628-2050 Phone and Fax

The Oak Tree
666 S. Findlay Avenue
Los Angeles, CA 90022
323/728-0915

Sidekick Guncart Company
7 Lyndeborough Road
Amherst, NH 03031-3040
603/673-4270
skguncarts@aol.com

GUNLEATHER

Aspen Sheepskin & Leather, Inc.
Bob Dunn Maker
PO Box 1420
117 Hillside Drive
Basalt, CO 81621-1420
970/927-3274

Bear Tooth Leather
22071? California Avenue, S.W. #1
Seattle, WA 98116
206/932-8012

Black Hills Leather
410 West Aurora
Laredo, TX 78041
877/712-9434
956/795-0224 Information only
956/712-8330 Fax
bhills@lmtonline.com
www.gunfighter.com/blackhills

Border States Leatherworks
1158 Apple Blossom Lane
Springdale, Arkansas 72762
501/361-2642
501/361-2851 Fax

Dennis A Yoder Custom Leather
525 Williams Street
Hamburg, PA 19526
610/562-8161

DKG Leather, LLC.
12016 La Crosse Avenue
Grand Terrace, CA 92313
909/370-3041

El Paso Saddlery
PO Box 27194
El Paso, TX 79926
915/544-2233
915/544-2535 Fax
www.epsaddlery.com

F.A. Meanea Company
Cheyenne Custom Cowboy
216 West 17th Street
Cheyenne, WY 82001
307/635-6608
307/634-2963 Fax
cowboyleather@wyoming.com
www.cowboyleather.com

Frontier Gun Leather
PO Box 2038
Rancho Mirage, CA 92270
619/321-6239
619/321-4139 Fax

Gila River Leather Co.
PO Box 42715
Phoenix, AZ 85080-2715
602/587-0936
gilariver@syspac.com
www.syspac.com/~gilarivr/

Galco International
2019 W. Quail Avenue
Phoenix, AZ 85027
602/258-8295
602/582-6854 Fax
800/874-2526

Hanel's Antiqued Leather Goods
17344 Ivy Lane
Sisters, OR 97759
541/548-2786

High Lonesome Plunder Custom Leather
B.K. Gore Maker
122 W. LaPorte Avenue
Fort Collins, CO 80524
970/481-0722

Hunter Company, Inc. (Leather)
3300 W. 71st Avenue
PO Box 467
Westminster, CO 80030-9977
303/427-4626
303/428-3980 Fax

JAX Leather Company
PO Box 937
Madera, CA 93639
559/675-1230
559/675-0475 Fax

Kirkpatrick Leather
PO Box 677
Laredo, TX 78042
956/723-6893
956/725-0672 Fax

Kicking Mule Outfitters (Leather Goods)
545 S. Main Street
PO Box 836
Camp Verde, AZ 86322
520/567-2501

Old West Reproductions, Inc.
446 Florence South Loop
Florence, MT 59833
406/273-2615

Rio Verde Saddlery
437 W. Gen. Crook Trail
PO Box 2293
Camp Verde, AZ 86322
888/746-8373
520/567-0427
saddles@sedona.net
www.rioverdesaddlery.com

Texas Gunslinger
2627 S. Cooper, C-21
Arlington, TX 76015
817/460-3840
817/543-0212 Fax

Wild Bill's Leather Goods
PO Box 13037
Burton, WA 98013
206/463-5738

Wolf Ears Equipment
702 S. Pine, Dept. C
Laramie, WY 82072
307/745-7135

GUNSMITHING

Accurate Plating and Weaponry, Inc.
940 Harbor Lake Drive
Safety Harbor, Florida 34695
727/796-5583
727/796-5943 Fax
www.apwcogan.com

Cylinder & Slide, Inc.
PO Box 937
Fremont, NE 68026-0937
402/721-4277
402/721-0263 Fax
800/448-1713
bill@cylinder-slide.com
www.cylinder-slide.com

James & Guns
5130 N. 19th Avenue Suite #9
Phoenix, AZ 85015
602/547-1942

King's Gun Works, Inc
1837 W. Glenoaks Blvd.
Glendale, CA 91201
Orders only: 800/282-9449
Fax orders: 818/548-8606
www.kingsgunworks.com

Lee's Gunsmithing
2777 Orange-Olive Road
Orange, CA 92865
714/921-9030
714/974-7356 Fax

Marble Arms/Poly-Choke
420 Industrial Park
PO Box 111
Gladstone, MI 49837
906/428-3710
906/428-3711 Fax
marble@up.net
www.marblearms.com

Oglesby & Oglesby Gunmakers, Inc.
744 W. Andrew Road
Springfield, IL 62707
217/487-7100
217/487-7980
Orders 888/800-6440

Paul's Precision Gunsmithing
2976 E. Los Angeles Avenue
Simi Valley, CA 93065
805/527-1090
805/527-0814 Fax

Peacemaker Specialists
PO Box 157
Whitmore, CA 96096
530/472-3438

Q'PR, Inc.
Qualite' Pistol & Revolver
5580 Havana, #6A
Denver, CO 80239
303/574-1765
888/762-3030
qpr@earthlink.net
www.qpr-inc.com

Smith Enterprises, Inc. (Gunsmiths)
1701 W. 10th Street Suite 14
Tempe, AZ 85281
480/964-1818
480/921-9987 Fax
www.smithenterprise.com

KNIVES

Bear Bone Knives
541/582-4144
ricksmith@echoweb.net
www.bearbone.com

Dixie Gun Works
PO Box 130, Highway 51 S.
Union City, TN 38261
901/885-0561
901/885-0440 Fax

Green River Knives
York Mountain Enterprises
RD#2
Box 272B
Pittsfield, PA 16340

Idaho Knife Works
PO Box 144
Spirit Lake, ID 83869
509/994-9394
www.idahoknifeworks.com

De La Ronde Forge
Box 84
Glorieta, NM 87535
505/757-6725

PUBLICATIONS

American Cowboy Magazine
PO Box 54555
Boulder, CO 80322-455
800/297-6933

The Cowboy Chronicle
The Journal of the Single Action Shooting
Society
23255 La Palma
Yorba Linda, CA 92887
714/694-1800
714/694-1813 Fax
sasschron@aol.com
www.sassnet.com

Guns of the Old West
C/O Harris Publications
1115 Broadway, 8th Floor
New York, NY 10010
888/226-6228

GUNS AND AMMO

Peterson Publishing Co
6420 Wilshire Blvd.
14th Floor
Los Angeles, CA 90048
323/782-2125
323/782-2867 Fax

Krause Publishing
700 East State Street
Iola, WI 54990
800/258-0929
www.krause.com

MLV Enterprises
Dept. #NPS
PO Box 914
Livingston, MT 59047
406/222-2659 Phone/Fax

The Rundown
Journal of the Cowboy Mounted Shooters
Association
Mike Minarsich
26825 N. 152nd Street
Scottsdale, AZ 85255
480/837-8322 x101
mminarsich@psn.net

Shoot! Magazine
1770 W. State Street
PMB 340
Boise, ID 83702
208/368-9920
208/338-8428 Fax
208/368-9920 Subscriptions
editor@shootmagazine.com

Shooting Times Magazine
PO Box 56777
Boulder, CO 80322-6777
800/727-4353

The Shootist
Journal of The National Congress of Old
West Shootist
PO Box 221
602 State Street
Cedar Falls, IA 50613
319/277-6839
319/277-6840 Fax
shootist@cfu-cybernet.net
www.swiftsite.com

True West Magazine
PO Box 8008
Cave Creek, AZ 85327
480/575-1881
480/575-1903 Fax
mail@truewestmagazine.com

Wild West Magazine
PO Box 420466
Palm Coast, FL 32141-0466

Wolfe Publishing Co.
6471 Airpark Dr.
Prescott, AZ 86301
520/445-7810
520/778-5124

Women & Guns Magazine
Second Amendment Foundation
PO Box 488
Buffalo, NY 14209
716/885-6408
716/884-4471 Fax

SADDLES

The Australian Stock Saddle Co.
PO Box 987
Malibu, CA 90265
818/889-6988
818/889-7271 Fax
dangaard@bigfoot.com
www.ausiesaddle.com

Constanza's Custom Saddles
516 Blue Grouse Lane
Stevensville, MT 59870
406/777-3506

G. D'Ambrose Custom Saddles
4305 E. Quail Track
Cave Creek, 85331
480/419-1863
www.deambrose.com

Old Pueblo Saddle
984 S. Charlo Drive
Pueblo West, CO 81007
719/547-0109

Rio Verde Saddlery
437 W. Gen. Crook Trail
PO Box 2293
Camp Verde, AZ 86322
888/740-8373
520/567-0427
saddles@sedona.net
www.rioverdesaddlery.com

San Pedro Saddlery co.
PO Box 542
Tombstone, AZ 85638-0542
520/457-3616
520/457-2265 Fax
sanpedro@primenet.com
www.sanpedrosaddlery.com

Sawtooth Saddle Company
8962 W. Castle Cove Road
Vernal, Utah 84078
435/789-5400

Stewart Saddlery
PO Box 1328
Ft. Gibson, OK 74434
918/478-4088

SHOOTING RANGES, ARENAS AND SCHOOLS

Agoura Hills Target Range, Inc.
5040 Cornell Road
Agoura Hills, CA 91301
818/899-0453 Range
818/706-1710 Guns
818/706-9944 Fax

**Ben Avery Shooting Range
(Winter Range)**
4044 W. Black Canyon Blvd.
Phoenix, AZ 85027
623/582-8313
623/582-5317 Fax

Black Water Training Center
850 Puddin Ridge Road
Moyock, NC 27958
877/425-5987
www.blackwaterlodge.com

Calico Ghost Town
PO Box 638
Yermo, CA 92398
760/254-2122
760/254-2047 Fax
calico@mscomm.com
www.calicotown.com

Gunsite
2900 W. Gunsite Road
Paulden, AZ 86334
520/636-4565
520/636-1236
www.gunsite.net

Leadville Shooting School
PO Box 93
Flatonia, TX 78941
515/865-9222 Phone/Fax
ryoung@fais.net

NRA Whittington Center
PO Box 700
Raton, NM 87740
505/445-3615
505/445-9418 Fax

National Festival of the West
PO Box 12966
Scottsdale, AZ 85267-2966
602/996-4387

SHOOTING CLUBS

CMSA
Cowboy Mounted Shooting Association
29317 N. 154th Place
Scottsdale, AZ 85262
480/471-0485
www.cowboymountedshooting.com
cmsa@futureone.com

NCOWS
The National Congress of Old West
Shootist, Inc.
PO Box 221
602 State Street
Cedar Falls, IA 50613
319/277-6839
319/277-6840 Fax
ncows@cfu.cybernet.net
shootist@cfu.cybernet.net
www.swiftsite.cows/ncows

NRA National Rifle Association
11250 Waples Mill Road
Fairfax, VA 22030
703/267-1585
703/267-3971
800/423-6894
www.nrahq.org

National Muzzle Loading Rifle
Association
NMLRA
PO Box 67
Friendship, Indiana 47021
812/667-5131

OWSA
Old West Shootist Association
712 James Street
Azle, TX 76020
817/444-2049
Bill Hahn: 760/433-1738

SASS
Single Action Shooting Society
23255 La Palma
Yorba Linda, CA 92887
714/694-1800
www.sassnet.com

The Great Basin BPCR Shooters
Pawnee Jack Maddox
62239 Cody Road
Bend, OR 97701
541/389-9673
tiyiyo@bendnet.com

Western Action Shootist Association
4719-G Quail Lakes Drive, Suite 140
Stockton, CA 95207
wasamail@wasaranch.com
www.wasaranch.com

SILVERSMITHS

Argent Express
PO Box 812
Waterford, CA 95386
209/874-2640

Bitterroot Bit n Spur
Frank and Vickie Shultz
431 Bear Creek Road
Victor, Montana 59875
406/642-3882 Phone and Fax
888/899-0930
bitspur@bitterroot.net
www.bitterroot.net/bitspur

SPUR MAKERS

Bitterroot Bit n Spur
Frank and Vickie Shultz
431 Bear Creek Road
Victor, Montana 59875
406/642-3882
888/899-0930
bitspur@bitterroot.net
www.bitterroot.net/bitspur

De La Ronde Forge
Box 84
Glorieta, NM 87535
505/757-6725

Lindholm Bros.
32425 Keno Springs Road
Bonanza, Oregon 97623
541/545-3120

Nailhead Spur Co. and Leather Works
305 Bessemer
Llano, TX 78643
915/247-2589
877/813-3811
www.nailheadspur.com

TARGETS

Arntzen Corp.
Rockford, IL 60105-0898
815/964-0045 Fax
ArntzenRM@aol.com

DS Welding
9438 Irondale Avenue
Chatsworth, CA 91311
818/727-9353
818/727-9378
dave@1stconnect.com
www.dswelding.com
www.steel-targets.com

MGM Targets
Mike Gibson Manufacturing
3554 N. 39th Street
Boise, Idaho 83703
208/368-9878
888/767-7371
208/368-9882 Fax

TIMERS

Competition Electronics, Inc.
34699 Precision Drive
Rockford, IL 61109
815/874-8001
815/874-8181 Fax
www.competitionelectronics.com

Pact, Inc.
PO Box 535025
Grand Prairie, TX 75053
800/722-8462
972/641-0049 in Texas
972/641-2641 Fax

Pegasus
1601 Chalk Hill Road
Dallas, TX 75212
214/339-2204
214/339-1585 Fax
peggo@peg-go.com
www.newmicros.com/pegasus/

WESTERN AMERICANA

Absaroka Western Designs
1416 Warm Springs Dr.
PO Box 777
Dubois, WY 82513
307/455-2440
307/455-3355 Fax
www.wy-biz.com/absarokawesternde-signs/index.html

Alias Images Productions, Inc.
PO Box 2697
Flagstaff, AZ 86003
520/714-1002
520/714-1032 Fax
877/246-8390
aliasinc.@earthlink.net
www.aliasimages.com

American West.com
Old West Merchandise and Auction Site
12691 Apple Valley Raod
Apple Valley, CA 92308
760/240-2401
townmayor@theamericanwest.com
www.theamericanwest.com

Bar H Productions
PO Box 4671
Sunland, CA 91041
818/353-7988
818/353-7988 Fax

B Bar 10 Ltd.
9685 Hwy. B
Amherst, WI 54406
800/852-2616
715/824-3750
715/824-2331 Fax
www.bbar10.com

Bitterroot Bit n Spur
Frank and Vickie Shultz
431 Bear Creek Road
Victor, Montana 59875
406/642-3882
888/899-0930
bitspur@bitterroot.net
www.bitterroot.net/bitspur

Buck Taylor (Actor & Artist)
Rte 2, Box 204
Phone/Fax: 940/433-5715
www.bucktaylor.com

Buckles by Mike
1225 Manzanta Street
Los Angeles, CA 90029-2233
323/663-6972

Buffalo Bayou Traders
927 Wycliffe
Houston, TX 77079
713/461-3502

Butler Bags
PO Box 609
Cedar City, Utah 84721
800/922-2247
cowboybedrolls@hotmail.com
www.butlerbags.com

Caswell Trading Co.
PO Box 359
Tehachapi, CA 93581
805/822-7770

Classic Era Cartridge Boxes
PO Box 28425
Dept. CC
Kansas City, MO 64188
816/413-9196
816/455-2859 Fax
cheyennepp@aol.com
www.cartridgeboxes.com

Coon Creek
Old West Reproductions
601 S. Desert Steppes
Tucson, AZ 85710
520/886-8273

Cowboy Land, Inc.
8711 E. Pinnacle Peak Rd. #368
Suite A-101
Scottsdale, AZ 85255
480/948-6851
480/473-7119 Fax
Jim Rogers 602/309-4390
Teal R. Henkel 602/571-8092

Cowboy Emporium (Pocket Watches)
1461 Oakwood
Sylvan Lake, MI 48320
248/682-4065
www.cemp.com

Don Donnelly Horseback Vacations
6010 S. Kings Ranch Road
Gold Canyon, AZ 85219
480/982-8895
480/982-8795 Fax
www.dondonnelly.com

The Frontier (Western Americana)
PO Box 1919
Boulder Creek, CA 95006
831/338-7790
831/338-7814 Fax
mgt1919@aol.com

Hart's Trading Post, Ltd.
555 Middle Line Road
Ballston Spa, NY 12020
518/885-4867

The Great Northwest Fur & Trading Post
PO Box 332
6100 Highway 95
Cocholalla, Idaho 83813
208/265-9592

James Country Mercantile
111 N. Main
Liberty, Missouri 64068
316/781-9473
Jamescntry@aol.com

Les Bois Brule
Meris Trading Company
PO Box 278
One Star Lane
Lodge Grass, Montana 59050
406/639-2298
406/639-9198 Fax

Lone Star Cowboy Gear
PO Box 721
Justin, TX 76247
940/648-3520
940/648-3525 Fax
garylplace@email.msn.com
www.lonestarcowboygear.com

Old Town Station, Ltd.
PO Box 14040-COW
Lenexa, KS 666285
913/492-3000
www.armchairgunshow.com

Pocket Watches
Terry Flynn
PO Box 550
Red Wing, MN 55066
651/388-6784

Ponderosa Ranch
100 Ponderosa Ranch Road
Incline Village, NV 89451
702/831-0691
702/831-0113 Fax

Red River Trade Co.
RR#1
Box 235
Earlham, Iowa 50072
515/758-2589

Renegade
Gunleather of the Old West
6324 West 600 South
New Palestine, IN 46163
317/861-6233
317/861-6338 Fax
Toll Free: 888/863-9494

RC Merrill, Cowboy Artist
PO Box 1843
Gilbert, AZ 852299-1843
602/813-9611

RMHA
Rocky Mountain Horseback Adventures
Ed Dabney
7696 Highway 287
Lander, WY 82520
800/408-9149
307/335-8626 Fax

SilverTip Originals
PO Box 278
Glorieta, NM 87535
505/757-6957

Spotted Owl Trade Goods
Banning, CA
909/922-9164

Tecumseh's Trading ost
140 W. Yellowstone Avenue
Cody, WY 82414
307/587-5362

The Cloak Drummer Company
257B East 29th St.
Loveland, CO 80538
970/495-3406

The Old West Shop
PO Box 5232
Vienna, WV 26105
304/295-3161
304/295-3143 Fax
oldwestshop@citynet.net
www.oldwestshop.com

Trail's End
10565 Lyon Road
Eric, KS 66733
316/244-5298
316/244-3545 Fax

Tumbleweed Hotel
PO Box 312
Cave Creek, AZ 85327
480/488-3668

Versatile Rack Company
5232 Alcoa Avenue
Vernon, CA 90058
323/588-0137
323/588-5067 Fax
www.versatilegunrack.com

Wild West Collectibles
33600 6th Avenue South
Federal Way, WA 98003
253/951-8000
253/815-8100
253/815-8992 Fax
boothill@wildwestguns.net

Vintage Cowboy
PO Box 501
360 Main Street
Old World Plaza #1
Hill City, SD 57745
605/574-4655
877/887-1884
vintage@blackhills.net

BIBLIOGRAPHY

Adler, Miller. *Colt Blackpowder Reproductions and Replicas: A Collectors and Shooter's Guide.* Minneapolis: Blue Book Publications, 1998.

Beatie, Russel, H. *Saddles.* Foreward by Dean Krakel. Norman, OK and London: University of Oklahoma Press, 1981.

Brothers Bloomingdale. *Bloomingdale's Illustrated 1886 Catalog: Fashions, Dry Goods and Housewares.* Intro. By Nancy Villa Bryk. New York: Dover Publications, Inc., 1988.

Capps, Benjamin. ed., *The Indians.* The Old West Series. New York: Time-Life-Books, 1975.

Cisneros, Jose. *Riders across the Centuries: Horsemen of the Spanish Borderlands.* El Paso: Texas Western Press, 1984.

Crandall, Judy. *Cowgirls: Early Images and Collectables with Price Guide.* Atglen, PA: Schiffer Publishing Ltd., 1994.

Crutchfield, et al. *Dixie Gunworks: The Cowboy Gazette.* Union City, Tennessee: Pioneer Press, 2000.

Dalrymle, Priscilla Harris. *American Victorian Costume in Early Photographs.* New York: Dover Publications, Inc. 1991.

De Voto, Bernard. *Across the Wide Missouri.* Boston: Houghton Mifflin Company, 1975.

Emmet, Boris. *Montgomery Ward & Co. Catalog and Buyers' Guide. No. 57, Spring and Summer.* An Unabridged reprint of the original edition. New York: Dover Publications, Inc., 1969.

Forbis, Wiliam, H., ed., *The Cowboys.* The Old West Series. New York: Time-Life Books, 1973.

Friedman, Michael. *Cowboy Culture: The Last Frontier of American Antiques.* rev. 2d. ed. Atglen, PA: Schiffer Publishing Ltd., 1999.

Gilbert, Bill,. ed., *The Trailblazers.* The Old West Series. New York: Time-Life Books, 1973.

Greener, W.W. *The Gun and Its Development.* Fairfax, VA: Odysseus Editions, Inc., 1995.

Gullet, Charly. *Cowboy Action Shooting.* Prescott, AZ: Wolfe Publishing Company, 1995.

Harrison, Julia D. *Metis: People between Two Worlds.* Vancouver and Toronto: The Glenbow-Alberta Institute, 1985.

Horn, Houston, ed., *The Pioneers.* The Old West Series. New York: Time-Life Books, 1974.

Hutchins, Dan and Sebie Hutchins. *Old Cowboy Saddles & Spurs: Identifying the Craftsmen Who Made Them.* Fifth Annual. Santa Fe, NM: Hutchins Publishing Co., 1995.

Jarrett, William S., ed., *Shooter's Bible No. 90 1999 edition.* Wayne, NJ : Stoeger Publishing Company, 1998.

Jordan, Marsh and Company. *Jordan, Marsh Illustrated Catalog of 1891: An Unabridged Reprint.* New York: The Athenaeum of Philadelphia and Dover Publications, Inc., 1991.

Kieft, Gary. *Beyond the Wild Bunch: The Fast-Growing Sport of Cowboy Action Shooting.* Photography by Nyle Latham. Scottsdale: Dillon Precision Products, Inc., 1999.

Laird, James R. *The Cheyenne Saddle.* 4th ed. Cheyenne: Vision Graphics, Inc., 1982.

Lindmier, Tom and Steve Mount. *I See by Your Outfit: Historic Cowboy Gear of the Northern Plains.* Glendo, WY: High Plains Press, 1996.

Madis, George. *The Winchester Book – 1 of 1000.* Brownsboro, TX: Art and Reference House, 1985.

Mails, Thomas E. *The Mystic Warrior of the Plains.* Garden City, NY: Doubleday & Company, Inc., 1972.

Manns, William and Elizabeth Clair Flood. *Cowboys & the Trappings of the Old West.* Santa Fe: Zon International Publishing Co., 1997.

Martin, N. and Jody Martin. *Bit and Spur Makers in the Vaquero Tradition: A Historical Perspective.* Nicasio, CA : Hawk Hill Press, 1997.

McDowell, R. Bruce. *A Study of Colt Conversions and Other Percussion Revolvers.* Iola, WI : Krause Publications, 1997.

Mora, Jo. *Californios: The Saga of the Hard Riding Vaqueros, America's First Cowboys.* 1946. Reprint. 2d ed. Ketchum, ID: Dober Hill Ltd. An Imprint of Stoecklein Publishing, 1994.

Moseman, C.M. and Brother. *Moseman's Illustrated Catalog of Home Furnishing Goods: An Unabridged Replication of the Fifth Edition.* New York: Dover Publications, Inc., 1987.

Nevin, David. ed., *The Ranchers.* The Old West Series. Alexandria , VA: Time Life Books, 1977.

_____, ed., *The Mexican War.* The Old West Series. Alexandria, VA: Time-Life Books, 1978.

Payne, Darwin. *Owen Wister: Chronicler of the West, Gentleman of the East.* Dallas: Southern Methodist University Press, 1985.

Rattenbury, Richard C. *Packing Iron: Gunleather of the Frontier West.* Santa Fe: Zon International Publishing Co. 1993.

Schwing, Ned. *2000 Standard Catalog of Firearms: The Collector's Price and Reference Guide – 10th Anniversary Edition.* Iola, WI: Krause Publications, 2000.

Stegner, Wallace. *Beyond the Hundreth Meridian: John Wesley Powell and The Second Opening of the West.* Intro. by Bernard De Voto. New York: Penguin Books, 1992.

Taffin, John. *Big Bore Sixguns.* Iola, WI: Krause Publications, 1997.

_____. *Action Shooting Cowboy Style: An In-Depth Look at America's Hottest New Shooting Game.* Iola, WI : Krause Publications, 1999.

Trachtman, Paul., ed., *The Gunfighters.* 1974. The Old West Series. Alexandria, VA: Time-Life Books, 1981.

Venturino, Mike. *Shooting Colt Single Action.* Livingston, MT: MLV Enterprises, 1995.

_____. *Six Guns of the Old West.* Livingston, MT: MLV Enterprises, 1997.

_____. *Shooting Lever Guns of the Old West.* Livingston, MT: MLV Enterprises, 2000.

Wheeler, Keith., ed., *The Scouts.* 1978. 2d ed. The Old West Series. Alexandria, VA: Time-Life Books, 1980.

Wilson, R. L. *The Book of Colt Firearms.* Minneapolis: Blue Book Publications, Inc., 1993.

_____. *The Peacemakers – Arms and Adventure in the American West.* Photography by Peter Beard, et al. New York: Random House, 1992.

_____. *Colt – An American Legend. Sequential Edition. The Official History of Colt Firearms from 1836 to the Present.* With Over 300 Illustrations in Full Color. New York/London: Artabras, 1985.

INDEX